GREAT AMERICAN SPEECHES

edited by

John Graham
UNIVERSITY OF VIRGINIA

GREAT AMERICAN SPEECHES
1898-1963
Texts and Studies

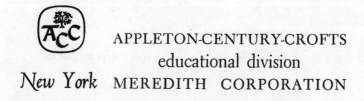

APPLETON-CENTURY-CROFTS
educational division
New York MEREDITH CORPORATION

PRINTED IN THE UNITED STATES OF AMERICA

390-37971-9

Preface

This collection puts into the reader's hands full and accurate texts of twenty-four great American speeches of the twentieth century, as well as over a dozen serious studies of five great speakers. Through the happy cooperation of Appleton-Century-Crofts and Caedmon Records, the reader can more closely approach the true dimension of public address by having not only the text but also the recording of each of these speeches in a single collection. A speech must be heard.

Designed for a general audience as well as for the student of public speaking, public address, and rhetorical criticism and theory, this collection can serve both as a text for speech or history courses (from the freshman year through graduate school) and as leisure reading.

In contrast to most, if not all, anthologies, the text of each speech in this volume is uncut, so that its full development can be appreciated. Minor exceptions to this basic rule are the selections from LaFollette and Darrow: they normally spoke for hours, and no great speech of theirs could be included in the confines of any anthology. These selections are, however, self-contained and unedited units—developed speeches in themselves, not unrepresentative purple passages.

The texts of early speeches were taken from the most authoritative sources, as indicated in the headnotes. When possible, the text was established for all speakers from live recordings by the speaker himself. (Faulkner's is a studio recording by the novelist, not recorded at the Nobel presentation in Sweden.) These texts then are of the speech as given, not as represented in an inaccurate press release. The recordings are seen as no autograph album of great men's voices: the man speaking is part of the form-and-content entity that makes a speech. For the scholar interested in the problems of an accurate text—or in the reasons for publishing an inaccurate one—references have been included to widely accepted printed versions.[1]

[1] There is a serious need for establishing definitive texts. See Robert W. Smith, "The 'Second' Inaugural Address of Lyndon Baines Johnson: A Definitive Text," *Speech Monographs* 34(1967):102–8.

The studies were carefully selected to illuminate the speeches themselves directly, and they were balanced to serve in a more general way both as descriptions of the nature of public speaking and as examples of varied approaches to scholarship and criticism. General studies directly concerned with the nature of speech or with speeches as history or methods of analysis were excluded, since these rather philosophical arguments are simply beyond the range of most students. The student needs first to experience the fact of many speeches before the larger issues can be fruitfully explored. These studies help build that experience while being within the grasp of the average college student.

JOHN GRAHAM

Contents

STUDIES

GREAT AMERICAN SPEECHES

Introduction

I

Some years ago leading authorities in history, law, and religion were asked to name the twenty most influential speakers in American history. The difficulty of establishing criteria prevented them from approaching anything like a consensus: eighty-four names were submitted and only half of the authorities agreed on the leading thirteen speakers. Surely literary critics on ranking American novelists or poets would never reveal so little agreement.

As the basic test for "the great speech," one might require that it be "influential," "successful," or "effective," since public address is surely a practical art. But the aim and method of a speech are multiple, so it may succeed greatly in the long history of mankind while failing to catch the moment. Edmund Burke, continually in opposition, was usually voted down, but surely he was a "great speaker."

Speeches of the past, whether distant or immediate, can be rated fairly, however, by a consideration of their content and their context. Many fine speeches gain their immediate objective brilliantly and force an audience to belief or action, yet much of their force depends on their context. By taking advantage of the context, they can serve as catalysts to cause or quicken the interaction among events, ideas, and emotions. But their shock of truth, derived through the audience's immediate involvement in events and conflicts, lessens rapidly as problems change. They are trapped in their own time and now have the diminished impact of clever political cartoons on forgotten issues.

The greater speech demands less recall of a conflict's particulars, since the issues rise from large movements in our culture—national expansion, World War I and democracy, the Great Depression, organized labor, World War II and fascism, continuing international stress in a "cold war," racial relations. The larger values implicit in the particular conflicts are evident to the most unsophisticated. One does not need to be a historian to

1

recognize the basis of the issues that, in one form or another, reveal themselves nakedly as the enduring problems of Western civilization. The contexts, if only in memory or through analogy, are always with us.

The greatest speeches develop their own contexts. Though often born mightily of a particular issue, such speeches image up a world of conflict within themselves and create, as does the poem or novel, a real place in which human values struggle, no matter what the actual time and place. It is a world of universal rights, of universal freedoms, of universal duties that arise from particular problems. Swift's *Gulliver's Travels* astonishes by its revelation of human values, not, except incidentally, by its exposure of the particular religious and political quarrels of the early eighteenth century. So, too, the greatest speeches of all types transcend national and temporal contexts and present the human condition. They are ultimately philosophical, since they are concerned with values themselves as much as the application of those values in a particular time or place. The good speech deals effectively with the particular, the great speech with the universal.

Perhaps, then, a definition of greatness in public address might be "enduring values well expressed in a time of need." This certainly distributes the credit to the ideals of a civilization and the speaker's recognition and expression of those traditions, as well as to the sweep of history that lifts him and his audience into a commitment to enduring values.

It is indeed a frustrating task to gather a slender book of great speeches. Readers and listeners will want more of Wilson, Franklin D. Roosevelt, and Stevenson, will prefer other speeches of Theodore Roosevelt, Hoover, and John F. Kennedy, or will want the speeches of great speakers not even represented—Eugene V. Debs, Alfred E. Smith, William E. Borah, John L. Lewis, and many others. Firm texts or permissions for use were simply not available. But this gathering is representative of the varieties of styles and positions that can serve as an introduction to the importance, the power, and the beauty of a man addressing his fellowmen.

II

Every speech both is and marks a beginning. The new president gives his inaugural, the new organization designs a manifesto, the new year calls for a State of the Union address. All, anticipating the future, are intrinsically optimistic, since they promise change or progression. Even the eulogy or memorial for the public figure is not only of death but of the continuing life, the evolution of principles and policies under a new generation. A speech is a thrust into the future, a new statement of values that should endure and guide.

To effect this beginning, a public address must be an active and flexible relationship of four elements: reality, language, speaker, and audience. The speaker studies and interprets reality and then casts it into a form acceptable to a particular audience at a particular time. Of unique importance, both speaker and audience reveal themselves to each other during the act of creation.

To analyze this creation, one can turn back to Aristotle's useful, though limited, "modes of proof." He saw every speech as a presentation of three elements, any one of which should compel the assent of the audience: "*Ethos* resides in the character of the speaker; *pathos* consists in producing a certain attitude in the hearer; *logos* appertains to the argument proper, in so far as it actually or seemingly demonstrates." In any speech these modes are inextricably intertwined though one may predominate.

On considering *logos*, or logic, the listener examines the accuracy and validity of evidence and reasoning. Evidence consists primarily of examples and statistics, or possibly the testimony of authority. Reasoning, both inductive and deductive, involves the relationship of the parts, especially through the use of generally accepted premises, such as statements of major cultural values. Franklin D. Roosevelt's "Four Freedoms" speech, with its axiom of freedom of speech and worship, freedom from want and fear, is an admirable example of the true function of the premise in reasoning: it serves as a common source from which many conclusions must flow.

The large clusters of principles that surround such key terms as "freedom," "progress," "rights," and "justice"—or *liberté, egalité, fraternité*—lead us from logic to *pathos* or emotions. In the history of a nation or an individual, these terms accrete meanings that trigger an audience's responses on a nonrational level. Self-interest and altruism, love and fear, pride and humility can, in fact, be logically defensible motivating concepts. But they often function emotionally—on the rim of consciousness and with a force disproportionate to the logic of a case. They can overwhelm both logic and our own principles—Darrow could make us love the guilty underdog. If the speaker suggests that our security is in danger because of legal restrictions or an armed enemy or disease or lack of money or social rejection, the power of his "argument" is greatly reinforced—or even made unnecessary. We are hurried emotionally—at least hopefully, perhaps desperately—to seize his solution to our dilemma.

In many areas of our lives, however, we have no evident basis, either logical or emotional, for our decisions; and short of a lifetime of study and experience, we would never be able to establish an acceptable base. We turn, then, to experts and have confidence, if not faith, in doctors, pilots, electricians, and carhops. To gain the confidence of his audience, the speaker must develop his *ethos* within his speech by demonstrating his intelligence and experience, his sound moral character, and his good will toward his audience. He must be, in Quintilian's view, "the good man speaking well" and must reveal that goodness while speaking. The logical appeal may be faulty, the emotional appeal weak, but if the speaker can present himself as the reliable source of facts and ideas, the speech can be a "success." The essential relationship of a man speaking with men is established.

Paradoxically, the audience must feel the speaker is addressing it both as a superior individual and as a member of the audience, both as a leader and as a man. The speaker must have done and be able to do the things he asks of his audience: vote, give time and money, have loyalty and conviction and wisdom. The preacher has the impossible task of urging his congregation to be saints and of being one himself—which is why we resent the preacher's "Do as I say, not as I do." The speaker's office always gives him more power over us but also demands more of him. At the same time the speaker must be one of the group, one who understands and feels the problems of mortal man. The salutation "My friends" or "My fellow Americans" is no casual greeting, and the orator's easy references to his boyhood, his wife, his children and are part of the calculated attempt to identify himself with the approved and the "normal."

And those normal humans have problems, want change, want the beginning that the speaker offers through his expression of reality and himself to that audience.

III

Great speeches, like great informal essays, testify to the truth of Samuel Johnson's dictum that "men more frequently require to be reminded than informed." Most political issues are points on an old continuum stretching between the extremes of dictatorship and anarchy, so that not many "original ideas" are offered in speeches, and if we insist on them, we ask the wrong thing of the speaker. But if the idea is not fresh in the mind of history, it is a translation, new in expression, new for the immediate problem. It thrusts a common idea into the field of action.

Although the great speaker builds a self-contained world within a speech, elements of that constructed world are constantly breaking out into the actual world, since the speech's immediate context must be met. A speech, like an epic, voices general national ideals and goals, but it must also use and give to a particular and important instance.

A speech, then, is never "complete" in itself. No set piece, it rises from and creates the context of an era, of particular events and men. La Follette's "Soldier's Pay" is an extract from a long-continued analysis of financing World War I; Darrow's "To the Jury" is the final note of a trial lasting months. But so, too, is Beveridge's "The March of the Flag" only a "part" of a running debate on America's role in world affairs, and the Truman Doctrine can be fully realized only in the historical context of the Monroe Doctrine. One could certainly argue that for any human act, "context is all." The ideas Roosevelt expresses in his First Inaugural may be there because of his beliefs, but they are there, in part, because of his audience's readiness to accept such thoughts at that particular time.

Form, as well as content, has a context, an audience expectation. There is language "appropriate to" the man, the occasion, and the audience—to the barracks room, the dinner party, and the podium. In Roosevelt's history-making speech there was the high level of biblical language and references to a war on economic problems, as well as recurring images of it. As simple a point as the length of a speech is dependent on the era. When there were few chances for public entertainment, people did not drive a buggy ten miles for a half-hour speech. They wanted and got a full afternoon of enlightenment and entertainment: a two- or three-hour speech was common. Delivery is also an essential part of that "form." The audience expectation of the "spread eagle" demanded that the speaker use inflated language, voice, and gesture, or he would disappoint that audience.

With the advent of radio, the speaker faced radically new problems of content and form. He had a far more varied audience, which made his adaptation of ideas and language more difficult, and time suddenly became costly and divided into neat quarter- and half-hour segments, so compression was essential. Furthermore, the majority of the audience listened at home without the excitement of the crowd. A conversational tone was the only one: a man cannot give an oration to a single person in an easy chair. A new audience and a new speaker had evolved.

But the great speaker transcends all contexts. Man, struggling to be rational, wants that the *logos*, the logical content of the speech, be the essential, and claims that it is. But after spending many pages analyzing the speaker's learning, preparation, and adaptability, his lines of argument and use of figures, learned critics with no little confusion regularly conclude "the really important factor was his personality." And we know how we react to a speaker. The negative test is telling: we read a speech, then hear it, and we are ready to accept Cicero's statement, "Delivery is the one dominant power in oratory." This admission tells us something more about speech than we may care to know; it shows us its darker side. It is Plato, then, who seems to have the final words: speech is a soul communicating with a soul. The ultimate surprise of delivery shocks us into the realization that the voice creates the immediacy, demands our attention and compliance, and mystically reveals the man within the idea. Finally, perhaps, a speech is merely a man trying to reveal himself.

The good speaker establishes *logos, pathos,* and *ethos,* but the great speaker goes much further. He creates a world of language that records and interprets the reality of an actual world, and that language world reflects his generative capacity, his raw energy. "Style is the man," style which can take the commonplace and stamp it as meaningful "now." The style-man forces the union of the world of thought with the world of action, the world of speaking.

The great speech, then, is both a great action by a man and, hopefully, prologue to great action by men.

SOURCES OF SPEECHES

The complete texts of most speeches are very hard to get. Too often newspapers "report" only fragments of even major addresses, and a speech by a representative of a minority or extremist group usually calls for an extended search. The best and most widely available source for contemporary speeches is the periodical *Vital Speeches,* issued every two weeks since 1934. The annual *Representative American Speeches* (1937–present) has excellent headnotes on the "occasion" of the speeches included; the general introductions by the editors, A. Craig Baird and Lester Thonssen, provide useful guidelines for reading speeches. The New York *Times* often carries significant addresses, and since it is indexed from early in the century, particular speeches can be located quickly. The *Congressional Record* appears more formidable than it is; selective reading can be both illuminating and entertaining, especially when major issues are debated by major figures. Particular speakers and issues can be located in the indexes.

SECONDARY MATERIAL

Some of the most substantial analyses of major American speakers in a variety of fields may be found in *American Public Speakers: Studies in Honor of Albert Craig Baird,* edited by Loren Reid (Columbia: University of Missouri Press, 1961) and in the Speech Association of America's *A History and Criticism of American Public Address,* Vols. 1 and 2 edited by William Norwood Brigance and Vol. 3 edited by Marie Hochmuth (New York: Russell & Russell, 1943, 1954). Reinhard Luthin's *American Demagogues: Twentieth Century* (Gloucester, Mass.: Peter Smith, 1959) and Charles W. Lomas' *The Agitator in American Society* (Englewood Cliffs, N.J.: Prentice-Hall, 1968) are both stimulating accounts of a kind of underworld. Further exploration of particular speakers and speeches may

be guided by *Rhetoric and Public Address: A Bibliography, 1947–1961,*
edited by James W. Cleary and Frederick W. Haberman (Madison: University of Wisconsin Press, 1964) and by the annual bibliographies in the
August issue of *Speech Monographs.*

For the systematic student of speech analysis, two paperbacks could
serve as brief introductions: Robert Cathcart's *Post Communication: Criticism and Evaluation* (Indianapolis: Bobbs-Merrill, 1966) and Anthony
Hillbrunner's *Critical Dimensions: The Art of Public Address Criticism*
(New York: Random House, 1966).

TEXTS

WILLIAM JENNINGS BRYAN

(1860–1925)

Naboth's Vineyard

1898

Bryan was a significant force in American politics for thirty years largely because of his sensitivity to the people's needs and because of his speaking ability. Not an original or logical thinker, he could, however, synthesize and express common ideas and present them sincerely and passionately. Believing that "persuasive speech is from heart to heart, not from mind to mind," he rarely developed extended arguments so much as made forceful assertions. Later generations may find his earnestness and simplistic view of intricate problems easy enough to mock, but, by doing so, we may be revealing our naiveté rather than our sophistication. A man who in the rough and tumble of national politics could regularly enthrall crowds of over fifteen thousand and win his party's presidential nomination three times must be listened to.

Some of Bryan's finest speeches were against America's involvement with the Philippines. He, Carl Schurz, and Bourke Cochran were leading spokesmen against the imperialism voiced by Beveridge, Lodge, and Roosevelt. For two or three years, these speakers heatedly attacked and refuted as they tried to define the nature of America's "destiny." "Naboth's Vineyard," one of Bryan's earliest challenges to colonialism, is very short but still typical in thought and presentation; he draws on the "god terms" of "freedom" and "liberty" and involves them with biblical morality to produce what could as well be called a sermon as a political speech.

OTHER IMPORTANT SPEECHES: "The Cross of Gold" (1896), "The Republic That Never Retreats" (1899), "America's Mission" (1899), "Imperialism" (1900), and Scopes Trial (1925).

TEXT SOURCE: William Jennings Bryan, *Speeches of William Jennings Bryan* (New York: Funk & Wagnalls, 1909), I, 6–8.

DISCOGRAPHY: Caedmon Record, TC 2031; playing time, 5:56.

11

The Bible tells us that Ahab, the king, wanted the vineyard of Naboth and was sorely grieved because the owner thereof refused to part with the inheritance of his fathers. Then followed a plot, and false charges were preferred against Naboth to furnish an excuse for getting rid of him.

"Thou shalt not covet!" "Thou shalt not bear false witness!" "Thou shalt not kill"—three commandments broken, and still a fourth, "Thou shalt not steal," to be broken in order to get a little piece of ground! And what was the result? When the king went forth to take possession, Elijah, that brave old prophet of the early days, met him and pronounced against him the sentence of the Almighty. "In the place where the dogs licked the blood of Naboth shall the dogs lick thy blood, even thine."

Neither his own exalted position nor the lowly station of his victim could save him from the avenging hand of outraged justice. His case was tried in a court where neither wealth, nor rank, nor power, could shield the transgressor.

Wars of conquest have their origin in covetousness, and the history of the human race has been written in characters of blood because rulers have looked with longing eyes upon the lands of others.

Covetousness is prone to seek the aid of false pretense to carry out its plans, but what it cannot secure by persuasion it takes by the sword.

Senator Teller's amendment to the intervention resolution saved the Cubans from the covetousness of those who are so anxious to secure possession of the island, that they are willing to deny the truth of the declaration of our own Congress, that "the people of Cuba are, and of right ought to be, free."

Imperialism might expand the nation's territory, but it would contract the nation's purpose. It is not a step forward toward a broader destiny; it is a step backward, toward the narrow views of kings and emperors.

Dr. Taylor has aptly exprest it in his "Creed of the Flag," when he asks:

> Shall we turn to the old world again
> With the penitent prodigal's cry?

I answer, never. This republic is not a prodigal son; it has not spent its substance in riotous living. It is not ready to retrace its steps and, with shamed face and trembling voice, solicit an humble place among the servants of royalty. It has not sinned against heaven, and God grant that the crowned heads of Europe may never have occasion to kill the fatted calf to commemorate its return from reliance upon the will of the people to dependence upon the authority which flows from regal birth or superior force.

We cannot afford to enter upon a colonial policy. The theory upon which a government is built is a matter of vital importance. The national idea has a controlling influence upon the thought and character of the people. Our national idea is self-government, and unless we are ready to abandon that idea forever we cannot ignore it in dealing with the Filipinos.

That idea is entwined with our traditions; it permeates our history; it is a part of our literature.

That idea has given eloquence to the orator and inspiration to the poet. Take from our national hymns the three words, free, freedom, and liberty, and they would be as meaningless as would be our flag if robbed of its red, white, and blue.

Other nations may dream of wars of conquest and of distant dependencies governed by external force; not so with the United States.

The fruits of imperialism, be they bitter or sweet, must be left to the subjects of monarchy. This is one tree of which the citizens of a republic may not partake. It is the voice of the serpent, not the voice of God, that bids us eat.

ALBERT
JEREMIAH
BEVERIDGE
(1862–1927)

The March
of the Flag
September 16, 1898

Beveridge was the most forceful and committed spokesman for America's "destiny" in the critical debates on imperialism. Convinced, even as a schoolboy, that oratory was the key to success, he practiced public speaking constantly and won many oratorical contests in college while taking a very active part in national politics. As the new senator from Indiana (1899–1905), he electrified his audience in a brilliant and solid maiden speech, "The Philippine Question" (1900), for which he had diligently prepared by six months' research in the islands. He remained very active in national politics almost until his death without gaining another major office, largely because of his uncertain party allegiance.

"The March of the Flag," with which he opened the Indiana Republican Convention of 1898, is a far more skillful and complicated speech than it first appears. It is obviously a speech of intense commitment, one filled with personal, national, and racial pride. Beveridge egotistically gloried in what he saw as America's God-given right and duty to take a place in international trade and so to bring liberty, peace, and "civilization" to the Philippines. His is not the quietly, even reluctantly, stated international position of a Wilson or a Truman. There is not the manly firmness or the cautious optimism of Kennedy's Inaugural Address. He presents his views dramatically by tracing America's "inevitable" westward expansion, raising the synecdoche of "the march of the flag" as a leitmotif.

But Beveridge's emotional flag-waving and his self-indulgence in stylistic effects, his occasional straining after parallelisms, balanced sentences, and antitheses, should not mislead us. Throughout the speech he is carefully building his own position through analogies with past and present history, while concurrently refuting his opponents by pressing their alternatives to the necessary and questionable conclusions. He is logically, as well as emotionally, calling America to what he believes to be its national and moral duty.

14

OTHER IMPORTANT SPEECHES: "Our Philippine Policy" (1900) and "The Star of Empire" (1900).
TEXT SOURCE: Albert J. Beveridge, *The Meaning of the Times and Other Speeches* (Indianapolis: Bobbs-Merrill, 1908), pp. 47–57.
DISCOGRAPHY: Caedmon Record, TC 2031; playing time, 21:24.

It is a noble land that God has given us; a land that can feed and clothe the world; a land whose coastlines would inclose half the countries of Europe; a land set like a sentinel between the two imperial oceans of the globe, a greater England with a nobler destiny.

It is a mighty people that He has planted on this soil; a people sprung from the most masterful blood of history; a people perpetually revitalized by the virile, man-producing working-folk of all the earth; a people imperial by virtue of their power, by right of their institutions, by authority of their Heaven-directed purposes—the propagandists and not the misers of liberty.   10

It is a glorious history our God has bestowed upon His chosen people; a history heroic with faith in our mission and our future; a history of statesmen who flung the boundaries of the Republic out into unexplored lands and savage wilderness; a history of soldiers who carried the flag across blazing deserts and through the ranks of hostile mountains, even to the gates of sunset; a history of a multiplying people who overran a continent in half a century; a history of prophets who saw the consequences of evils inherited from the past and of martyrs who died to save us from them; a history divinely logical, in the process of whose tremendous reasoning we find ourselves to-day.   20

Therefore, in this campaign, the question is larger than a party question. It is an American question. It is a world question. Shall the American people continue their march toward the commercial supremacy of the world? Shall free institutions broaden their blessed reign as the children of liberty wax in strength, until the empire of our principles is established over the hearts of all mankind?

Have we no mission to perform, no duty to discharge to our fellow-man? Has God endowed us with gifts beyond our deserts and marked us as the people of His peculiar favor, merely to rot in our own selfishness, as men and nations must, who take cowardice for their companion and   30
self for their deity—as China has, as India has, as Egypt has?

Shall we be as the man who had one talent and hid it, or as he who had ten talents and used them until they grew to riches? And shall we reap the reward that waits on our discharge of our high duty; shall we occupy new markets for what our farmers raise, our factories make, our merchants sell—aye, and, please God, new markets for what our ships shall carry?

Hawaii is ours; Porto Rico is to be ours; at the prayer of her people Cuba finally will be ours; in the islands of the East, even to the gates of

Asia, coaling stations are to be ours at the very least; the flag of a liberal government is to float over the Philippines, and may it be the banner that Taylor unfurled in Texas and Frémont carried to the coast.

The Opposition tells us that we ought not to govern a people without their consent. I answer, The rule of liberty that all just government derives its authority from the consent of the governed, applies only to those who are capable of self-government. We govern the Indians without their consent, we govern our territories without their consent, we govern our children without their consent. How do they know that our government would be without their consent? Would not the people of the Philippines prefer the just, humane, civilizing government of this Republic to the savage, bloody rule of pillage and extortion from which we have rescued them?

And, regardless of this formula of words made only for enlightened, self-governing people, do we owe no duty to the world? Shall we turn these peoples back to the reeking hands from which we have taken them? Shall we abandon them, with Germany, England, Japan, hungering for them? Shall we save them from those nations, to give them a self-rule of tragedy?

They ask us how we shall govern these new possessions. I answer: Out of local conditions and the necessities of the case methods of government will grow. If England can govern foreign lands, so can America. If Germany can govern foreign lands, so can America. If they can supervise protectorates, so can America. Why is it more difficult to administer Hawaii than New Mexico or California? Both had a savage and an alien population; both were more remote from the seat of government when they came under our dominion than the Philippines are to-day.

Will you say by your vote that American ability to govern has decayed; that a century's experience in self-rule has failed of a result? Will you affirm by your vote that you are an infidel to American power and practical sense? Or will you say that ours is the blood of government; ours the heart of dominion; ours the brain and genius of administration? Will you remember that we do but what our fathers did—we but pitch the tents of liberty farther westward, farther southward—we only continue the march of the flag?

The march of the flag! In 1789 the flag of the Republic waved over 4,000,000 souls in thirteen states, and their savage territory which stretched to the Mississippi, to Canada, to the Floridas. The timid minds of that day said that no new territory was needed, and, for the hour, they were right. But Jefferson, through whose intellect the centuries marched; Jefferson, who dreamed of Cuba as an American state; Jefferson, the first Imperialist of the Republic—Jefferson acquired that imperial territory which swept from the Mississippi to the mountains, from Texas to the British possessions, and the march of the flag began!

The infidels to the gospel of liberty raved, but the flag swept on! The title to the noble land out of which Oregon, Washington, Idaho and Montana have been carved was uncertain; Jefferson, strict constructionist of constitutional power though he was, obeyed the Anglo-Saxon impulse within him, whose watchword then and whose watchword throughout the world to-day is, "Forward!"; another empire was added to the Republic, and the march of the flag went on!

Those who deny the power of free institutions to expand urged every argument, and more, that we hear, to-day; but the people's judgment approved the command of their blood, and the march of the flag went on! 10

A screen of land from New Orleans to Florida shut us from the Gulf, and over this and the Everglade Peninsula waved the saffron flag of Spain; Andrew Jackson seized both, the American people stood at his back, and, under Monroe, the Floridas came under the dominion of the Republic, and the march of the flag went on! The Cassandras prophesied every prophecy of despair we hear, to-day, but the march of the flag went on.

Then Texas responded to the bugle calls of liberty, and the march of the flag went on! And, at last, we waged war with Mexico, and the flag swept over the southwest, over peerless California, past the Gates of Gold to Oregon on the north, and from ocean to ocean its folds of glory blazed. 20

And, now, obeying the same voice that Jefferson heard and obeyed, that Jackson heard and obeyed, that Grant heard and obeyed, that Harrison heard and obeyed, our President to-day plants the flag over the islands of the seas, outposts of commerce, citadels of national security, and the march of the flag goes on!

Distance and oceans are no arguments. The fact that all the territory our fathers bought and seized is contiguous, is no argument. In 1819 Florida was farther from New York than Porto Rico is from Chicago to-day; Texas, farther from Washington in 1845 than Hawaii is from Boston in 1898; California, more inaccessible in 1847 than the Philippines are now. 30 Gibraltar is farther from London than Havana is from Washington; Melbourne is farther from Liverpool than Manila is from San Francisco.

The ocean does not separate us from lands of our duty and desire—the oceans join us, rivers never to be dredged, canals never to be repaired. Steam joins us; electricity joins us—the very elements are in league with our destiny. Cuba not contiguous! Porto Rico not contiguous! Hawaii and the Philippines not contiguous! The oceans make them contiguous. And our navy will make them contiguous.

But the Opposition is right—there is a difference. We did not need the western Mississippi Valley when we acquired it, nor Florida, nor 40 Texas, nor California, nor the royal provinces of the far northwest. We had no emigrants to people this imperial wilderness, no money to develop it, even no highways to cover it. No trade awaited us in its savage fast-

nesses. Our productions were not greater than our trade. There was not
one reason for the land-lust of our statesmen from Jefferson to Grant,
other than the prophet and the Saxon within them. But, to-day, we are
raising more than we can consume, making more than we can use. Therefore we must find new markets for our produce.

And so, while we did not need the territory taken during the past century at the time it was acquired, we do need what we have taken in 1898,
and we need it now. The resources and the commerce of these immensely
rich dominions will be increased as much as American energy is greater
10   than Spanish sloth. In Cuba, alone, there are 15,000,000 acres of forest
unacquainted with the ax, exhaustless mines of iron, priceless deposits of
manganese, millions of dollars' worth of which we must buy, today, from
the Black Sea districts. There are millions of acres yet unexplored.

The resources of Porto Rico have only been trifled with. The riches
of the Philippines have hardly been touched by the finger-tips of modern
methods. And they produce what we consume, and consume what we produce—the very predestination of reciprocity—a reciprocity "not made with
hands, eternal in the heavens." They sell hemp, sugar, coconuts, fruits of
the tropics, timber of price like mahogany; they buy flour, clothing, tools,
20   implements, machinery and all that we can raise and make. Their trade
will be ours in time. Do you indorse that policy with your vote?

Cuba is as large as Pennsylvania, and is the richest spot on the globe.
Hawaii is as large as New Jersey; Porto Rico half as large as Hawaii; the
Philippines larger than all New England, New York, New Jersey and Dela-
ware combined. Together they are larger than the British Isles, larger than
France, larger than Germany, larger than Japan.

If any man tells you that trade depends on cheapness and not on government influence, ask him why England does not abandon South Africa,
Egypt, India. Why does France seize South China, Germany the vast
30   region whose port is Kaouchou?

Our trade with Porto Rico, Hawaii and the Philippines must be as
free as between the states of the Union, because they are American territory, while every other nation on earth must pay our tariff before they can
compete with us. Until Cuba shall ask for annexation, our trade with her
will, at the very least, be like the preferential trade of Canada with England. That, and the excellence of our goods and products; that, and the
convenience of traffic; that, and the kinship of interests and destiny, will
give the monopoly of these markets to the American people.

The commercial supremacy of the Republic means that this Nation is
40   to be the sovereign factor in the peace of the world. For the conflicts of
the future are to be conflicts of trade—struggles for markets—commercial
wars for existence. And the golden rule of peace is impregnability of position and invincibility of preparedness. So, we see England, the greatest

strategist of history, plant her flag and her cannon on Gibraltar, at
Quebec, in the Bermudas, at Vancouver, everywhere.

So Hawaii furnishes us a naval base in the heart of the Pacific; the
Ladrones another, a voyage further on; Manila another, at the gates of
Asia—Asia, to the trade of whose hundreds of millions American mer-
chants, manufacturers, farmers, have as good right as those of Germany or
France or Russia or England; Asia, whose commerce with the United
Kingdom alone amounts to hundreds of millions of dollars every year;
Asia, to whom Germany looks to take her surplus products; Asia, whose
doors must not be shut against American trade. Within five decades the   10
bulk of Oriental commerce will be ours.

No wonder that, in the shadows of coming events so great, free-silver
is already a memory. The current of history has swept past that episode.
Men understand, to-day, that the greatest commerce of the world must be
conducted with the steadiest standard of value and most convenient
medium of exchange human ingenuity can devise. Time, that unerring rea-
soner, has settled the silver question. The American people are tired of
talking about money—they want to make it. Why should the farmer get a
half-measure dollar of money any more than that he should give a half-
measure bushel of grain?   20

Why should not the proposition for the free coinage of silver be as
dead as the proposition of irredeemable paper money? It is the same proposition in a different form. If the Government stamp can make a piece of
silver, which you can buy for 45 cents, pass for 100 cents, the Government
stamp can make a piece of pewter, worth one cent, pass for 100 cents, and
a piece of paper, worth a fraction of a cent, pass for 100 cents. Free-silver
is the principle of fiat money applied to metal. If you favor fiat silver, you
necessarily favor fiat paper.

If the Government can make money with a stamp, why does the Government borrow money? If the Government can create value out of noth-   30
ing, why not abolish all taxation?

And if it is not the stamp of the Government that raises the value,
but the demand which free coinage creates, why has the value of silver
gone down at a time when more silver was bought and coined by the Government than ever before? Again, if the people want more silver, why do
they refuse what we already have? And if free silver makes money more
plentiful, how will *you* get any of it? Will the silver-mine owner give it to
you? Will he loan it to you? Will the Government give or loan it to you?
Where do you or I come in on this free-silver proposition?

The American people want this money question settled for ever. They   40
want a uniform currency, a convenient currency, a currency that grows as
business grows, a currency based on science and not on chance.

And now, on the threshold of our new and great career, is the time

permanently to adjust our system of finance. The American people have
the mightiest commerce of the world to conduct. They can not halt to
unsettle their money system every time some ardent imagination sees a
vision and dreams a dream. Think of Great Britain becoming the commercial monarch of the world with her financial system periodically assailed!
Think of Holland or Germany or France bearing their burdens, and, yet,
sending their flag to every sea, with their money at the mercy of politicians-
out-of-an-issue. Let us settle the whole financial system on principles so
sound that no agitation can shake it. And then, like men and not like
children, let us on to our tasks, our mission and our destiny.

There are so many real things to be done—canals to be dug, railways
to be laid, forests to be felled, cities to be builded, fields to be tilled, markets to be won, ships to be launched, peoples to be saved, civilization to be
proclaimed and the flag of liberty flung to the eager air of every sea. Is this
an hour to waste upon triflers with nature's laws? Is this a season to give
our destiny over to word-mongers and prosperity-wreckers? No! It is an
hour to remember our duty to our homes. It is a moment to realize the
opportunities fate has opened to us. And so it is an hour for us to stand
by the Government.

Wonderfully has God guided us. Yonder at Bunker Hill and Yorktown
His providence was above us. At New Orleans and on ensanguined seas
His hand sustained us. Abraham Lincoln was His minister and His was the
altar of freedom the Nation's soldiers set up on a hundred battle-fields.
His power directed Dewey in the East and delivered the Spanish fleet into
our hands, as He delivered the elder Armada into the hands of our English
sires two centuries ago. The American people can not use a dishonest
medium of exchange; it is ours to set the world its example of right and
honor. We can not fly from our world duties; it is ours to execute the purpose of a fate that has driven us to be greater than our small intentions.
We can not retreat from any soil where Providence has unfurled our
banner; it is ours to save that soil for liberty and civilization.

MARK TWAIN

(1835–1910)

Public Education Association

November 23, 1900

Mark Twain, the literary child of the tradition of oral storytelling, loved to "talk" in his books and later from the lecture platform. In Roughing It and Innocents Abroad especially can be found his favorite guise, or persona, as speaker—the greenhorn. Uneducated, inexperienced, imperceptive, and certainly not dangerous to anyone but himself, the greenhorn accepts any subject, any occasion, and any audience—and talks. Twain seems to be deliberately reducing his ethos as a speaker, but the ultimate control and the style reveal the good sense. He is the clown on the tightrope. Superficially he is the incompetent attempting to imitate the heroic acrobat and failing ingloriously: he has no grace, no poise, no dignity. He is about to collapse because of his own presumption, and so we laugh. But slowly we realize that he is not failing, that he continues to be on the wire, that in his own chaotic way he is mastering chaos.

Twain's little talk is touched with mockery of self and praise for his audience and their goals. It is as circular in its form as a graceful essay, returning quietly to the beginning and pretending to have gone nowhere. The middle third must be called a digression. But he knits with great skill his major theme of the importance of education to this concern with the Boxer Rebellion, so much an international affair that summer, and with the general problem of a nation's right to self-determination. The section could easily get too intense, but his light phrasing keeps the argument penetrating (his nimble definition of a patriot) without his becoming combative. In a key very different from speakers more "respectable," he offers equally significant moral, political, and economic points.

21

OTHER IMPORTANT SPEECHES: "Whittier Birthday Speech" (1877) and "Seven-
tieth Birthday Speech" (1905).
TEXT SOURCE: Samuel Langhorne Clemens [Mark Twain], *Mark Twain's
Speeches*, Introduction by William Dean Howells (New York: Harper &
Brothers, 1910), pp. 144–46.
DISCOGRAPHY: Caedmon Record, TC 2031; playing time, 3:45.

I don't suppose that I am called here as an expert on education, for that
would show a lack of foresight on your part and a deliberate intention to
remind me of my shortcomings.

As I sat here looking around for an idea it struck me that I was called
for two reasons. One was to do good to me, a poor unfortunate traveller on
the world's wide ocean, by giving me a knowledge of the nature and scope
of your society and letting me know that others beside myself have been of
some use in the world. The other reason that I can see is that you have
called me to show by way of contrast what education can accomplish if
10   administered in the right sort of doses.

Your worthy president said that the school pictures, which have
received the admiration of the world at the Paris Exposition, have been
sent to Russia, and this was a compliment from the Government—which
is very surprising to me. Why, it is only an hour since I read a cablegram
in the newspapers beginning "Russia Proposes to Retrench." I was not
expecting such a thunderbolt, and I thought what a happy thing it will be
for Russians when the retrenchment will bring home the thirty thousand
Russian troops now in Manchuria, to live in peaceful pursuits. I thought
this was what Germany should do also without delay, and that France and
20   all the other nations in China should follow suit.

Why should not China be free from the foreigners, who are only
making trouble on her soil? If they would only all go home, what a pleasant place China would be for the Chinese! We do not allow Chinamen to
come here, and I say in all seriousness that it would be a graceful thing to
let China decide who shall go there.

China never wanted foreigners any more than foreigners wanted Chinamen, and on this question I am with the Boxers every time. The Boxer
is a patriot. He loves his country better than he does the countries of other
people. I wish him success. The Boxer believes in driving us out of his
30   country. I am a Boxer too, for I believe in driving him out of our country.

When I read the Russian dispatch further my dream of world peace
vanished. It said that the vast expense of maintaining the army had made

it necessary to retrench, and so the Government had decided that to support the army it would be necessary to withdraw the appropriation from the public schools. This is a monstrous idea to us. We believe that out of the public school grows the greatness of a nation.

It is curious to reflect how history repeats itself the world over. Why, I remember the same thing was done when I was a boy on the Mississippi River. There was a proposition in a township there to discontinue public schools because they were too expensive. An old farmer spoke up and said if they stopped the schools they would not save anything, because every time a school was closed a jail had to be built.

10

It's like feeding a dog on his own tail. He'll never get fat. I believe it is better to support schools than jails.

The work of your association is better and shows more wisdom than the Czar of Russia and all his people. This is not much of a compliment, but it's the best I've got in stock.

THEODORE
ROOSEVELT

(1858–1919)

The Man with the Muck-rake

April 14, 1906

Most historians consider Theodore Roosevelt's dominant characteristic to have been his compulsion to polarize problems in moral terms: one side was good, the other evil. He saw American wars as ones of "righteousness," the manly energy of the good smiting the ultimately weak evil. To love or desire peace was no virtue; one had to fight for it. Owen Wister called him "the preacher militant," and throughout his speeches he demands that Americans be dutiful, honest, and honorable, be both physically and morally robust. The worldly good of the country could follow from the energies of good men. In an 1899 speech he said, "The doctrine that I preach . . . is a doctrine that teaches us that men shall prosper as long as they do their duty to themselves and their neighbors alike."

The carefully prepared "The Man with the Muck-rake" speech illustrates well Roosevelt's qualities, attitudes, and speechmaking. His call is for honesty, sanity, and broad human sympathy in all men. Although he discusses the function of the national government, the relation of wealth to the common good, and especially the responsibility of the press, all these points are but loosely focused on his hope for unity of all classes under a moral code. He urges a philosophy of life; he does not attempt to argue a program of economic or political reform.

OTHER IMPORTANT SPEECHES: "The Strenuous Life" (1899) and "Madison Square Garden" (1912).

TEXT SOURCE: *The Works of Theodore Roosevelt: National Edition* (New York: Charles Scribner's Sons, 1926), XVI, 415–24.

DISCOGRAPHY: Caedmon Record, TC 2031; playing time, 26:55.

Over a century ago Washington laid the corner-stone of the Capitol in what was then little more than a tract of wooded wilderness here beside the Potomac. We now find it necessary to provide great additional buildings for the business of the government. This growth in the need for the housing of the government is but a proof and example of the way in which the nation has grown and the sphere of action of the National Government has grown. We now administer the affairs of a nation in which the extraordinary growth of population has been outstripped by the growth of wealth and the growth in complex interests. The material problems that face us to-day are not such as they were in Washington's time, but the underlying facts of human nature are the same now as they were then. Under altered external form we war with the same tendencies toward evil that were evident in Washington's time, and are helped by the same tendencies for good. It is about some of these that I wish to say a word   10 to-day.

In Bunyan's "Pilgrim's Progress" you may recall the description of the Man with the Muck-rake, the man who could look no way but downward, with the muck-rake in his hand; who was offered a celestial crown for his muck-rake, but who would neither look up nor regard the crown he was offered, but continued to rake to himself the filth of the floor.

In "Pilgrim's Progress" the Man with the Muck-rake is set forth as the example of him whose vision is fixed on carnal instead of on spiritual things. Yet he also typifies the man who in this life consistently refuses to see aught that is lofty, and fixes his eyes with solemn intentness only on   20 that which is vile and debasing. Now, it is very necessary that we should not flinch from seeing what is vile and debasing. There is filth on the floor and it must be scraped up with the muck-rake; and there are times and places where this service is the most needed of all the services that can be performed. But the man who never does anything else, who never thinks or speaks or writes, save of his feats with the muck-rake, speedily becomes, not a help to society, not an incitement to good, but one of the most potent forces for evil.

There are, in the body politic, economic and social, many and grave evils, and there is urgent necessity for the sternest war upon them. There   30 should be relentless exposure of and attack upon every evil man whether politician or business man, every evil practice, whether in politics, in business, or in social life. I hail as a benefactor every writer or speaker, every man who, on the platform, or in book, magazine, or newspaper, with merciless severity makes such attack, provided always that he in his turn remembers that the attack is of use only if it is absolutely truthful. The liar is no whit better than the thief, and if his mendacity takes the form of slander, he may be worse than most thieves. It puts a premium upon knavery untruthfully to attack an honest man, or even with hysterical exaggeration to assail a bad man with untruth. An epidemic of indiscriminate   40 assault upon character does not good, but very great harm. The soul of every scoundrel is gladdened whenever an honest man is assailed, or even when a scoundrel is untruthfully assailed.

Now, it is easy to twist out of shape what I have just said, easy to affect to misunderstand it, and, if it is slurred over in repetition, not difficult really to misunderstand it. Some persons are sincerely incapable of understanding that to denounce mud-slinging does not mean the indorse-ment of whitewashing; and both the interested individuals who need whitewashing, and those others who practice mud-slinging, like to encour-age such confusion of ideas. One of the chief counts against those who make indiscriminate assault upon men in business or men in public life, is that they invite a reaction which is sure to tell powerfully in favor of the unscrupulous scoundrel who really ought to be attacked, who ought to be exposed, who ought, if possible, to be put in the penitentiary. If Aristides is praised overmuch as just, people get tired of hearing it; and overcensure of the unjust finally and from similar reasons results in their favor.

Any excess is almost sure to invite a reaction; and, unfortunately, the reaction, instead of taking the form of punishment of those guilty of the excess, is very apt to take the form either of punishment of the unoffend-ing or of giving immunity, and even strength, to offenders. The effort to make financial or political profit out of the destruction of character can only result in public calamity. Gross and reckless assaults on character, whether on the stump or in newspaper, magazine, or book, create a morbid and vicious public sentiment, and at the same time act as a profound deterrent to able men of normal sensitiveness and tend to prevent them from entering the public service at any price. As an instance in point, I may mention that one serious difficulty encountered in getting the right type of men to dig the Panama Canal is the certainty that they will be exposed, both without, and, I am sorry to say, sometimes within, Congress, to utterly reckless assaults on their character and capacity.

At the risk of repetition let me say again that my plea is, not for immunity to but for the most unsparing exposure of the politician who betrays his trust, of the big business man who makes or spends his fortune in illegitimate or corrupt ways. There should be a resolute effort to hunt every such man out of the position he has disgraced. Expose the crime, and hunt down the criminal; but remember that even in the case of crime, if it is attacked in sensational, lurid, and untruthful fashion, the attack may do more damage to the public mind than the crime itself. It is because I feel that there should be no rest in the endless war against the forces of evil that I ask that the war be conducted with sanity as well as with resolution. The men with the muck-rakes are often indispensable to the well-being of society; but only if they know when to stop raking the muck, and to look upward to the celestial crown above them, to the crown of worthy endeavor. There are beautiful things above and roundabout them; and if they gradually grow to feel that the whole world is nothing but muck, their power of usefulness is gone. If the whole picture is painted black there remains no hue whereby to single out the rascals for distinction from their fellows. Such painting finally induces a kind of moral color-blindness; and people affected by it come to the conclusion that no man is really black, and no man really white, but they are all gray. In other words, they neither believe in the truth of the attack, nor in the honesty of the man who is attacked; they grow as suspicious of the accusation as of the offense; it becomes well-nigh hopeless to stir them either to wrath against wrong-doing or to enthusiasm for what is right; and such a mental attitude in the public gives hope to every knave, and is the despair of honest men.

To assail the great and admitted evils of our political and industrial life with such crude and sweeping generalizations as to include decent men in the general condemnation means the searing of the public conscience. There results a general attitude either of cynical belief in and indifference to public corruption or else of a distrustful inability to discriminate between the good and the bad. Either attitude is fraught with untold damage to the country as a whole. The fool who has not sense to discriminate between what is good and what is bad is well-nigh as dangerous as the man who does discriminate and yet chooses the bad. There is nothing more distressing to every good patriot, to every good American, than the hard, scoffing spirit which treats the allegation of dishonesty in a public man as a cause for laughter. Such laughter is worse than the crackling of thorns under a pot, for it denotes not merely the vacant mind, but the heart in which high emotions have been choked before they could grow to fruition.

There is any amount of good in the world, and there never was a time when loftier and more disinterested work for the betterment of mankind was being done than now. The forces that tend for evil are great and terrible, but the forces of truth and love and courage and honesty and generosity and sympathy are also stronger than ever before. It is a foolish and timid, no less than a wicked, thing to blink the fact that the forces of evil are strong, but it is even worse to fail to take into account the strength of the forces that tell for good. Hysterical sensationalism is the very poorest weapon wherewith to fight for lasting righteousness. The men who with stern sobriety and truth assail the many evils of our time, whether in the public press, or in magazines, or in books, are the leaders and allies of all engaged in the work for social and political betterment. But if they give good reason for distrust of what they say, if they chill the ardor of those who demand truth as a primary virtue, they thereby betray the good cause, and play into the hands of the very men against whom they are nominally at war.

In his "Ecclesiastical Polity" that fine old Elizabethan divine, Bishop Hooker, wrote: "He that goeth about to persuade a multitude that they are not so well governed as they ought to be, shall never want attentive and favorable hearers; because they know the manifold defects whereunto every kind of regimen is subject, but the secret lets and difficulties, which in public proceedings are innumerable and inevitable, they have not ordinarily the judgment to consider."

This truth should be kept constantly in mind by every free people desiring to preserve the sanity and poise indispensable to the permanent success of self-government. Yet, on the other hand, it is vital not to permit this spirit of sanity and self-command to degenerate into mere mental stagnation. Bad though a state of hysterical excitement is, and evil though the results are which come from the violent oscillations such excitement invariably produces, yet a sodden acquiescence in evil is even worse. At this moment we are passing through a period of great unrest—social, political, and industrial unrest. It is of the utmost importance for our future that this should prove to be not the unrest of mere rebelliousness against life, of mere dissatisfaction with the inevitable inequality of conditions, but the unrest of a resolute and eager ambition to secure the betterment of the individual and the nation. So far as this movement of agitation throughout the country takes the form of a fierce discontent with evil, of a determination to punish the authors of evil, whether in industry or politics, the feeling is to be heartily welcomed as a sign of healthy life.

If, on the other hand, it turns into a mere crusade of appetite against appetite, of a contest between the brutal greed of the "have-nots" and the brutal greed of the "haves," then it has no significance for good, but only for evil. If it seeks to establish a line of cleavage, not along the line which divides good men from bad, but along that other line, running at right angles thereto, which divides those who are well off from those who are less well off, then it will be fraught with immeasurable harm to the body politic.

We can no more and no less afford to condone evil in the man of capital than evil in the man of no capital. The wealthy man who exults because there is a failure of justice in the effort to bring some trust magnate to an account for his misdeeds is as bad as, and no worse than, the so-called labor leader who clamourously strives to excite a foul class feeling on behalf of some other labor leader who is implicated in murder. One attitude is as bad as the other, and no worse; in each case the accused is entitled to exact justice; and in neither case is there need of action by others which can be construed into an expression of sympathy for crime.

It is a prime necessity that if the present unrest is to result in permanent good the emotion shall be translated into action, and that the action shall be marked by honesty, sanity, and self-restraint. There is mighty little good in a mere spasm of reform. The reform that counts is that which comes through steady, continuous growth; violent emotionalism leads to exhaustion.

It is important to this people to grapple with the problems connected with the amassing of enormous fortunes, and the use of those fortunes, both corporate and individual, in business. We should discriminate in the

sharpest way between fortunes well-won and fortunes ill-won; between those gained as an incident to performing great services to the community as a whole, and those gained in evil fashion by keeping just within the limits of mere law-honesty. Of course no amount of charity in spending such fortunes in any way compensates for misconduct in making them. As a matter of personal conviction, and without pretending to discuss the details or formulate the system, I feel that we shall ultimately have to consider the adoption of some such scheme as that of a progressive tax on all fortunes, beyond a certain amount either given in life or devised or bequeathed upon death to any individual—a tax so framed as to put it out   10
of the power of the owner of one of these enormous fortunes to hand on more than a certain amount to any one individual; the tax, of course, to be imposed by the National and not the State Government. Such taxation should, of course, be aimed merely at the inheritance or transmission in their entirety of those fortunes swollen beyond all healthy limits.

Again, the National Government must in some form exercise supervision over corporations engaged in interstate business—and all large corporations are engaged in interstate business—whether by license or otherwise, so as to permit us to deal with the far-reaching evils of overcapitalization. This year we are making a beginning in the direction of serious effort to   20
settle some of these economic problems by the railway-rate legislation. Such legislation, if so framed, as I am sure it will be, as to secure definite and tangible results, will amount to something of itself; and it will amount to a great deal more in so far as it is taken as a first step in the direction of a policy of superintendence and control over corporate wealth engaged in interstate commerce, this superintendence and control not to be exercised in a spirit of malevolence toward the men who have created the wealth, but with the firm purpose both to do justice to them and to see that they in their turn do justice to the public at large.

The first requisite in the public servants who are to deal in this shape   30
with corporations, whether as legislators or as executives, is honesty. This honesty can be no respecter of persons. There can be no such thing as unilateral honesty. The danger is not really from corrupt corporations; it springs from the corruption itself, whether exercised for or against corporations.

The eighth commandment reads: "Thou shalt not steal." It does not read: "Thou shalt not steal from the rich man." It does not read: "Thou shalt not steal from the poor man." It reads simply and plainly: "Thou shalt not steal." No good whatever will come from that warped and mock morality which denounces the misdeeds of men of wealth and forgets the   40
misdeeds practiced at their expense; which denounces bribery, but blinds itself to blackmail; which foams with rage if a corporation secures favors by improper methods, and merely leers with hideous mirth if the corporation is itself wronged. The only public servant who can be trusted honestly

to protect the rights of the public against the misdeed of a corporation is that public man who will just as surely protect the corporation itself from wrongful aggression. If a public man is willing to yield to popular clamor and do wrong to the men of wealth or to rich corporations, it may be set down as certain that if the opportunity comes he will secretly and furtively do wrong to the public in the interest of a corporation.

But, in addition to honesty, we need sanity. No honesty will make a public man useful if that man is timid or foolish, if he is a hot-headed zealot or an impracticable visionary. As we strive for reform we find that it is not at all merely the case of a long up-hill pull. On the contrary, there is almost as much of breeching work as of collar work; to depend only on traces means that there will soon be a runaway and an upset. The men of wealth who to-day are trying to prevent the regulation and control of their business in the interest of the public by the proper government authorities will not succeed, in my judgment, in checking the progress of the movement. But if they did succeed they would find that they had sown the wind and would surely reap the whirlwind, for they would ultimately provoke the violent excesses which accompany a reform coming by convulsion instead of by steady and natural growth.

On the other hand, the wild preachers of unrest and discontent, the wild agitators against the entire existing order, the men who act crookedly, whether because of sinister design or from mere puzzle-headedness, the men who preach destruction without proposing any substitute for what they intend to destroy, or who propose a substitute which would be far worse than the existing evils—all these men are the most dangerous opponents of real reform. If they get their way they will lead the people into a deeper pit than any into which they could fall under the present system. If they fail to get their way they will still do incalculable harm by provoking the kind of reaction which, in its revolt against the senseless evil of their teaching, would enthrone more securely than ever the very evils which their misguided followers believe they are attacking.

More important than aught else is the development of the broadest sympathy of man for man. The welfare of the wage-worker, the welfare of the tiller of the soil, upon these depend the welfare of the entire country; their good is not to be sought in pulling down others; but their good must be the prime object of all our statesmanship.

Materially we must strive to secure a broader economic opportunity for all men, so that each shall have a better chance to show the stuff of which he is made. Spiritually and ethically we must strive to bring about clean living and right thinking. We appreciate also that the things of the soul are immeasurably more important. The foundation-stone of national life is, and ever must be, the high individual character of the average citizen.

CLARENCE SEWARD DARROW

(1857–1938)

To the Jury: Self-defense

August 14–15, 1912

Clarence Darrow is undoubtedly the best-known trial lawyer in American history. It is estimated that he was active in over two thousand trials, many of which dramatically reflected major social and philosophical issues in a changing America. A brilliant impromptu courtroom pleader, he varied his speeches by massing evidence, by portraying the lives and plights of the accused, and, most important, by arguing broad issues of labor and management, science and religion, determinism and free will. His strong, frank language and his obviously sincere involvement were revealed whether he defended Debs, Loeb and Leopold, or Scopes—or himself. His summations were long—eleven hours in the Haywood case—and always based on a single principle: "Jurymen seldom convict a person they like, or acquit one they dislike. The main work of a trial lawyer is to make a jury like or, at least, to feel sympathy for him. Facts regarding the crime are relatively unimportant. I try to get a jury with little education but much human sympathy."

Darrow's "To the Jury: Self-defense" is the closing section of his trial for bribery in the earlier McNamara case. Worn out before the trial started, Darrow nevertheless fought his way through ninety days in the summer's heat and defended his honor. Using no notes, he spoke for a day and a half, summarizing his life and thought as well as the case itself. Throughout one can hear the thread of his belief in determinism.

Given the general principle that the jury must sympathize with the accused, Darrow is more emotional than logical. He is trying to reveal a person more than a case. He has already finished with his logical arguments—three months of evidence and cross-examination—and is now attempting to move the jury to action. Many of the two thousand in the packed courtroom wept openly, as did Darrow himself, and he was acquitted in twenty minutes.

31

OTHER IMPORTANT SPEECHES: Haywood Trial (1907), Leopold-Loeb Trial (1924), and Scopes Trial (1925).

TEXT SOURCE: Clarence Darrow, *The Darrow Bribery Trial*, edited by Patrick H. Ford (Whittier, Calif.: Western Printing Co., 1956), pp. 57–60. Courtesy of William G. Sharp, Clerk of the Superior Court, County of Los Angeles.

DISCOGRAPHY: Caedmon Record, TC 2031; playing time, 12:07.

I have been a busy man. I have never had to look for clients, they have come to me. I have been a general attorney of a big railroad. I have been the attorney several different times, and general counsel, as it were, of the great City of Chicago. I have represented the strong and the weak—but never the strong against the weak. I have been called into a great many cases for labor unions. I have been called into a great many arbitration cases. I believe if you went to my native town, that the rich would tell you that they could trust not only my honor, but my judgment, and my sense of justice and fairness. More than once have they left their disputes with the laboring men with me to settle and I have settled them as justly as I could, without giving the working man as much as he ought to have. It will be many and many a long year before he will get all he ought to have. That must be reached step by step. But every step means more in the progress of the world.

This McNamara case came like a thunderclap upon the world. What was it? A building had been destroyed, and twenty lives had been lost. It shocked the world. Whether it was destroyed by accident or violence no one knew, and yet everyone had an opinion. How did they form that opinion? Everybody who sympathized with the corporations believed it was dynamite. Everyone who sympathized with the workingman believed it was something else. All had opinions. Society was in open rupture. Upon the one hand all the powerful forces thought, "Now we have these men by the throat, and we will strangle them to death. Now we will reach out the strong arm of money and the strong arm of the law, and we will destroy the labor unions of America."

On the other hand were the weak, and the poor, and the workers, whom I had served; these were rallying to the defense of the unions and to the defense of their homes. They called on me. I did not want to go. I urged them to take someone else, but I had to lay aside my own preferences and take the case.

There was a direct cleavage in society. Upon the one hand, those who hated, growing fiercer and bitterer day by day. It was a class struggle, gentlemen of the jury, filled with all the venom and bitterness born of a class struggle. These two great contending armies were meeting in almost mortal combat. No one could see the end.

I have loved peace, all my life. I have taught it all my life. I believe that love does more than hatred. I believe that both sides have gone about the settlement of these difficulties in the wrong way. The acts of the one have caused the acts of the other, and I blame neither. Men are not perfect. They had an imperfect origin, and they are imperfect today, and the long struggle of the human race from darkness to comparative civilization has been filled with clash and discord and murder and war, and violence and wrong, and it will be, for years and years to come. But ever we are going onward and upward toward the sunshine, where the hatred and war and cruelty and violence of the world will disappear.

Men were arrayed here in two great forces—the rich and the poor. None could see the end. They were trying to cure hate with hate.

I know I could have tried the McNamara case, and that a large class of the working people of America would honestly have believed, if these men had been hanged, that they were not guilty. I could have done this and have saved myself. I could have made money had I done this—if I had wanted to get money in that way. I know if you had hanged these men and the other men, you would have changed the opinion of scarcely a man in America and you would have settled in the hearts of a great mass of men a hatred so deep, so profound, that it would never die away.

And I took the responsibility, gentlemen. Maybe I did wrong, but I took it, and the matter was disposed of and the questions set at rest. Here and there I got praise for what you called an heroic act, although I did not deserve the praise, for I followed the law of my being—that was all. I acted out the instincts that were within me. I acted according to the teachings of the parents who reared me, and according to the life I had lived. I did not deserve praise, but where I got one word of praise, I got a thousand words of blame! and I have stood under that for nearly a year.

This trial has helped clear up the McNamara case. It will all finally be cleared up, if not in time for me to profit by it, in time for my descendants to know. Some time we will know the truth. But I have gone on about my way as I always have regardless of this, without asking anything of anybody who lived, and I will go on that way to the end.

I know the mob. In one way I love it, in another way I despise it. I know the unreasoning, unthinking mass. I have lived with men and worked with them. I have been their idol and I have been cast down and trampled beneath their feet. I have stood on the pinnacle, and I have heard the cheering mob sound my praises. I have gone down to the depths of the valley, where I have heard them hiss my name—this same mob—but I have summoned such devotion and such courage as God has given me, and I have gone on—gone on my path unmoved by their hisses or their cheers.

I have tried to live my life and to live it as I see it, regarding neither praise nor blame, both of which are unjust. No man is judged rightly by his fellowman. Some look upon him as an idol, and forget that his feet are clay, as are the feet of every man. Others look upon him as a devil and can see no good in him at all. Neither is true. I have known this, and I have tried to follow my conscience and my duty the best I could and to do it faithfully; and here I am today in the hands of you twelve men who will one day say to your children, and they will say to their children, that you passed on my fate.

Gentlemen, there is not much more to say. You may not agree with all my views of philosophy. I believe we are all in the hands of destiny, and if it is written in the book of destiny that I shall go on to the penitentiary, that you twelve men before me shall send me there, I will go. If it is written that I am now down to the depths and that you twelve men shall liberate me, then, so it will be. We go here and there, and we think we control our destinies, and our lives, but above us and beyond us and around us, are unseen hands, and unseen forces that move us at their will.

I am here and I can look back to the forces that brought me here, and I can see that I had nothing whatever to do with it, and could not help it, any more than any of you twelve men had to do with or could help passing on my fate. There is not one of you that would have wished to judge me, unless you could do it in a way to help me in my sore distress, I know that. We have little to do with ourselves.

As one poet has expressed it,[1]

> Life is a game of whist. From unknown sources
> The cards are shuffled and the hands are dealt.
> Blind are our efforts to control the forces
> That though unseen are no less strongly felt.
> I do not like the way the cards are shuffled,
> But still I like the game and want to play
> And through the long, long night, I play unruffled
> The cards I get until the break of day.

I have taken the cards as they came. I have played the best I could. I have tried to play them honestly, manfully, doing for myself and for my fellow the best I could, and I will play the game to the end, whatever that end may be.

Gentlemen, I came to this city as a stranger. Misfortune has beset me, but I never saw a place in my life with greater warmth and kindness and love than Los Angeles. Here to a stranger have come hands to help me, hearts to beat with mine, words of sympathy to encourage and cheer, and though a stranger to you twelve men and a stranger to this city, I am will-

---

[1] Attributed to Eugene Fitch Ware ("Ironquill"), American poet (1841–1911), "Whist." [Ed.]

ing to leave my case with you. I know my life, I know what I have done. My life has not been perfect. It has been human, too human. I have felt the heart beats of every man who lived. I have tried to be the friend of every man who lived. I have tried to help in the world. I have not had malice in my heart. I have had love for my fellowman. I have done the best I could. There are some people who know it. There are some who do not believe it. There are people who regard my name as a byword and a reproach, more for the good I have done than for the evil.

There are people who would destroy me. There are people who would lift up their hands to crush me down. I have enemies powerful and strong. 10 There are honest men who misunderstand me and doubt me; and still I have lived a long time on earth, and I have friends—I have friends in my old home who have gathered around to tell you as best they could of the life I have lived. I have friends who have come to me here to help me in my sore distress. I have friends throughout the length and breadth of the land, and these are the poor and the weak and the helpless, to whose cause I have given voice. If you should convict me, there will be people to applaud the act. But if in your judgment and your wisdom and your human- ity, you believe me innocent, and return a verdict of not guilty in this case, I know that from thousands and tens of thousands and yea, perhaps 20 hundreds of thousands, of the weak and the poor and the helpless through- out the world will come thanks to this jury for saving my liberty and my name.

ROBERT M. LA FOLLETTE

(1855–1925)

Soldier's Pay

September 10, 1917

Cited by a Senate committee in 1959 as one of the five outstanding senators—along with Clay, Calhoun, Webster, and Taft—La Follette aggressively served as a conscience during his twenty years (1905–1925) in the Senate. Whether "Fighting Bob" is labeled a progressive or a Progressive, there is no doubt that he, though not an original thinker, led the way to many economic and political reforms. He was perhaps the perfect example of "the loyal and enlightened opposition"; proposals he made—and saw rejected—were almost invariably adopted ten or fifteen years later whether they related to trusts or tariffs, railroads or public rights. His basic concerns were national; he was easy to caricature as a "Midwestern isolationist" and fought America's involvement in World War I, rejected the Versailles Treaty, and saw the League of Nations as a hazard.

Faced with a generally hostile press both within and without his party, he had to rely on his public speaking, his energy, and his eagerness to go personally to the people to get a hearing for his ideas. This speechmaking was no casual thing for La Follette. His biography reveals the intensity and depth to which he pursued his material. In his speeches he was prepared and willing to develop solid and pertinent arguments with a mass of statistics and examples. But he always spoke to specific audiences with the data relevant to their lives as his proof, and that audience was willing to stay with him.

Although he basically felt America should have no part in a European war, La Follette deliberated responsibly the issues once we entered World War I. He was concerned particularly with finance, and "Soldier's Pay," part of a running debate in Congress, is his support of extra pay for overseas duty. His argument here is probably as much emotional as logical and reveals openly his deep concern for the common man and his sharp distrust of the rich. Of

36

particular interest stylistically is the number of long and, I am certain, im-promptu sentences, built of modifying clauses, which dramatically suspend their meaning until the end. His closing remarks on the insertion of the roll call refer to a significant innovation—La Follette was the first to disturb the complacency of his fellow senators by regularly making each man's vote a matter of public record. (The other speakers in this section of the debate were Hardwick of Georgia and Vardaman of Mississippi.)

OTHER IMPORTANT SPEECHES: "On War Revenues: 1917" (August 21, September 1, September 3, and September 10), "Freedom of Speech in War-time" (October 6, 1917), and "Congress and the Presidency" (March 4, 1919).

TEXT SOURCE: U.S., Congress, Senate, *Congressional Record*, 65th Congress, 1st sess., 1917, 55, pt. 7: 6856–57.

DISCOGRAPHY: Caedmon Record, TC 2031; playing time, 11:20.

Mr. LA FOLLETTE. Mr. President, I want to say just a few words about that amendment, and I will be just as expeditious as I possibly can. Senators who voted for that amendment have been arraigned in this body as having done an unworthy thing. The Senator from Georgia [Mr. Hardwick], who moved that amendment, has been criticized before the Senate as seeking to create dissatisfaction among the troops to be sent to foreign shores to prosecute this war.

Mr. President, can it be possible that the Senate of the United States is to permit any other country engaged in this war against Germany to pay more money to soldiers fighting in Europe than the United States pays to her soldiers fighting in Europe? If it can be called Hessianizing the American troops to add $50 a month to the pay of soldiers who leave their homes and leave those dependent upon them for subsistence in these trying times, when the cost of living is going beyond the reach of every family of moderate income, if that is to be denounced as disloyal to the country, then, Mr. President, I beg to say that there is a standard of loyalty in this country to which the great body of the people will never subscribe.

Mr. President, it was not considered Hessianizing the troops of this country to double their pay less than a year ago when it was not expected or suggested that our soldiers were to be sent abroad. Now that they are being taken away from their families, with the cost of subsistence for those families mounting every day, now that they are ordered to a foreign country, strange to them in language and in surroundings, when there is proposed an additional pay for those soldiers in an amount that will relieve their minds of anxiety as to their families, that will make them feel that the loved ones at home under this extra pay will be reasonably taken care of, is it to be taken as a measure of wishing to create dissension and disloyalty in this country and dissension and dissatisfaction among the troops to vote for and to sustain such an amendment?

Sir, it ought to be received as an evidence of a desire to put those troops into the best fighting spirit, not solely because of the advantage which the increase in pay would be to them individually but because of what it will enable them to do for their families at home. They are the husbands of wives, they are the sons of fathers and mothers many of whom are hard pressed to live. They receive $33 as the rate now stands. They would receive $50 or more under this proposed amendment. That would bring their pay about to the level of what policemen and firemen receive in first-class cities.

Canada pays her troops $33 a month for foreign service, just as we pay $33 per month for service abroad; and on top of that Canada gives from $20 to $60, known in her law as separation allowance, for every family.

Mr. HARDWICK. Mr. President—

Mr. LA FOLLETTE. Wait just a moment. It begins at $20, ranging up, taking corporals and sergeants and lieutenants and captains and majors and lieutenant colonels, and when it reaches lieutenant colonels the separate family allowance is $60 in addition to the regular pay. Shame upon this country! Shame upon anybody who votes against giving as much to the men whom we are to send to wallow in the mire and blood of the trenches in a foreign country as Canada gives to her troops in that same service!

Mr. HARDWICK. Mr. President—

Mr. LA FOLLETTE. I will yield in just a moment. Mr. President, what makes an effective army? Freeing them from every consideration except getting at the enemy, relieving their minds of any apprehension regarding the old folks, their wives, or their little ones at home.

In God's name, is a man to be arraigned here as a traitor who would put the troops of this great country at least in something approaching as good a position as the troops of Canada? Read, Senators, the account of the battles in Europe. Who are the men who carry the flag farthest into the enemy's lines? Who are the men who are free to forget everything except that for which they are fighting? The Canadian troops. The report of every battle gives you that record. Will you not be willing to do as much for our troops?

Will it put a 10 per cent additional charge upon small incomes? No, no; this additional tax is to be raised from incomes in excess of $25,000, and we just take the additional amount of 10 per cent out of those incomes. When men with an income of $25,000, and from that up to those with incomes of from one to ten million dollars, can not give out of such incomes 10 per cent to provide this tax to put our soldiers not just on a par with Canada, but on a little better basis than Canada, Mr. President, I can not understand it. I can not understand the spirit which prevailed in the Senate when an amendment of that kind was offered here and is derided and denounced as disloyal. It seems to me that every Senator should have risen in his place and that this amendment should have been adopted by the unanimous vote of this body.

I beg pardon of the Senator from Georgia. I yield to him.

Mr. HARDWICK. I merely wish to suggest to the Senator the fact that I have discovered since the debate the other day that the State of Minnesota pays a bounty of something over $3 a day to secure enlistment of members of the National Guard at the present moment.

Mr. LA FOLLETTE. I thank the Senator.

Mr. President, I have not done with Canada. Providing a separate   10
allowance of from $20 to $60 per month is not all that Canada has done for her soldiers. In addition to that there is provided a life insurance on which the premiums are not taken out of the soldier's pay, as is proposed in this country, where fortunes are considered more precious than human life, but in Canada they provide for their enlisted men a life insurance on which the premiums are paid by the municipalities. They do not stop there. There is a Canadian Patriotic Fund.

This fund was incorporated in August, 1914, to render financial assist-ance to dependent relatives of men in active service. It is intended that this assistance shall be given to those whose income from all sources,   20
including the assigned pay and the separate allowance provided by law, is insufficient to enable the family to live according to a standard which would provide a reasonable amount of comfort. It is supported by volun-tary contributions, appropriations by some of the Provinces and grants from cities, counties, and other political subdivisions. Take the case of a Canadian private with a wife and three children: that family will receive as an assignment of a portion of the father's pay $15, from the separate allow-ance fund $20, and from the Canadian patriotic fund $25—a total of $65.

Canada did not wait to be driven to make this provision. It adopted it right at the beginning of the war. That country recognized from the start   30
its obligation to its soldiers and their dependents and it patriotically made the most liberal provision for them ever written into the law of any coun-try. It contributed in no small degree to stimulate a popular response to the call for men. The men who were responsible for that legislation in Canada were not reviled as disloyal nor accused of attempting to make the war unpopular.

Mr. President, I have not said it here, but it has been said in the course of this debate, that this war is unpopular in this country. If this great, rich country, with its incomes and war profits exceeding any country on earth, is to deal penuriously, grudgingly, stingily by its soldiers, if when   40
an amendment is offered in the interest of our soldiers who are to be sent abroad, such as that offered by the Senator from Georgia, we are to have on the floors of Congress men rise and denounce it as disloyal, as they

have denounced everything attempted throughout the consideration of this bill that sought to impose a just tax upon wealth, then I assert that if the war is unpopular you are aiding directly to make it more unpopular by that course.

Mr. VARDAMAN. I wish to remind the Senator that when the law was passed appropriating $50 a month for the support of the dependent families of the soldiers serving on the border last summer there was little or no protest against it. There might have been a few Senators who opposed it.

Mr. LA FOLLETTE. Ah, Mr. President—

Mr. VARDAMAN. If the Senator will permit me one moment, I want to say that when the measure was proposed some months ago doubling the pay of the private soldier there was little or no protest, but the difference between that question and the one before the Senate now is this: The soldier was to be paid out of money taken from the general fund, whereas he is to be paid $50 per month under the pending proposition, which money is to be derived from taxes levied upon the incomes of the rich. The people in this country with incomes of $25,000 per year are to be taxed to give this pittance to the man who offers his life for the flag in a foreign land. That is the vital difference and may probably account for the furious and unwarranted assault made by distinguished Senators upon those of us who favored the proposition a day or two ago.

Mr. LA FOLLETTE. Yes. And, Mr. President, there is one other difference. Those propositions came before the election and just before the election, and that sometimes makes a difference to Senators and to Members of the other House when they come to a vote. I regret to say that, but every man in his place here knows that that is true.

I fear the Senator from New Mexico [Mr. Jones] will think I am not keeping my word with him. I leave that matter for the present, just closing with this summary of it. Why is it regarded unpatriotic to offer an amendment to vote extra pay to the soldiers who go abroad?

I have lying on my desk an account of four suicides which have already occurred in Pershing's army since we began to land our men on the other side. I do not know, and the dispatches do not disclose, what caused those suicides, but, oh, Mr. President, with new surroundings, in a strange land, cut off from communication with everybody but their immediate comrades, the thoughts of these men turn to home; they think about the loved ones gathered around the family board and about the fireside in the evening, and the worry that comes at the end of the month in these times when they must pay the bills. Will you not do at least this much to relieve the minds of those soldier boys, of whom we are only permitted to know, that they are "Somewhere in France"?

Will you not help them to take a little better care of themselves over there by making this small addition to their pay?

Will it not enable them to allot to their dependent loved ones here who are deprived of their services a part of this extra pay to meet the excessive cost of living which war brings to their families?

Is not that a desirable provision to make for those boys—those husbands, fathers, sons 4,000 miles from home?

Will it not take a burden, an anxiety, off their minds to know that they can assign a part of that $50 every month to their families?

Is it not an exhibition of a greater regard for the surplus incomes of the overrich than for the soldiers of our country wallowing in the mire and blood of the trenches to vote against an amendment which would grant 10 those soldiers this extra $50 a month?

Now, Mr. President, I hope that I shall have a better roll call to insert in the *Record* upon the amendment offered by the Senator from Georgia [Mr. Hardwick] when the roll is called in the Senate of the United States than we had in Committee of the Whole. I prefer to insert that roll call rather than the one that was had.

WOODROW WILSON
(1856–1924)

Fourteen Points

January 8, 1918

Woodrow Wilson studied law, then history, and after teaching history for over fifteen years, was elected President of Princeton in 1902. It was not until 1910 that he entered politics, first as the Governor of New Jersey, then as President for two terms. His tenure of office was incredibly difficult, filled with political conflict and large-scale war. The pressures on America to enter the war were constant, but Wilson used the weapons of official protests to preserve U.S. neutrality and could run for reelection in 1916 on the slogan, "He kept us out of war." But by 1917, in the face of increased German U-boat activity, he was forced to present his Declaration of War to Congress and then return to the White House to weep over the significance of his own act.

One of Wilson's major efforts to restore peace was his "Fourteen Points" speech, in which, in the even tones of a lawyer and a historian, he offered a specific plan for an armistice. A cohesive element throughout is Wilson's general sense of the unity—or possible unity—of the whole world under principles of the equality and integrity of every people, with liberty, justice, and peace as the ultimate goals. The impact of the speech was great on the people of every land, especially the Germans, who ached for a quick end to the slaughter. But the Allied leaders, differing over the objectives of World War I, could not accept the plan. The war dragged on for another ten months.

OTHER IMPORTANT SPEECHES: "Declaration of War" (1917) and "For the League of Nations" (September 6, 1919).

TEXT SOURCE: U.S., Congress, Joint, *Congressional Record*, 65th Congress, 2nd session, 1918, 56, pt. 1: 680–81.

DISCOGRAPHY: Caedmon Record, TC 2031; playing time, 16:02.

Gentlemen of the Congress. Once more, as repeatedly before, the spokesmen of the Central Empires have indicated their desire to discuss the
objects of the war and the possible bases of a general peace. Parleys have
been in progress at Brest-Litovsk between Russian representatives and representatives of the Central Powers, to which the attention of all the bellig-
erents has been invited for the purpose of ascertaining whether it may be
possible to extend these parleys into a general conference with regard to
terms of peace and settlement. The Russian representatives presented not
only a perfectly definite statement of the principles upon which they
would be willing to conclude peace, but also an equally definite programme   10
of the concrete application of those principles. The representatives
of the Central Powers, on their part, presented an outline of settlement
which, if much less definite, seemed susceptible of liberal interpretation
until their specific programme of practical terms was added. That programme proposed no concessions at all either to the sovereignty of Russia
or to the preferences of the populations with whose fortunes it dealt, but
meant, in a word, that the Central Empires were to keep every foot of territory their armed forces had occupied,—every province, every city, every
point of vantage,—as a permanent addition to their territories and their
power. It is a reasonable conjecture that the general principles of settle-   20
ment which they at first suggested originated with the more liberal statesmen of Germany and Austria, the men who have begun to feel the force
of their own peoples' thought and purpose, while the concrete terms of
actual settlement came from the military leaders who have no thought but
to keep what they have got. The negotiations have been broken off. The
Russian representatives were sincere and in earnest. They cannot entertain
such proposals of conquest and domination.

The whole incident is full of significance. It is also full of perplexity.
With whom are the Russian representatives dealing? For whom are the
representatives of the Central Empires speaking? Are they speaking for the   30
majorities of their respective parliaments or for the minority parties, that
military and imperialistic minority which has so far dominated their whole
policy and controlled the affairs of Turkey and of the Balkan states which
have felt obliged to become their associates in the war? The Russian representatives have insisted, very justly, very wisely, and in the true spirit of
modern democracy, that the conferences they have been holding with the
Teutonic and Turkish statesmen should be held within open, not closed,
doors, and all the world has been audience, as was desired. To whom have
we been listening, then? To those who speak the spirit and intention of
the Resolutions of the German Reichstag of the ninth of July last, the   40
spirit and intention of the liberal leaders and parties of Germany, or to
those who resist and defy that spirit and intention and insist upon con-

quest and subjugation? Or are we listening, in fact, to both, unreconciled and in open and hopeless contradiction? These are very serious and pregnant questions. Upon the answer to them depends the peace of the world.

But, whatever the results of the parleys at Brest-Litovsk, whatever the confusions of counsel and of purpose in the utterances of the spokesmen of the Central Empires, they have again attempted to acquaint the world with their objects in the war and have again challenged their adversaries to say what their objects are and what sort of settlement they would deem just and satisfactory. There is no good reason why that challenge should not be responded to, and responded to with the utmost candor. We did not wait for it. Not once, but again and again, we have laid our whole thought and purpose before the world, not in general terms only, but each time with sufficient definition to make it clear what sort of definitive terms of settlement must necessarily spring out of them. Within the last week Mr. Lloyd George has spoken with admirable candor and in admirable spirit for the people and Government of Great Britain. There is no confusion of counsel among the adversaries of the Central Powers, no uncertainty of principle, no vagueness of detail. The only secrecy of counsel, the only lack of fearless frankness, the only failure to make definite statement of the objects of the war, lies with Germany and her Allies. The issues of life and death hang upon these definitions. No statesman who has the least conception of his responsibility ought for a moment to permit himself to continue this tragical and appalling outpouring of blood and treasure unless he is sure beyond a peradventure that the objects of the vital sacrifice are part and parcel of the very life of Society, and that the people for whom he speaks think them right and imperative as he does.

There is, moreover, a voice calling for these definitions of principle and of purpose which is, it seems to me, more thrilling and more compelling than any of the many moving voices with which the troubled air of the world is filled. It is the voice of the Russian people. They are prostrate and all but helpless, it would seem, before the grim power of Germany, which has hitherto known no relenting and no pity. Their power, apparently, is shattered. And yet their soul is not subservient. They will not yield either in principle or in action. Their conception of what is right, or what it is humane and honorable for them to accept, has been stated with a frankness, a largeness of view, a generosity of spirit, and a universal human sympathy which must challenge the admiration of every friend of mankind; and they have refused to compound their ideals or desert others that they themselves may be safe. They call to us to say what it is that we desire, in what, if in anything, our purpose and our spirit differ from theirs; and I believe that the people of the United States would wish me to respond, with utter simplicity and frankness. Whether their present leaders believe it or not, it is our heartfelt desire and hope that some way may be opened whereby we may be privileged to assist the people of Russia to attain their utmost hope of liberty and ordered peace.

It will be our wish and purpose that the processes of peace, when they are begun, shall be absolutely open and that they shall involve and permit henceforth no secret understandings of any kind. The day of conquest and aggrandizement is gone by; so is also the day of secret covenants entered into in the interest of particular governments and likely at some unlooked-for moment to upset the peace of the world. It is this happy fact, now clear to the view of every public man whose thoughts do not still linger in an age that is dead and gone, which makes it possible for every nation whose purposes are consistent with justice and the peace of the world to avow now or at any other time the objects it has in view.

We entered this war because violations of right had occurred which touched us to the quick and made the life of our own people impossible unless they were corrected and the world secured once for all against their recurrence. What we demand in this war, therefore, is nothing peculiar to ourselves. It is that the world be made fit and safe to live in; and particularly that it be made safe for every peace-loving nation which, like our own, wishes to live its own life, determine its own institutions, be assured of justice and fair dealing by the other peoples of the world as against force and selfish aggressions. All the peoples of the world are in effect partners in this interest, and for our own part we see very clearly that unless justice be done to others it will not be done to us. The programme of the world's peace, therefore, is our programme; and that programme, the only possible programme, as we see it, is this:

I. Open covenants of peace, openly arrived at, after which there shall be no private international understanding of any kind but diplomacy shall proceed always frankly and in the public view.

II. Absolute freedom of navigation upon the seas, outside territorial waters, alike in peace and in war, except as the seas may be closed in whole or in part by international action for the enforcement of international covenants.

III. The removal, so far as possible, of all economic barriers and the establishment of an equality of trade conditions among all the nations consenting to the peace and associating themselves for its maintenance.

IV. Adequate guarantees given and taken that national armaments will be reduced to the lowest point consistent with domestic safety.

V. A free, open-minded, and absolutely impartial adjustment of all colonial claims, based upon a strict observance of the principle that in determining all such questions of sovereignty the interests of the populations concerned must have equal weight with the equitable claims of the government whose title is to be determined.

VI. The evacuation of all Russian territory and such a settlement of

all questions affecting Russia as will secure the best and freest cooperation
of the other nations of the world in obtaining for her an unhampered and
unembarrassed opportunity for the independent determination of her own
political development and national policy and assure her of a sincere welcome into the society of free nations under institutions of her own choosing; and, more than a welcome, assistance also of every kind that she may
need and may herself desire. The treatment accorded Russia by her sister
nations in the months to come will be the acid test of their good will, of
their comprehension of her needs as distinguished from their own interests, and of their intelligent and unselfish sympathy.

VII. Belgium, the whole world will agree, must be evacuated and
restored, without any attempt to limit the sovereignty which she enjoys in
common with all other free nations. No other single act will serve as this
will serve to restore confidence among the nations in the laws which they
have themselves set and determined for the government of their relations
with one another. Without this healing act the whole structure and validity
of international law is forever impaired.

VIII. All French territory should be freed and the invaded portions
restored, and the wrong done to France by Prussia in 1871 in the matter of
Alsace-Lorraine, which has unsettled the peace of the world for nearly fifty
years, should be righted, in order that peace may once more be made
secure in the interest of all.

IX. A readjustment of the frontiers of Italy should be effected along
clearly recognizable lines of nationality.

X. The peoples of Austria-Hungary, whose place among the nations
we wish to see safeguarded and assured, should be accorded the freest
opportunity of autonomous development.

XI. Rumania, Serbia, and Montenegro should be evacuated; occupied
territories restored; Serbia accorded free and secure access to the sea; and
the relations of the several Balkan states to one another determined by
friendly counsel along historically established lines of allegiance and
nationality; and international guarantees of the political and economic
independence and territorial integrity of the several Balkan states should
be entered into.

XII. The Turkish portions of the present Ottoman Empire should be
assured a secure sovereignty, but the other nationalities which are now
under Turkish rule should be assured an undoubted security of life and an
absolutely unmolested opportunity of autonomous development, and the
Dardanelles should be permanently opened as a free passage to the ships
and commerce of all nations under international guarantees.

XIII. An independent Polish state should be erected which should
include the territories inhabited by indisputably Polish populations, which
should be assured a free and secure access to the sea, and whose political

and economic independence and territorial integrity should be guaranteed by international covenant.

XIV. A general association of nations must be formed under specific covenants for the purpose of affording mutual guarantees of political independence and territorial integrity to great and small states alike.

In regard to these essential rectifications of wrong and assertions of right we feel ourselves to be intimate partners of all the governments and peoples associated together against the Imperialists. We cannot be separate in interest or divided in purpose. We stand together until the end.

For such arrangements and covenants we are willing to fight and to continue to fight until they are achieved; but only because we wish the right to prevail and desire a just and stable peace such as can be secured only by removing the chief provocations to war, which this programme does remove. We have no jealousy of German greatness, and there is nothing in this programme that impairs it. We grudge her no achievement or distinction of learning or of pacific enterprise such as have made her record very bright and very enviable. We do not wish to injure her or to block in any way her legitimate influence or power. We do not wish to fight her either with arms or with hostile arrangements of trade if she is willing to associate herself with us and the other peace-loving nations of the world in covenants of justice and law and fair dealing. We wish her only to accept a place of equality among the peoples of the world,—the new world in which we now live,—instead of a place of mastery.

Neither do we presume to suggest to her any alteration or modification of her institutions. But it is necessary, we must frankly say, and necessary as a preliminary to any intelligent dealings with her on our part, that we should know whom her spokesmen speak for when they speak to us, whether for the Reichstag majority or for the military party and the men whose creed is imperial domination.

We have spoken now, surely, in terms too concrete to admit of any further doubt or question. An evident principle runs through the whole programme I have outlined. It is the principle of justice to all peoples and nationalities, and their right to live on equal terms of liberty and safety with one another, whether they be strong or weak. Unless this principle be made its foundation no part of the structure of international justice can stand. The people of the United States could act upon no other principle; and to the vindiction of this principle they are ready to devote their lives, their honor, and everything that they possess. The moral climax of this the culminating and final war for human liberty has come, and they are ready to put their own strength, their own highest purpose, their own integrity and devotion to the test.

OLIVER WENDELL HOLMES, JR.

(1841–1935)

On His Ninetieth Birthday

March 7, 1931

During his long and distinguished career as a lawyer and judge, Oliver Wendell Holmes, Jr., gave many addresses, especially on ceremonial occasions such as commencements and dedications. He had continued his undergraduate interest in philosophy—he was a classmate and close friend of William James—and such public platforms gave him an opportunity to voice his general views on man. He rarely offered long and carefully reasoned arguments, but, as he himself characterized his speeches, "chance utterances of faith and doubt." He quite simply voiced his commitments rather than attempted argument or persuasion. He was, in the best sense, more interested in himself than in his audience, since he believed "absolute truth is a mirage" and that each man must find and act on his own sense of reality.

This delicate yet manly speech, "On His Ninetieth Birthday," is his dignified response to the warm and high praise given by many prominent figures during a special radio program. The little allegory of the race is characteristic. As he said in his "John Marshall Speech," symbols stimulate men to thought and he preferred to do that rather than dictate conclusions. The dialogue and Latin tag, besides adding to the quiet drama through the statement and counterstatement, elevate the address and make it peculiarly appropriate to the near-mythic speaker and occasion.

OTHER IMPORTANT SPEECHES: "Soldier's Faith" (1895), "John Marshall" (1901), and "Law and the Court" (1913).

PUBLISHED VERSION: Mr. Justice Holmes, edited by Felix Frankfurter (New York: Coward-McCann, 1931).

DISCOGRAPHY: Caedmon Record, TC 2033; playing time, 1:23.

In this symposium my part is only to sit in silence. To express one's feelings as the end draws near is too intimate a task.

But I may mention one thought that comes to me as a listener-in. The riders in a race do not stop short when they reach the goal. There is a little finishing canter before coming to a standstill. There is time to hear the kind voice of friends and to say to oneself, "The work is done."

But just as one says that, the answer comes, "The race is over, but the work never is done while the power to work remains."

The canter that brings you to a standstill need not be only coming to rest. It cannot be, while you still live, for to live is to function. That is all there is in living. 10

And so I end with a line from a Latin poet who uttered the message more than fifteen hundred years ago: "Death, death, plucks my ear and says, 'Live—I am coming.'"

FRANKLIN DELANO ROOSEVELT

(1882–1945)

First Inaugural Address

March 4, 1933

By the time Franklin Delano Roosevelt was inaugurated President of the United States he was already considered one of the finest speakers of his day. His immersion in national politics had begun in 1910, and in spite of the severe attack of infantile paralysis which forced a three-year retirement, he was constantly speaking to the voter both through personal appearances and over the radio. During his governorship of New York, he regularly used that new tool of communication to explain his position, so that by the time he was ready to seek the Presidency, he had tested the medium's value, learned to use it with admirable effectiveness, and created a new and intimate mode of public address. The spread-eagle oration was displaced by the low-keyed talk, or, to use Roosevelt's term, "the fireside chat." Roosevelt wanted a dialogue between the people and the President—he repeatedly asked for letters, for reports, from the worker, the farmer, the small businessman; in turn, the leader talked with the people, reported to them. As he said in his important "Commonwealth Club" address (September 23, 1932), "the greatest duty of the statesman is to educate." The constantly expressed interdependence of President and people, based on mutual trust and good will, was a basic element of Roosevelt's speeches.

The roaring twenties ended, and there was a nation of men without jobs, families without food. There is little question that Roosevelt was voted in "to do something." When he accepted the nomination, he had promised "a new deal for the American people," so his Inaugural Address was awaited with hope and concern. What could be done? And if too little had been done by the conservative Hoover, would too much be done by his successor? Italy and Germany were revealing their answers to similar dilemmas. Perhaps the most important theme of Roosevelt's Inaugural Address is that the seriousness of the situation was

admitted, but it was recognized as not the necessary course of events. "We are
stricken by no plague of locusts . . . nature still offers her bounty." In this
philosophy of man's freedom and capacity to form his life rests the hope
expressed in the speech.

OTHER IMPORTANT SPEECHES: Campaign Speeches, "Commonwealth Club"
(1932) and "Teamster's Union" (1944); Fireside Chats, "Accomplishments
of the New Deal" (1934) and "A Plea for Neutrality" (1939); others,
"New Instruments for Public Power" (1936), "Jackson Day" (1936), and
"Four Freedoms" (1941).

PUBLISHED VERSION: "Inaugural Address: March 4, 1933." In *Inaugural Ad-*
dresses of the Presidents of the United States from George Washington
1789 to John F. Kennedy 1961 (Washington: U.S. Government Printing
Office, 1961).

DISCOGRAPHY: Caedmon Record, TC 2033; playing time, 18:37.

President Hoover, Mr. Chief Justice, my friends. This is a day of national
consecration, and I am certain that on this day my fellow Americans
expect that on my induction into the Presidency I will address them with
a candor and a decision which the present situation of our people impels.
This is preeminently the time to speak the truth, the whole truth, frankly
and boldly. Nor need we shrink from honestly facing conditions in our
country today. This great nation will endure as it has endured, will revive,
and will prosper. So, first of all, let me assert my firm belief that the only
thing we have to fear is fear itself—nameless, unreasoning, unjustified
terror which paralyzes needed efforts to convert retreat into advance.   10
    In every dark hour of our national life, a leadership of frankness and
of vigor has met with that understanding and support of the people themselves which is essential to victory. And I am convinced that you will again
give that support to leadership in these critical days.
    In such a spirit on my part and on yours we face our common difficul-
ties. They concern, thank God, only material things. Values have shrunk to
fantastic levels, taxes have risen, our ability to pay has fallen, government
of all kinds is faced by serious curtailment of income, the means of
exchange are frozen in the currents of trade, the withered leaves of industrial enterprise lie on every side, farmers find no markets for their produce,   20
and the savings of many years in thousands of families are gone. More
important, a host of unemployed citizens face the grim problem of existence, and an equally great number toil with little return. Only a foolish
optimist can deny the dark realities of the moment.
    And yet our distress comes from no failure of substance. We are
stricken by no plague of locusts. Compared with the perils which our forefathers conquered, because they believed and were not afraid, we have still
much to be thankful for. Nature still offers her bounty, and human efforts
have multiplied it. Plenty is at our doorstep, but a generous use of it languishes in the very sight of the supply. Primarily, this is because the rulers   30
of the exchange of mankind's goods have failed through their own stub-

bornness and their own incompetence, have admitted their failure, and have abdicated. Practices of the unscrupulous money-changers stand indicted in the court of public opinion, rejected by the hearts and minds of men.

True, they have tried, but their efforts have been cast in the pattern of an outworn tradition. Faced by failure of credit, they have proposed only the lending of more money. Stripped of the lure of profit by which to induce our people to follow their false leadership, they have resorted to exhortations, pleading tearfully for restored confidence. They only know the rules of a generation of self-seekers. They have no vision, and when there is no vision the people perish.

Yes, the money-changers have fled from their high seats in the temple of our civilization. We may now restore that temple to the ancient truths. The measure of that restoration lies in the extent to which we apply social values more noble than mere monetary profit. Happiness lies not in the mere possession of money; it lies in the joy of achievement, in the thrill of creative effort. The joy, the moral stimulation, of work no longer must be forgotten in the mad chase of evanescent profits. These dark days, my friends, will be worth all they cost us if they teach us that our true destiny is not to be ministered unto but to minister to ourselves, to our fellowmen.

Recognition of that falsity of material wealth as the standard of success goes hand in hand with the abandonment of the false belief that public office and high political position are to be valued only by the standards of pride of place and personal profit. And there must be an end to a conduct in banking and in business which too often has given to a sacred trust the likeness of callous and selfish wrongdoing. Small wonder that confidence languishes, for it thrives only on honesty, on honor, on the sacredness of obligations, on faithful protection, and on unselfish performance. Without them, it cannot live.

Restoration calls, however, not for changes in ethics alone. This nation is asking for action, and action now.

Our greatest primary task is to put people to work. This is no unsolvable problem if we face it wisely and courageously. It can be accomplished in part by direct recruiting by the government itself, treating the task as we would treat the emergency of a war but at the same time, through this employment, accomplishing great—greatly needed projects to stimulate and reorganize the use of our great natural resources.

Hand in hand with that we must frankly recognize the overbalance of population in our industrial centers and by engaging on a national scale in a redistribution endeavor to provide a better use of the land for those best fitted for the land. Yes, the task can be helped by definite efforts to raise the values of agricultural products and with this the power to purchase the output of our cities. It can be helped by preventing realistically the tragedy of the growing loss through foreclosure of our small homes and our farms.

It can be helped by insistence that the Federal, the state, and the local governments act forthwith on the demand that their cost be drastically reduced. It can be helped by the unifying of relief activities which today are often scattered, uneconomical, unequal. It can be helped by national planning for and supervision of all forms of transportation and of communications and other utilities that have a definitely public character. There are many ways in which it can be helped, but it can never be helped by merely talking about it.

We must act, and we must act quickly.

And finally, in our progress towards a resumption of work we require 10 two safeguards against a return of the evils of the old order. There must be a strict supervision of all banking and credits and investments. There must be an end to speculation with other people's money. And there must be provision for an adequate but sound currency.

These, my friends, are the lines of attack. I shall presently urge upon a new Congress, in special session, detailed measures for their fulfillment, and I shall seek the immediate assistance of the forty-eight states.

Through this program of action we address ourselves to putting our own national house in order and making income balance outgo. Our international trade relations, though vastly important, are in point of time and 20 necessity secondary to the establishment of a sound national economy. I favor as a practical policy the putting of first things first. I shall spare no effort to restore world trade by international economic readjustment, but the emergency at home cannot wait on that accomplishment. The basic thought that guides these specific means of national recovery is not nationally—narrowly nationalistic. It is the insistence, as a first consideration, upon the interdependence of the various elements in and parts of the United States of America, a recognition of the old and permanently important manifestation of the American spirit of the pioneer. It is the way to recovery. It is the immediate way. It is the strongest assurance that recov- 30 ery will endure.

In the field of world policy I would dedicate this nation to the policy of the "good neighbor"—the neighbor who resolutely respects himself and, because he does so, respects the rights of others—the neighbor who respects his obligations and respects the sanctity of his agreements in and with a world of neighbors.

If I read the temper of our people correctly, we now realize as we have never realized before our interdependence on each other, that we cannot merely take but we must give as well, that if we are to go forward, we must move as a trained and loyal army, willing to sacrifice for the good 40 of a common discipline, because without such discipline no progress can be made, no leadership becomes effective. We are, I know, ready and willing to submit our lives and our property to such discipline because it makes possible a leadership which aims at the larger good. This I propose to offer, pledging that the larger purposes will bind upon us, bind upon us all as a sacred obligation, with a unity of duty hitherto evoked only in times of armed strife.

With this pledge taken, I assume unhesitatingly the leadership of this great army of our people dedicated to a disciplined attack upon our common problems.

Action in this image, action to this end, is feasible under the form of government which we have inherited from our ancestors. Our constitution is so simple, so practical, that it is possible always to meet extraordinary
10   needs by changes in emphasis and arrangement without loss of essential form. That is why our constitutional system has proved itself the most superbly enduring political mechanism the modern world has ever seen. It has met every stress of vast expansion of territory, of foreign wars, of bitter internal strife, of world relations. And it is to be hoped that the normal balance of executive and legislative authority may be wholly equal, wholly adequate, to meet the unprecedented task before us. But it may be that an unprecedented demand and need for undelayed action may call for temporary departure from that normal balance of public procedure. I am prepared under my constitutional duty to recommend the measures that a
20   stricken nation in the midst of a stricken world may require. These measures, or such other measures as the Congress may build out of its experience and wisdom, I shall seek within my constitutional authority to bring to speedy adoption. But in the event that the Congress shall fail to take one of these two courses, in the event that the national emergency is still critical, I shall not evade the clear course of duty that will then confront me. I shall ask the Congress for the one remaining instrument to meet the crisis: broad executive power to wage a war against the emergency, as great as the power that would be given to me if we were in fact invaded by a foreign foe.
30   For the trust reposed in me I return the courage and the devotion that befit the time. I can do no less.

We face the arduous days that lie before us in the warm courage of national unity, with the clear consciousness of seeking old and precious moral values, with the clean satisfaction that comes from the stern performance of duty by old and young alike. We aim at the assurance of a rounded, a permanent national life. We do not distrust the essen—the future of essential democracy. The people of the United States have not failed. In their need they have registered a mandate that they want direct, vigorous action. They have asked for discipline and direction under leader-
40   ship. They have made me the present instrument of their wishes. In the spirit of the gift, I take it.

In this dedication, in this dedication of a nation, we humbly ask the blessing of God. May he protect each and every one of us. May he guide me in the days to come.

WILL ROGERS

(1879–1935)

Morgenthau's Plan

April 28, 1935

Mark Twain both lived and created American dreams: in fact and fiction he was a Mississippi River pilot, a gold miner, and a newspaper man. But Will Rogers stepped into the middle of the American myth of the cowboy as hero and complicated it by being a talker. He reacted strongly to an audience—his radio talks without an audience are strained—and he often went on and on for hours, talking common sense. The famous alarm clock that rings at the end of this speech is not a comedian's prop; it is a necessary barrier that forces this great talker to acknowledge time.

Will Rogers was the political and social common man who regularly claimed, "All I know is what I read in the newspaper." But he was no innocent. He walked around a subject, testing it, chipping off a piece here and there until the façade was gone and the essential structure was left—if there had been any to begin with.

Superficially he was a model of the poor speaker: he would get stuck, repeat himself, throw out irrelevancies, interrupt himself. His speeches were choked with voiced pauses and loaded with grammatical errors. His candidness could be labeled simple-minded tactlessness as he mocked America, prominent public figures, and himself. But while he slowly wound his way toward a point, his audience saw a man unable to conceal his thoughts, a man who honestly and tenaciously sought the human interpretation, the sensible solution to a problem. His art was the concealment of art.

This recording of a typical weekly radio talk, "Morgenthau's Plan," exemplifies Rogers' rambling commentary on national events. He touches on many facets of American life, ranging from the inheritance tax and the soldiers' bonus to movie stars and fishing. It is indeed a mass of unrelated points, but they are held together by a point of view and a style. He is constantly calling for a sense of proportion and for practicality and confidence. He sees the

55

major economic and social problems of a nation as caused by the same kind of muddied thinking and vanity that holds as "important" Garbo's secretiveness, Mae West's marital entanglements, and the publicity shots of Presidential fishing exploits. His wit is achieved essentially by extending ideas to absurdity and by stating complex problems with a simplicity that shocks. This is no mere jokester. Rogers' laughing about railroad grade crossings near the end of this speech is the same statement—and just as serious a one—as Roosevelt's well-known line in his First Inaugural Address, "The only thing we have to fear is fear itself."

OTHER IMPORTANT SPEECHES: "Arms Conference" (April 6, 1930), "Prohibition" (June 8, 1930), "Roosevelt: Hollywood Bowl" (September 23, 1932), and "Plan Day" (April 21, 1935).
PUBLISHED VERSION: None.
DISCOGRAPHY: Caedmon Record, TC 2033; playing time, 16:07.

Thank you very much. We—we—we're here an hour earlier today. It seems kind of funny to be ... With everybody advised to spend and the government spending and everything, and then ... It seems sort of funny for somebody to save a little daylight nowadays. Put a little of it on the budget or something.

Do you remember my act on the radio last Sunday night? Well, even if you don't remember it, don't, I mean, it don't matter very much. Fact, I'd about forgot it myself. But as well as I can remember it, I introduced a plan, it was a plan—it was a plan to end all plans. That's what it was.

10   Well, it looks like it had the very—it had the very opposite effect. This last week has been one of the biggest plan weeks I've known of in anything. It's the biggest plan week the country has suffered in years—this last one. In fact, I think they could have named it "Plan Week." Now one of the big things that President Roosevelt made his original hit with was when he said, "If I'm wrong, I'll be the first to admit it." So when I say we should end all plans, it looks like I'm wrong and I'm the first to admit it.

So, it looks like we've got to have plans, and I've really got to get busy on one, I won't give it to you today, but I'm gonna dig one up. If you want a plan, brother, I can sure give you one now. I presented facts and
20   figures to show you that plans didn't work. Now I did that last Sunday, see. Do you think that discouraged the planners? Nope. Not on your life. It just seemed to encourage them, looks like.

Right on top of my advice to not plan—well, there come a plan from Secretary Morgenthau, who's Secretary of the Treasury. His father used to be the Ambassador to Turkey, and a fine old gentleman and a good friend of mine. But this Morgenthau, the young fellow, a very able man—he come out with a plan to put a bigger and better tax on these big estates, these tremendous big, a inheritance tax, it is, to be exact that is, a man who died. And on an estate of say ten million dollars, why the government will take just take about ninety percent of it, and then giving the offspring ten and . . . and . . . after Mr. Morgenthau gets through with him. And then on estates of a hundred—a hundred million and two hundred million, a billion, and like that . . . well, well, the government just takes all of that and notifies the heirs. . . . Says, your father died a pauper here today. And he died a pauper here today, and he's being buried by the . . . let's see, it'd be MEBA, the MEBA, that is—the Millionaires' Emergency   10 Burial Association. It's a kind of branch of the RFC.

Now mind you, mind you . . . I'm not telling all this—I don't hold any brief or any great grief either for a man that dies and leaves a million millions and hundreds of millions and billions. . . . I don't mean that. But I don't believe Mr. Morgenthau's plan will work, because he gives figures in there that shows what this new inheritance tax would bring in every year. He says—in 1936 we get so much, and 1938 . . . oh, right along, see. He gives these figures to show what it'd bring in every year—that is, as long as the Democrats stay in—and he seems to know—he seems to know just who's going to die each year. And how much they're going to leave.   20 Now brother, that's planning, ain't it, when you can figure out that! Now suppose, now suppose for instance, he's got scheduled to die J. P. Morgan. He's got him scheduled to die on a certain year. And you can bet, if they can arrange it, they'll have him die while the Democrats are in . . . so . . . so they can get the benefit . . . so they get the benefit of that estate anyhow, see? Now, according to plans, J. P. Morgan, he's got to die in order for Mr., for Mr. Morgenthau to reach his quota for that year. Now while I think Mr. Morgan is a nice man—I never met him but once, that was a time when he was on trial in Washington and he had the midget on his knee and . . . I met him there, but he's a very nice fellow, very able,   30 nice fellow . . . and I don't hear from him but very seldom. But I think his patriotism maybe would compare with some of the rest of us, but, but whether he'd be patriotic enough to want to die on this year scheduled or not—just to make Morgenthau's budget balance . . . I mean, I mean that's asking a good deal of a man to just die right off just so I can balance my budget. He might be rather unreasonable and not want to do it. As I say, old men is contrary—you know what I mean. And rich old men is awful contrary. They've had their own way so long that you can't . . . So in order for Mr. Morgenthau's plan to work out, I—well, I'd say if it's to work out a hundred percent he's got to bump these wealthy guys off, or something.   40 Well, now, that's . . . the government's doing everything else but, you know, but there is a humane society, I mean.

Now a . . . you know, there was another—there was another big plan

developed during the week. Did you read about Aimee McPherson meeting Gandhi in India? Yes, yes, sir, Aimee met . . . Sister Aimee . . . she had
a date with the Mahatma over there. Yes, she had a date with him. It was
what the French call a . . . a rendezvous. I'd like to have had the talking
movie rights to the conversation between Mahatma and Aimee. I'd of love
to heard, heard, what they said, you know. I . . . I think the Mahatma
wanted her to stay in India and help him with the untouchables, and
Aimee says . . . Brother Mahatma, you ought to come to Hollywood, and,
you know, and try and get near Garbo, and meet some of our unapproach-
10   ables . . . and . . .

    Well, speaking of plans, I will say this for old Huey. He didn't break
out with any . . . He didn't hatch any new plans during the week. He's just
settin' on the same eggs he was.

    And now a little later on, folks, I want to tell you . . . A little later on
. . . To be exact, I think it's seven o'clock our time out here, and I guess
that makes about four hours' difference—eleven hours in the East . . . oh
well, you know what time it is. But tonight later on, the President of our
United States is going to be on the air. He hasn't spoken to us since last
September. He's spoke to a lot of people, but not us, I mean. And he must
20   have something important to say because he don't just go shooting off
every time he sees a microphone like these other candidates do. They can't
pass a microphone without yowling in it.

    And I don't know what he's going to talk about. Maybe he'll be talk-
ing about Mae West, everybody else is. In fact, I bet he'd rather talk
about Mae than some of the things—some of the things that he'll feel
obliged to talk on tonight. You could explain Mae's husbands easier than
they could the NRA, I'll bet . . . and . . . You know, speaking of Mae, I'll
bet there's nothing that would embarrasses a successful person, you know,
any more than having some old husbands show up on you at the wrong
30   time. Just when she thought she had him in Brooklyn, he showed up.

    The President is liable to talk about catching fish off the Astors'
yacht. . . . He's been down there, but I bet he don't talk on that, for he
never did catch anything on that old tub. There's fish in the ocean, but
that yacht gets theirs out of the fish market. They used to have photographers . . . remember, they used to have photographers, just they did nothing but just follow our presidents around just to get pictures of 'em when
they fished, you know. Remember that? All around, just catching fish. Even
Mr. Coolidge used to drag in a little inoffensive little perch now and again.
Poor little fish—he'd drag him in just for the Sunday supplement. And Mr.
40   Hoover would go out and hook some old mudcat for a hungry lens sometimes. But there's been three photographers starved to death during Roosevelt's administration waiting for this Astor's yacht to approach even a
crawdad anywhere. They ought to put skis on that Astor yacht and go fur

hunting. That's his racket . . . much obliged. You remember your history, don't you? You remember how some of our big estates were founded.

He might talk about the bonus, the President might. He's kind of switched over on that. He has a plan of paying it. I never saw as many schemes put forward, you know. They want to pay it, all of them, the soldiers want to receive it, but it's just the way, everybody's got their own way and want to do it. I don't know how they can have so many different schemes when it's paying, it's paying the same bunch of men and the same bunch of money. Seems to me like they'll have to do with the bonus like we have to do with everything else now to get anybody to take it. They'll 10 have to wrap it in cellophane.

But he may speak on that. And I'll touch lightly on it because I don't want to interfere with anything that he would say. Mine is just a—mine is just a little preliminary introductory remarks to his.

Of course, he's liable to touch on some of these new schemes to spend this five billion dollars. You can't you know, you can't spend five . . . Now there's something you've got to have a plan for. You can't spend five billion dollars in the old-fashioned way. I'll bet you couldn't put a strong man in the treasury warehouse full of, full of hundred-dollar bills and give him a scoop shovel, and he couldn't shovel out that much money in the 20 rest of his life, you know.

We used to . . . we couldn't spell a billion dollars, much less to realize it, or count it or anything. But we now—now we're a nation, we learn awful fast, and it won't be long now till we'll be working on the word trillion—trillion—that follows billion and then trillion. You'll read in the papers—Congress has just been asked to appropriate two trillion dollars to relieve the descendants of a race of people called Wall Streeters. The paper will go further on to say—this is a worthy cause and no doubt this small appropriation will be made, as these are descendants of a once-proud—proud—race—a once-proud race—and after all, they're wards of 30 the government.

Then they've got another plan, now they've got another plan. They've figured out that what's the matter with this country is—I'll bet you couldn't guess it in a million years. You couldn't guess this plan they've figured out what's the matter with the country, and they're going to spend a half a billion dollars on it. I'll bet you couldn't figure out what it is. Well, you know what it is? Well, it's that the people try to cross a railroad track without looking both ways. That's what it is. They're going to fix the grade crossings—that's what that is. Well, you'll say—well, the problem is to teach the people to look both ways. Drive up to the track and look up 40 and down and then cross. Yes, well that's exactly what's the matter with, with us . . . even when, when it don't apply to railroad trains. Everybody's—everybody looks one way. In 1928 and '29, around there.

That's when the train hit all of us, remember? There wasn't a ... there wasn't a soul—there wasn't a soul in the United States that looked both ways then. We certainly, now, now we've gone to the other extreme. We're so scared now that we drive up to the track and we won't do anything. We're just standing there. We just stand there and look, and look, and we won't cross the track at all. We even won't trust our own eyesight. If a train goes by and it looks like everything is O.K. and we might be able to cross, we won't do it. We're, we're so scared that we think it might turn around and come back and hit us again.

That's what the President is liable to talk on. It's to try to get us to quit standing there looking and shaking and being scared that something's going to happen to us. And he'll tell us it's the same, it's the same track, you know—it's the same old track, and the same ... you know you've been crossing it for years, and all we have to do is just to use some judgment and carry on just as we have been for years. But we won't believe him. He's got to go to work—and now he's got to build a runway over the top of all these, of all these railroads—either over the top or under the bottom, and get that under there. To build it. They get that all done ... of course, I think it's a good plan. Mind you, I'm not against it. I think it's a fine plan, and it will give a lot of people work and do a lot of things, although I don't think that it will do everything it is supposed to do. I don't think it will save all the lives, because I think this grade-crossing thing ... You'll just rush right over the grade crossing and right on down to the ... and get hit at the first intersection by a bus. That's what you'll do. See? That's one thing about buses. You know, there's one thing about a bus—they're bigger than trains are now, and death is more certain with a bus when you get hit with that. There's no lingering illness with that at all. And the buses, and the buses come so much oftener than trains do anyhow, you know. A lot of times—a lot of times people have had to wait pretty near a day to get hit by a train—you know, you know they come so seldom, but buses are, you know, there's so many of them why you can just get hit pretty nearly any time. And I'll bet you never did read, too, of a, of a train ever hitting a car with just one person in it, just the driver in it, you know, just one lone passenger, nope. No, they just wait—they just wait till the car gets loaded, and then they hit everybody, and ... Oh here, wait a minute. I ain't through yet. Now next Sunday I'm going to try and dig you up ... I gonna have ... If you want plans, brother, I've got one. Good night and thank you.

HERBERT HOOVER

(1874–1964)

War Comes to Europe

September 1, 1939

During the 1920's Herbert Hoover was recognized as a brilliant and widely traveled engineer who had ably directed war relief programs and then performed superbly as Secretary of Commerce. But in popular history he is the colorless man who was President when the market crashed in 1929, an event ranked with the world wars for its international disruptive force.

An uninspired orator as President, Hoover developed quickly as a forceful speaker challenging the direction of the New Deal. His speeches of the middle 30's have the urgency of a fighter for principles—principles held as a very personal and basic credo. Again·and again he attacked centralized government and warned of the erosion of liberty.

Then the German army rolled into Poland. As with an anticipated death, no amount of preparation eased the shock of the widening conflict. Having seen the devastation of World War I, the former President sorrowfully, hesitantly, speculates on the course and duration of the new fury, unable to imagine the sudden fall of France, the monumental slaughter of Stalingrad, the fearful aerial bombardment of Coventry and London, of Dresden and Hamburg, or the overwhelming revelation of Auschwitz and Buchenwald.

A Gallup Poll of 1937 revealed that 70 percent of those questioned believed that America should not have entered World War I, and toward the end of this short speech Hoover summarizes the isolationists' position that had been passionately stated during the 30's by such brilliant speakers as William E. Borah (see especially his speech of March 25, 1939): America could best serve peace, freedom, and democracy by keeping herself economically strong and politically free from the centralized power and the ever-expanding censorship necessary for a country at war.

OTHER IMPORTANT SPEECHES: "California Republican Assembly" (1935), "The
   American Bill of Rights" (September 17, 1935), "Republican National
   Convention" (1936), and "A Non-Communist United Nations" (1950).
PUBLISHED VERSION: Herbert Hoover, "War in Europe." *Vital Speeches*, Sep-
   tember 15, 1939, p. 736.
DISCOGRAPHY: Caedmon Record, TC 2033; playing time, 2:50.

Fellow Americans of the radio audience. This is one of the saddest weeks
that has come to humanity in a hundred years. A senseless war seems inevitably forced upon hundreds of millions of people. The whole world still
prays for some miracle that might deliver us. For war means the killing of
millions of the best and the most courageous of men who might contribute something to human progress. It means the killing and the starvation
of millions of women and children. It means another quarter of a century
of impoverishment for the whole world.

     And it will likely be a long war. It is possible that the brave people of
10 Poland may be overrun in a few months, but there seems no point of
access from which an overwhelming attack can be delivered from the British and French on one side to the Germans on the other, which might
quickly end this war. It is likely to be a war of slow attrition, and the
fate of Poland will depend upon its ending.

     The land defenses of France and England, their greatly superior naval
strength, their manpower and resources, their resolution, make it certain
that they can defend themselves. And it is true that vast fleets of airplanes
on both sides contribute a new and uncertain factor. But there is nothing
which proves that even the superiority in airplanes can win the war. And
20 while assurances have been given that there will be no bombing of women
and children, there may come a time of desperation when all restraints go
to the winds. It is likely to be the most barbarous war that we have ever
known.

     This situation in the world today is not the act of the German people
themselves. It is the act of a group who hold them in subjection. The
whole Nazi system is repugnant to the American people. The most of
American sympathies will be with the democracies. But whatever our sympathies are, we cannot solve the problems of Europe. America must keep
out of this war. The President and the Congress should be supported in
30 their every effort to keep us out. We can keep out if we have the resolute
national will to do so. We can be of more service to Europe and to
humanity if we preserve the vitality and strength of the United States for
use in the period of peace which must some time come. And we must keep
out if we are to preserve for civilization the very foundations of democracy
and of free men.

WENDELL L. WILLKIE
(1892–1944)

A Loyal Opposition

November 11, 1940

In the late 30's Wendell L. Willkie became the foremost critic of Roosevelt's domestic policies and was nominated as the Republican candidate for the Presidency in 1940. Constant themes in his speeches were freedom from government control and unity of all elements of society.

Fond of quoting Lincoln's "with malice toward none," this business executive turned politician constantly argued that there was enough for all, that the quarrels between labor and management were based on appearance, not reality. During the war he developed his concept of "one world," while revealing himself as particularly alert to the Far East and the rejection of colonialism. Ultimately his speeches were of a piece—the unity of all men in a free, stable, and prosperous society.

In the election just completed before this speech, Willkie lost handily, but the popular vote was the closest since 1916. Richard Nixon, whose last official duty as Vice President was to announce to Congress the results of the very close 1960 election, spoke firmly and well on the problem of narrow victories (January 6, 1961): "In our campaigns, no matter how hard fought they may turn out to be, those who lose accept the verdict, and support those who win ... in a cause that is bigger than any man's ambition, greater than any party. It is the cause of freedom, of justice and peace for all mankind." Willkie argues much the same point of unity but insists that "a vital element in the balanced operation of democracy is a strong, alert, and watchful opposition." He carefully guides his audience with particulars of the opposition he campaigned for and wants continued, as well as the limits beyond which the defense of America will not permit "a vigorous, loyal, and public-spirited opposition party" to go. This speech is both a graceful ending and an aggressive beginning.

63

OTHER IMPORTANT SPEECHES: "America, the League, and the Future" (May 11,
    1942), Report on "One World" (October 26, 1942), and "Objectives of
    War and Peace" (November 17, 1942).
PUBLISHED VERSION: Wendell L. Willkie, "Cooperation But Loyal Opposition,"
    Vital Speeches, December 1, 1940, pp. 103–6.
DISCOGRAPHY: Caedmon Record, TC 2033; playing time, 25:45.

People of America. Twenty-two years ago today a great conflict raging on
the battlefields of Europe came to an end. The guns were silent. A new era
of peace began and for that era the people of our Western world, our democratic world, held the highest hopes. Those hopes have not been fulfilled.
The democratic way of life did not become stronger; it became weaker.
The spirit of constitutional government flickered like a dying lamp, and
within the last year or so the light from that lamp has disappeared entirely
upon the continent of Europe. We in America watched darkness fall
upon Europe, and as we watched there approached an important time for
10 us, the national election of 1940.

    In that election, and in our attitudes after that election, the rest of
the world would see an example of democracy in action, an example of a
great people faithful to their Constitution and to their elected representatives. The campaign preceding this election stirred us deeply. Millions
upon millions of us who had never been active in politics took part in it.
The people flocked to the polling places in greater numbers than ever
before in history.

    Nearly fifty million people exercised on November 5th the right of
the franchise, the precious right which we inherited from our forefathers
20 and which we must cherish and pass on to future generations. Thus it
came about that although constitutional government had been blotted out
elsewhere, here in America men and women kept it triumphantly alive.

    No matter which side you were on, on that day, remember that this
great free expression of our faith in the free system of government must
have given hope to millions upon millions of others—on the heroic island
of Britain—in the ruined cities of France and Belgium—yes, perhaps even
to people in Germany and in Italy. It has given hope wherever man hopes
to be free.

    In the campaign preceding this election serious issues were at stake.
30 People became bitter. Many things were said, which in calmer moments,
might have been left unsaid, or might have been worded more thoughtfully. But we Americans know that the bitterness is a distortion, not a true
reflection, of what is in our hearts. I can truthfully say that there is no bitterness in mine. I hope there is none in yours.

    We have elected Franklin Roosevelt President. He is your President.

He is my President. We all of us owe him the respect due to his high office. We give him that respect. We will support him with our best efforts for our country, and we pray that God may guide his hand during the next four years in the supreme task of administering the affairs of the people.

It is a fundamental principle of the democratic system that the majority rules. The function of the minority, however, is equally fundamental. It is about the function of that minority—22 million people, nearly half of our electorate—that I wish to talk to you tonight.

A vital element in the balanced operation of democracy is a strong, 10 alert, and watchful opposition. That is our task for the next four years. We must constitute ourselves a vigorous, loyal, and public-spirited opposition party.

It has been suggested that in order to present a united front to a threatening world the minority should now surrender its convictions and join the majority. This would mean that in the United States of America there would be only one dominant party, only one economic philosophy, only one political philosophy of life. This is a totalitarian idea. It is a slave idea. It must be rejected utterly.

The British people are unified with a unity almost unexampled in his- 20 tory for its endurance and its valor. Yet that unity coexists with an unimpaired freedom of criticism and of suggestion.

In the continual bates—debates of the House of Commons and the House of Lords, all of the government's policies, its taxation, its expenditures, its military and naval policies, its basic economic policies are brought under steady, friendly, loyal, critical review. Britain survives free. Les—Let us Americans choose no lesser freedom.

In Britain some opposition party leaders are member—members of the government and some say that a similar device should be adopted here. That is a false conception of our Government. When a leader of the 30 British Liberal Party or a member of the British Labor Party becomes a member of the Churchill cabinet, he becomes, from the British parliamentary point of view, an equal of Mr. Churchill's. This is because the British cabinet is a committee of the Houses of Parliament. It is a committee of equals, wherein the Prime Minister is chairman, a lofty chairman indeed, and yet but a chairman. The other members are his colleagues.

With us, the situation, as you well know, is different. Our executive branch is not a committee of our legislative branch. Our President is independent of our congress. The members of his cabinet are not his colleagues. They are his administrative subordinates. They are subject to his 40 orders.

An American President could fill his whole Cabinet with leaders of the opposition party, and still our administration would not be a two-party administration. It would be an administration of a majority President, giving orders to minority representatives of his own choosing. These representatives must concur in the President's convictions. If they do not they have no alternative, except to resign.

Clearly no such device as this can give us in this country any self-respecting agreement between majority and minority for concerted effort toward the national welfare. Such a plan for us would be but the shadow, not the substance, of unity. Our American unity cannot be made with words or with gestures. It must be forged between the ideas of the opposi-
10   tion and the practices and the policies of the Administration. Ours is a government of principles and not one merely of men. Any member of the minority party, though willing to die for his country, still retains the right to criticize the policies of the government. This right is imbedded in our constitutional system.

We, who stand ready to serve our country behind our Commander-in-Chief, nevertheless retain the right, and I will say the duty, to debate the course of our government. Ours is a two-party system. Should we ever permit one party to dominate our lives entirely, democracy would collapse, and we would have dictatorship.
20   Therefore, to you who have so sincerely given yourselves to this cause, which you chose me to lead, I say, your function during the next four years is that of the loyal opposition. You believe deeply in the principles that we stood for in the recent election. And principles are not like a football suit to be put on in order to play a game and then taken off when the game is over.

It is your constitutional duty to debate the policies of this or any other administration and to express yourselves freely and openly to those who represent you in your state and national government.

Now let me, however, raise a single warning. Ours is a very powerful
30   opposition. On November 5th, we were a minority by only a few million votes. Let us not, therefore, fall into the partisan error of opposing things just for the sake of opposition. Ours must not be an opposition against, it must be an opposition for, an opposition for a strong America, a productive America, for only the productive can be strong and only the strong can be free.

Let me remind you of some of the principles for which we fought and which we hold as sincerely today as we did yesterday. We do not believe in unlimited spending of borrowed money by the Federal government, the piling up of bureaucracy, the control of our electorate by political
40   machines, however successful, the usurpation of powers reserved to Congress, the subjugation of the courts, the concentration of enormous authority in the hands of the executive, the discouragement of enterprise, and the continuance of economic dependence for millions of our citizens upon government. Nor do we believe in verbal provocations to war.

On the other hand, we stand for a free America, an America of opportunity created by the enterprise and imagination of its citizens. We believe that this is the only kind of an America in which democracy can in the long run exist. This is the only kind of an America that offers hope for our youth and an expanding life for all our people. Under our philosophy, the primary purpose of government is to serve its people and to keep them from hurting one another. For this reason our Federal government has regulatory laws and commissions. For this reason we must fight for the rights of labor, for assistance to the farmers, and for protection for the unemployed, the aged, and the physically handicapped.

But while our government must thus regulate and protect us, it must not dominate our lives. We, the people, are the masters. We, the people, must build this country, and we, the people, must hold our elected representatives responsible to us for the care they take of our national credit, our democratic institutions, and the fundamental laws of the land. It is in the light of these principles, and not of petty partisanship or of politics, that our opposition must be conducted. It is in the light of these principles that we must join in debate, without selfishness and also without fear.

Let me take as an example the danger that threatens us through our national debt. Two days after the election, this Administration recommended that the national debt limit be increased from $49 billion to $65 billion. Immediately after that announcement, prices on the New York Stock Exchange, and other exchanges, jumped sharply upward. This was not a sign of health, but a sign of fever. Those who are familiar with these things agreed unanimously that the announcement of the Treasury indicated a danger, sooner or later, of inflation. Now you all know what inflation means. You have lately watched its poisonous course in Europe. It means a rapid decline in the purchasing power of money, a decline in what the dollar will buy. Or stated the other way around, inflation means a rise in the price of everything—food, rent, clothing, amusements, automobiles, necessities, and luxuries. Invariably these prices rise faster than wages, with the result that the workers suffer and the standard of living declines.

Now, no man is wise enough to say exactly how big the national debt can become before—be—causing serious inflation. But some sort of limit certainly exists, beyond which lies financial chaos. Such chaos would inevitably mean the loss of our social gains, the destruction of our savings, the ruin of every little property owner, and the creation of vast unemployment and hardships. It would mean finally the rise of dictatorship. Those have been the results of financial collapse in every country in the history of the world. The only way that we can avoid them is to remain sound and solvent.

It is not incumbent upon any American to remain silent concerning such a danger. I shall not be silent, and I hope you will not be. This is one of your functions as a member of the minority. But in fulfilling our duties as an opposition party, we must be careful to be constructive. We must help to show the way. Thus, in order to counteract the threat of inflation and to correct some of our economic errors, I see five steps for our government to take immediately.

First, all Federal expenditures, except those for national defense and necessary relief, ought to be cut to the bone and below the bone. Work relief, obviously, has to be maintained, but every effort should be made to substitute for relief, productive jobs.

Second, the building of new plants and new machinery for the defense program should be accomplished, as far as possible, by private capital. There should be no nationalization under the guise of defense of any American industry, with a consequent outlay of Federal funds.

Third, taxes should be levied so as to approach as nearly as possible the pay-as-you-go plan. Obviously, we cannot hope to pay for all the defense program as we go. But we must do our best. That is part of the sacrifice that we must make to defend this democracy.

Fourth, taxes and government restrictions should be adjusted to take the brakes off private enterprise so as to give it freedom under wise regulation, to release new investments and new energies, and thus to increase the national income. I do not believe we can hope to bear the debt and taxes arising out of this defense program with a national income of less than $100 billion—our present national income is only $70 billion—unless we lower the standard of living of every man and woman who works. But if we can increase our national income to $100 billion, we can pay for this defense program out of the increase and that increase can readily be produced if we free private enterprise, not for profiteering, but for natural development.

Fifth, and finally, our government must change its punitive attitude toward both big and little business. Regulations there must be. We of the opposition have consistently recommended that. But the day of witch-hunting must be over.

If this administration has the unity of America really at heart, and I assume it has, it must consider without prejudice and with an open mind such recommendations of the opposition. National unity can only be achieved by recognizing and giving serious weight to the viewpoint of the opposition. Such a policy can come only from the administration itself. It will be from the suppression of the opposition that discord and disunity will arise. The administration has the ultimate power to force us apart or to bind us together.

And now a word about the most important immediate task that confronts this nation. On this, all Americans are of one purpose. There is no disagreement among us about the defense of America. We stand united behind the defense program. But here particularly, as a minority party, our role is an important one. It is to be constantly watchful to see that America is effectively safeguarded and that the vast expenditure of funds which we have voted for that purpose is not wasted.

And in so far as I have the privilege to speak for you, I express once more the hope that we help to maintain the rim of freedom in Britain and elsewhere by supplying those defenders with materials and equipment. This should be done to the limit of our ability but with due regard to our own defense. On this point, I think I can say without boast that never in the history of American presidential campaigns has a candidate gone further than I did in attempting to create a united front. However, I believe that our aid should be given by constitutional methods and with the approval, accord, and ratification of Congress. Only thus can the people determine, from time to time, the course they wish to take and the hazards they wish to run.

Mr. Roosevelt and I both promised the people in the course of the campaign that if we were elected we would keep this country out of war unless attacked. Mr. Roosevelt was reelected, and this solemn pledge for him I know will be fulfilled, and I know the American people desire him to keep it sacred.

Since November 5th I have received thousands and thousands of letters. As a matter of fact, tens of thousands of them. I have personally read a great portion of these messages. I am profoundly touched. They come from all parts of our country and from all kinds of people. They come from Catholics and Protestants, Jews and Christians, colored people and white people. They come from workers and farmers and clerks and businessmen, men and women of all the occupations that make up our American life. All of these letters and telegrams, almost without exception, urge that the cause that we have been fighting for be carried on.

In your enthusiasm for our cause, you've founded thousands of organizations. They are your own organizations, financed by you and directed by you. It is very appropriate for you to continue them if you feel so inclined. I hope you do continue them. It is not, however, appropriate to continue these organizations in my name. I do not want this great cause to be weakened by even a semblance of any personal advantage to any individual. I feel too deeply about it for that. Nineteen hundred and forty-four will take care of itself. It is of the very essence of my belief that democracy is fruitful of leadership.

I want to see all of us dedicate ourselves to the principles for which we fought. My fight for those principles has just begun. I shall advocate them in the future as ardently and as confidently as I have in the past. As Woodrow Wilson once said, "I would rather lose in a cause that I know some day will triumph, than to triumph in a cause that I know some day will fail." Whatever I may undertake in the coming years, I shall be working shoulder to shoulder with you for the defense of our free way of life, for the better understanding of our economic system, and for the development of that new America whose vision lies within every one of us.

Meanwhile, let us be proud, let us be happy in the fight that we have made. We have brought our cause to the attention of the world. Millions have welcomed it. As time goes on, millions more will find in it the hope that they are looking for. We can go on from here with the words of Abraham Lincoln in our hearts, "With malice toward none, with charity for all, with firmness in the right as God gives us to see the right, let us finish the work we are in, to bind up the nation's wounds, to do all which may achieve and cherish a just and lasting peace among ourselves and with all nations."

Good night, and God bless and keep every one of you.

FRANKLIN
DELANO
ROOSEVELT

(1882–1945)

Declaration

of War

December 8, 1941

For over two years Americans had watched the gigantic European struggle with uncertainty. Sympathetic with the Allied forces to the point of declaring "economic war" through the Lend-Lease Act, we nevertheless stood back uneasily from the edge of war. The sudden and effective Japanese attack on Pearl Harbor turned us around—we were confused and fearful, angry and united. Yet, paradoxically and horribly, we were relieved, since the freedom of judgment was lifted and decision was thrust upon us.

Roosevelt's speech calling for a declaration of war on Japan held no surprises in terms of raw meaning: we were, in fact, at war and we knew it. But in the speech the President acknowledged and reflected the psychological state of the Union and by articulating that state made it bearable and permitted us to regroup for action.

One rather curious section of the speech warrants particular comment. Roosevelt's blunt, seemingly clumsy listing of the many Japanese military actions was a necessary recapitulation of the news that had been crackling in for twenty-four hours. We needed to know what the physical situation was, and Roosevelt needed to tell us that the attack on Hawaii was neither accidental nor isolated. This "material" was reinforced by the "form" he chose: the parallel structure and repetition of words (anaphora) hammered home the size and seriousness, "the repetition" of the continuing Japanese action.

PUBLISHED VERSION: U.S., Congress, Joint, *Congressional Record*, 77th Congress, 1st session, 1941, 87, pt. 9: 9519–20.
DISCOGRAPHY: Caedmon Record, TC 2033; playing time, 7:05.

Yesterday, December 7th, 1941—a date which will live in infamy—the United States of America was suddenly and deliberately attacked by naval and air forces of the Empire of Japan.

71

The United States was at peace with that nation and, at the solicitation of Japan, was still in conversation with its government and its Emperor, looking toward the maintenance of peace in the Pacific. Indeed, one hour after Japanese air squadrons had commenced bombing in the American island of Oahu, the Japanese Ambassador to the United States and his colleague delivered to our Secretary of State a formal reply to a recent American message. And while this reply stated that it seemed useless to continue the existing diplomatic negotiations, it contained no threat or hint of war or of armed attack.

10   It will be recorded that the distance of Hawaii from Japan makes it obvious that the attack was deliberately planned many days or even weeks ago. During the intervening time the Japanese government has deliberately sought to deceive the United States by false statements and expressions of hope for continued peace.

The attack yesterday on the Hawaiian Islands has caused severe damage to American naval and military forces. I regret to tell you that very many American lives have been lost. In addition, American ships have been reported torpedoed on the high seas between San Francisco and Honolulu.

20   Yesterday the Japanese government also launched an attack against Malaya.

Last night Japanese forces attacked Hong Kong.

Last night Japanese forces attacked Guam.

Last night Japanese forces attacked the Philippine Islands.

Last night the Japanese attacked Wake Island.

And this morning the Japanese attacked Midway Island.

Japan has, therefore, undertaken a surprise offensive extending throughout the Pacific area. The facts of yesterday and today speak for themselves. The people of the United States have already formed their

30   opinions and well understand the implications to the very life and safety of our nation.

As Commander-in-Chief of the Army and Navy, I have directed that all measures be taken for our defense.

But always will our whole nation remember the character of the onslaught against us.

No matter how long it may take us to overcome this premeditated invasion, the American people in their righteous might will win through to absolute victory.

I believe that I interpret the will of the Congress and of the people

40   when I assert that we will not only defend ourselves to the uttermost but will make it very certain that this form of treachery shall never again endanger us.

Hostilities exist. There is no blinking at the fact that our people, our territory, and our interests are in grave danger.

With confidence in our armed forces, with the unbounding determination of our people, we will gain the inevitable triumph—so help us God.

I ask that the Congress declare that since the unprovoked and dastardly attack by Japan on Sunday, December 7th, 1941, a state of war has existed between the United States and the Japanese Empire.

DWIGHT D. EISENHOWER

(1890–1969)

Order of the Day

June 6, 1944

A career army officer, Dwight D. Eisenhower rose to the rank of General of the Army and Supreme Commander of the Allied Expeditionary Force during World War II. In the spring of 1944 he was in England, commander of a great invasion army, prepared to attempt a Channel crossing that had blocked Napoleon in one century and Hitler in his own. Anxious about wind and weather, secrecy and morale, he finally gave the order to attack.

Although generally undistinguished as a speaker during his Presidency—he seemed trapped in the gray organization prose of reports—Eisenhower's "Order of the Day" is a ceremonial of the high rank demanded in committing thousands to battle. Simply and confidently he asserts their strength and unity and the necessity and nobility of their cause. The language and thought is elevated yet not emotional. He and his listeners are under too constant a stress to release that emotion—as might a crowd at a political rally. The climactic action is too great, the self too involved, for the comparative luxury of exposed emotion. Fear must now be released in the form of action for principles. "The Order of the Day" reaffirms those principles, makes possible the act.

OTHER IMPORTANT SPEECHES: "England and America" (1945), "First Inaugural" (1953), and "Geneva" (1955).

PUBLISHED VERSION: Dwight D. Eisenhower, The New York *Times*, June 6, 1944, p. 3, col. 6.

DISCOGRAPHY: Caedmon Record, TC 2033; playing time, 1:45.

Soldiers, sailors, and airmen of the Allied Expeditionary Force. You are about to embark upon the great crusade, toward which we have striven these many months. The eyes of the world are upon you. The hopes and prayers of liberty-loving people everywhere march with you.

In company with our brave Allies and brothers-in-arms on other fronts, you will bring about the destruction of the German war machine, the elimination of Nazi tyranny over the oppressed peoples of Europe, and security for ourselves in a free world.

74

Your task will not be an easy one. Your enemy is well trained, well equipped, and battle-hardened. He will fight savagely. But this is the year 1944. Much has happened since the Nazi triumphs of 1940–41. The United Nations have inflicted upon the Germans great defeats in open battle, man to man. Our air offensive has seriously reduced their strength in the air and their capacity to wage war on the ground. Our home fronts have given us an overwhelming superiority in weapons and munitions of war and placed at our disposal great reserves of trained fighting men.

The tide has turned. The free men of the world are marching together to victory. I have full confidence in your courage, devotion to duty, and 10 skill in battle. We will accept nothing less than full victory. Good luck, and let us all beseech the blessing of Almighty God upon this great and noble undertaking.

HARRY S. TRUMAN

(1884–   )

The Truman Doctrine

March 12, 1947

Roosevelt's death in the spring of 1945, less than four months before the end of World War II, shocked the nation in that time of universal shock. The colorful, patrician wartime leader was succeeded by Harry S. Truman, simply "a man of the people." After years of the Easterner's sophistication, the bluntness of the Missourian needed more than a little getting used to, but he grew under the critical and intricate trials of the postwar Presidency, its complexity of hopes and hopes dashed, and he was able to project his sincerity and intensity. Even his hot temper worked in his favor—he spoke, seemingly artlessly, man to man—and he was at his best, though dangerously so, in extempore speaking.

Truman's most significant speech demanded immediate and firm action from a recalcitrant Congress. Postwar relations between America and Russia had deteriorated steadily and "the bitter internal strife" in Greece—strife supported by Communist countries to the north—had to be resolved. His call was for aid to support the objectives of World War II by continuing the fight against totalitarianism and to reveal, again and clearly, America's commitment. In his Memoirs he wrote

The key sentence . . . read "I believe that it should be the policy of the United States [to support peoples who are resisting attempted subjugation by armed minorities or by outside pressures]." I took my pencil, scratched out "should" and wrote in "must." In several other places I did the same thing. I wanted no hedging in this speech. This was America's answer to the surge of expansion of Communist tyranny. It had to be clear and free of hesitation and double talk. . . . [The Truman Doctrine] was, I believe, the turning point in America's foreign policy.

Large bipartisan congressional majorities quickly approved of and implemented the policy ultimately so significant for Korea and Vietnam.

76

OTHER IMPORTANT SPEECHES: First Address to Congress (1945), Acceptance of
    Nomination (1948), Inaugural Address (1949), and "On the Presidency and
    the Legislature" (1954).
PUBLISHED VERSION: U.S., Congress, Joint, *Congressional Record*, 80th Con-
    gress, 1st session, 1947, 93, pt. 2: 1980–81.
DISCOGRAPHY: Caedmon Record, TC 2033; playing time, 18:37.

Mr. President, Mr. Speaker, Members of the Congress of the United
States. The gravity of the situation which confronts the world today neces-
sitates my appearance before a joint session of the Congress. The foreign
policy and the national security of this country are involved.

One aspect of the present situation, which I present to you at this
time for your consideration and decision, concerns Greece and Turkey.

The United States has received from the Greek government an urgent
appeal for financial and economic assistance. Preliminary reports from the
American economic mission now in Greece and reports from the American
Ambassador in Greece corroborate the statement of the Greek government   10
that assistance is imperative if Greece is to survive as a free nation. I do
not believe that the American people and the Congress wish to turn a deaf
ear to the appeal of the Greek government.

Greece is not a rich country. Lack of sufficient natural resources has
always forced the Greek people to work hard to make both ends meet.
Since 1940, this industrious, peace-loving country has suffered invasion,
four years of cruel enemy occupation, and bitter internal strife.

When forces of liberation entered Greece, they found that the retreat-
ing Germans had destroyed virtually all the railways, roads, port facilities,
communications, and merchant marine. More than a thousand villages   20
had been burned. Eighty-five percent of the children were tubercular.
Livestock, poultry, and draft animals had almost disappeared. Inflation had
wiped out practically all savings. As a result of these tragic conditions, a
militant minority, exploiting human want and misery, was able to create
political chaos which, until now, has made economic recovery impossible.

Greece is today without funds to finance the importation of those
goods which are essential to bare subsistence. Under these circumstances,
the people of Greece cannot make progress in solving their problems of
reconstruction. Greece is in desperate need of financial and economic
assistance to enable it to resume purchases of food, clothing, fuel, and   30
seeds. These are indispensable for the subsistence of its people and are
obtainable only from abroad. Greece must have help to import the goods
necessary to restore internal order and security so essential for economic
and political recovery.

The Greek government has also asked for the assistance of experienced American administrators, economists, and technicians to insure
that the financial and other aid given to Greece shall be used effectively in

creating a stable and self-sustaining economy and in improving its public administration.

The very existence of the Greek state is today threatened by the terrorist activities of several thousand armed men, led by Communists, who defy the government's authority at a number of points, particularly along the northern boundaries. A commission appointed by the United Nations Security Council is at present investigating disturbed conditions in northern Greece and alleged border violations along the frontiers between Greece on the one hand and Albania, Bulgaria, and Yugoslavia on the other.

10   Meanwhile, the Greek government is unable to cope with the situation. The Greek army is small and poorly equipped. It needs supplies and equipment if it is to restore authority to the government throughout Greek territory.

Greece must have assistance if it is to become a self-supporting and self-respecting democracy.

The United States must supply this assistance. We have already extended to Greece certain types of relief and economic aid, but these are inadequate.

There is no other country to which democratic Greece can turn. No 20 other nation is willing and able to provide the necessary support for a democratic Greek government. The British government, which has been helping Greece, can give no further financial or economic aid after March 31. Great Britain finds itself under the necessity of reducing or liquidating its commitments in several parts of the world, including Greece.

We have considered how the United Nations might assist in this crisis. But the situation is an urgent one, requiring immediate action, and the United Nations and its related organizations are not in a position to extend help of the kind that is required.

It is important to note that the Greek government has asked for our 30 aid in utilizing effectively the financial and other assistance we may give to Greece and in improving its public administration. It is of the utmost importance that we supervise the use of any funds made available to Greece, in such a manner that each dollar spent will count toward making Greece self-supporting and will help to build an economy in which a healthy democracy can flourish.

No government is perfect. One of the chief virtues of a democracy, however, is that its defects are always visible and under democratic processes can be pointed out and corrected. The government of Greece is not perfect. Nevertheless, it represents 85 percent of the members of the Greek 40 parliament who were chosen in an election last year. Foreign observers, including 692 Americans, considered this election to be a fair expression of the views of the Greek people.

The Greek government has been operating in an atmosphere of chaos and extremism. It has made mistakes. The extension of aid by this country does not mean that the United States condones everything that the Greek government has done or will do. We have condemned in the past, and we condemn now, extremist measures of the right or the left. We have in the past advised tolerance, and we advise tolerance now.

Greece's neighbor, Turkey, also deserves our attention. The future of Turkey as an independent and economically sound state is clearly no less important to the freedom-loving peoples of the world than the future of Greece. The circumstances in which Turkey finds itself today are consider- 10 ably different from those of Greece. Turkey has been spared the disasters that have beset Greece, and during the war the United States and Great Britain furnished Turkey with material aid. Nevertheless, Turkey now needs our support.

Since the war, Turkey has sought additional financial assistance from Great Britain and the United States for the purpose of effecting that modernization necessary for the maintenance of its national integrity. That integrity is essential to the preservation of order in the Middle East. The British government has informed us that, owing to its own difficulties, it can no longer extend financial or economic aid to Turkey. 20

As in the case of Greece, if Turkey is to have the assistance it needs, the United States must supply it. We are the only country able to provide that help.

I am fully aware of the broad implications involved if the United States extends assistance to Greece and Turkey, and I shall discuss these implications with you at this time.

One of the primary objectives of the foreign policy of the United States is the creation of conditions in which we and other nations will be able to work out a way of life free from coercion. This was a fundamental issue in the war with Germany and Japan. Our victory was won over coun- 30 tries which sought to impose their will, and their way of life, upon other nations. To insure the peaceful development of nations, free from coercion, the United States has taken a leading part in establishing the United Nations. The United Nations is designed to make possible lasting freedom and independence for all its members. We shall not realize our objectives, however, unless we are willing to help free peoples to maintain their free institutions and their national integrity against aggressive movements that seek to impose upon them totalitarian regimes. This is no more than a frank recognition that totalitarian regimes imposed upon free peoples, by direct or indirect aggression, undermine the foundations of international 40 peace and hence the security of the United States.

The peoples of a number of countries of the world have recently had totalitarian regimes forced upon them against their will. The government of the United States has made frequent protests against coercion and intimidation, in violation of the Yalta agreement, in Poland, Rumania, and Bulgaria. I must also state that in a number of other countries there have been similar developments.

At the present moment in world history nearly every nation must choose between alternative ways of life. The choice is too often not a free one. One way of life is based upon the will of the majority and is distinguished by free institutions, representative government, free elections, guarantees of individual liberty, freedom of speech and religion, and free-
10   dom from political oppression. The second way of life is based upon the will of a minority forcibly imposed upon the majority. It relies upon terror and oppression, a controlled—controlled press and radio, fixed elections, and the suppression of personal freedoms.

I believe that it must be the policy of the United States to support free peoples who are resisting attempted subjugation by armed minorities or by outside pressures. I believe that we must assist free peoples to work out their own destinies in their own way.

I believe that our help should be primarily through economic and financial aid which is essential to economic stability and orderly political
20   processes.

The world is not static, and the *status quo* is not sacred, but we cannot allow changes in the *status quo* in violation of the charter of the United Nations by such methods as coercion or by subterfuges, such subterfuges as political infiltration. In helping free and independent nations to maintain their freedom, the United States will be giving effect to the principles of the charter of the United Nations.

It is necessary only to glance at a map to realize that the survival and integrity of the Greek nation are of grave importance in a much wider situation. If Greece should fall under the control of an armed minority, the
30   effect upon its neighbor, Turkey, would be immediate and serious. Confusion and disorder might well spread throughout the entire Middle East. Moreover, the disappearance of Greece as an independent state would have a profound effect upon those countries in Europe whose peoples are struggling against great difficulties to maintain their freedoms and their independence while they repair the damages of war.

It would be an unspeakable tragedy if these countries, which have struggled so long against overwhelming odds, should lose that victory for which they sacrificed so much. Collapse of free institutions and loss of independence would be disastrous not only for them but for the world.
40   Discouragement and possibly failure would quickly be the lot of neighboring peoples striving to maintain their freedom and independence.

Should we fail to aid Greece and Turkey in this fateful hour, the effect will be far-reaching to the West as well as to the East. We must take immediate and resolute action.

I therefore ask the Congress to provide authority for assistance to Greece and Turkey in the amount of $400 million for the period ending June 30, 1948. In requesting these funds, I have taken into consideration the maximum amount of relief assistance which would be furnished to Greece out of the $350 million which I recently requested that the Congress authorize for the prevention of starvation and suffering in countries devastated by the war.

In addition to funds, I ask the Congress to authorize the detail of American civilian and military personnel to Greece and Turkey, at the request of those countries, to assist in the tasks of reconstruction and for the purpose of supervising the use of such financial and material assistance as may be furnished. I recommend that authority also be provided for the instruction and training of selected Greek and Turkish personnel.

Finally, I ask that the Congress provide authority which will permit the speediest and most effective use, in terms of needed commodities, supplies, and equipment, of such funds as may be authorized.

If further funds, or further authority, should be needed for the purposes indicated in this message, I shall not hesitate to bring the situation before the Congress. On this subject the executive and legislative branches of the Government must work together.

This is a serious course upon which we embark. I would not recommend it except that the alternative is much more serious. The United States contributed—The United States contributed $341 billion toward winning World War II. This is an investment in world freedom and world peace. The assistance that I am recommending for Greece and Turkey amounts to a little more than one-tenth of one percent of this investment. It is only common sense that we should safeguard this investment and make sure that it was not in vain.

The seeds of totalitarian regimes are nurtured by misery and want. They spread and grow in the evil soil of poverty and strife. They reach their full growth when the hope of a people for a better life has died. We must keep that hope alive.

The free peoples of the world look to us for support in maintaining their freedom. If we falter in our leadership, we may endanger the peace of the world, and we shall surely endanger the welfare of this nation.

Great responsibilities have been placed upon us by the swift movement of events. I am confident that the Congress will face these responsibilities squarely.

GEORGE CATLETT MARSHALL

(1880–1959)

The Marshall Plan

June 5, 1947

As Chief of Staff during World War II, General Marshall is credited with organizing the greatest military force in history, a force that rocketed from 187,000 men in 1939 to over 4,000,000 by 1944. He became Secretary of State under President Truman and, still later, Secretary of Defense. His speeches are models of "the plain style"—direct, unadorned, clear. His early interest was in practical problems, their causes and effects, their questions and solutions. Almost all his speeches as an officer involved army planning or the progress of the war and as a statesman concerned the Marshall Plan, so that he was constantly explaining and justifying expenditures to Congress and the people. In his later speeches, however, his drive for large principles heightened and enriched his expression and delivery.

The Marshall Plan was a major policy statement, since following the Truman Doctrine, it reinforced America's commitment to an international position. The speech is not a vivid one, but Marshall's talents, experience, attitude, and voice worked to underline the enormous significance of his essentially informative statement. Republican Senator Arthur Vandenberg said in a great speech supporting the plan in its final form, "In the name of peace, stability, and freedom it deserves prompt passage. In the name of intelligent American self-interest it envisions a mighty undertaking worthy of our faith" (March 1, 1948). In 1953 George C. Marshall, a career military officer, received the Nobel Peace Prize for the Marshall Plan.

OTHER IMPORTANT SPEECHES: "American Aid and the Foreign Press" (July 1, 1947), "European Recovery Program" (January 8, 1948), and "The United Nations" (September 23, 1948).

PUBLISHED VERSION: George C. Marshall, "European Unity," Vital Speeches, July 1, 1947, pp. 553–54.

DISCOGRAPHY: Caedmon Record, TC 2033; playing time, 12:23.

Mr. President, Dr. Conant, Members of the Board of Overseers, Ladies and Gentlemen. I'm profoundly grateful, touched, by the great distinction and honor, great confidence, accorded me by the authorities of Harvard this morning. I'm overwhelmed, as a matter of fact, and I'm rather fearful of my inability to maintain such a high rating that you've been generous enough to accord to me. In these historic and lovely surroundings, this perfect day, and this very wonderful assembly, it is a tremendously impressive thing to an individual in my position.

But to speak more seriously.

I need not tell you that the world situation is very serious. That must   10
be apparent to all intelligent people. I think one difficulty is that the problem is one of such enormous complexity that the very mass of facts, presented to the public by press and radio, make it exceedingly difficult for the man in the street to reach a clear appraisement of the situation. Furthermore, the people of this country are distant from the troubled areas of the earth and it is hard for them to comprehend the plight and consequent reactions of the long-suffering peoples of Europe and the effect of those reactions on their governments in connection with our efforts to promote peace in the world.

In considering the requirements for the rehabilitation of Europe, the   20
physical loss of life, the visible destruction of cities, factories, mines, and railroads was correctly estimated. But it has become obvious during recent months that this visible destruction was probably less serious than the dislocation of the entire fabric of European economy. For the past ten years conditions have been highly abnormal. The feverish preparation for war and the more feverish maintenance of the war effort engulfed all aspects of national economies. Machinery has fallen into disrepair or is entirely obsolete. Under the arbitrary and destructive Nazi rule, virtually every possible enterprise was geared into the German war machine. Long-standing commercial ties, private institutions, banks, insurance companies, and shipping   30
companies disappeared, through loss of capital, absorption through nationalization, or by simple destruction. In many countries, confidence in the local currency has been severely shaken. The breakdown of the business structure of Europe during the war was complete. Recovery has been seriously retarded by the fact that two years after the close of hostilities a peace settlement with Germany and Austria has not been agreed upon. But even given a more prompt solution of these difficult problems, the rehabilitation of the economic structure of Europe, quite evidently, will require a much longer time and greater effort than had been foreseen.

There is a phase of this matter which is both interesting and serious.   40
The farmer has always produced the foodstuffs to exchange with the city dweller for the other necessities of life. This division of labor is the basis of modern civilization. At the present time, it is threatened with breakdown.

The town and city industries are not producing adequate goods to exchange with the food-producing farmer. Raw materials and fuel are in short supply. Machinery, as I have said, is lacking or worn out. The farmer or the peasant cannot find the goods for sale which he desires to purchase, so the sale of his farm produce for money which he cannot use seems to him an unprofitable transaction. He therefore has withdrawn many fields from crop cultivation and is using them for grazing. He feeds more grain to stock and finds for himself and his family an ample supply of food, however short he may be on clothing and the other ordinary gad-
10 gets of civilization. Meanwhile, people in the cities are short of food and fuel and in some places approaching the starvation limit. So the governments are forced to use their foreign money and credits to procure these necessities abroad. This process exhausts funds which are urgently needed for reconstruction. Thus, a very serious situation is rapidly developing which bodes no good for the world. The modern system of the division of labor, upon which the exchange of products is based, is in danger of breaking down.

The truth of the matter is that Europe's requirements for the next three or four years of foreign food and other essential products, principally
20 from America, are so much greater than her present ability to pay that she must have substantial additional help or face economic, social, and political deterioration of a very grave character.

The remedy seems to lie in breaking the vicious circle and restoring the confidence of the European people in the economic future of their own countries and of Europe as a whole. The manufacturer and the farmer throughout wide areas must be able and willing to exchange their products for currencies the continuing value of which is not open to question.

Aside from the demoralizing effect on the world at large and the possi-
30 bilities of disturbances arising as a result of the desperate—desperation of the people concerned, the consequences to the economy of the United States should be apparent to all. It is logical that the United States should do whatever it is able to do to assist in the return of normal economic health in the world, without which there can be no political stability and no assured peace. Our policy is directed not against any country or doctrine but against hunger, poverty, desperation, and chaos. Its purpose should be the revival of a working economy in the world so as to permit the emergence of political and social conditions in which free institutions can exist.

40 Such assistance, I am convinced, must not be on a piecemeal basis, as various crises develop. Any assistance that this government may render, in the future, should provide a cure rather than a mere palliative. Any government that is willing to assist in the task of recovery will find full coopera-

tion, I am sure, on the part of the United States government. Any government which maneuvers to block the recovery of other countries cannot expect help from us. Furthermore—furthermore, governments, political parties, or groups which seek to perpetuate human misery in order to profit therefrom politically, or otherwise, will encounter the opposition of the United States.

It is already evident that, before the United States government can proceed much further in its efforts to alleviate the situation and help start the European world on its way to recovery, there must be some agreement among the countries of Europe as to the requirements of the situation and   10 the part those countries themselves will take in order to give a proper effect to whatever action might be undertaken by this government. It would be neither fitting nor efficacious for our government to undertake to draw up unilaterally a program designed to place Europe on its feet economically. This is the business of the Europeans. The initiative, I think, must come from Europe. The role of this country should consist of friendly aid in the drafting of a European program and of later support of such a program, so far as it may be practicable for us to do so. The program should be a joint one, agreed to by a number, if not all European nations.

An essential part of any successful action on the part of the United   20 States is an understanding on the part of the people of America of the character of the problem and the remedies to be applied. Political passion and prejudice should have no part. With foresight, and a willingness on the part of our people to face up to the vast responsibility which history has clearly placed upon our country, the difficulties I have outlined can and will be overcome.

I am sorry that on each occasion I have said something publicly in regard to our international situation, I have been forced, by the necessities of the case, to enter into rather technical discussions. But, to my mind it is of vast importance that our people reach some general understanding of   30 what the complications really are, rather than react from a passion or a prejudice or an emotion of the moment. As I said more formally a moment ago, we are remote from the scene of these troubles. It is virtually impossible, at this distance, merely by reading or listening or even seeing photographs and motion pictures, to grasp at all the real significance of the situation. And yet, the whole world of the future hangs on a proper judgment. It hangs, I think to a large extent, on the realization of the American people of just what are the very dominant factors, what are the reactions of the people, what are the justifications of those reactions, what are the sufferings, what is needed, what can best be done, what must be done.   40

Thank you very much.

WILLIAM FAULKNER
(1897–1962)

Nobel Prize
Speech

December 10, 1950

A reluctant speaker with a soft, thin voice, William Faulkner is a perfect indication of the wide variety of greatness in speaking. With something that needed saying and a long-exercised sense of paragraph rhythm, Faulkner could passionately and sincerely bring into play the thought, feelings, music, images, and wit revealed in his prose. He was a great speaker far removed from the popular stereotype of a man on a podium.

By 1950 the cold war had gone on and on, and the Korean War threatened to involve China and become the last war. Faulkner in his brief Nobel Prize Speech shocks with his blunt summary: "There is only the question: When will I be blown up?" But equally aggressively he offers an alternative to immobilizing fear and calls on man to remember "the old universal truths." Speaking directly to the young writer, he defines the writer's—or speaker's—human role: "It is his privilege to help man endure by lifting his heart, by reminding him of the courage and honor and hope and pride and compassion and pity and sacrifice which have been the glory of his past." I can think of no higher calling and no greater statement of that calling.

OTHER IMPORTANT SPEECHES: Funeral Sermon for Mammy Caroline Barr (1940), Address to the Delta Council (1952), and "A Word to Virginians" (1958).

DISCOGRAPHY: Caedmon Record, TC 2035; playing time, 3:00. [The recording of which this text is a transcription was made after the actual speech in Sweden when Faulkner received the Nobel Prize for Literature.]

I feel that this award was not made to me as a man, but to my work, a life's work in the agony and sweat of the human spirit, not for glory and least of all for profit, but to create out of the materials of the human spirit

[Reprinted by permission. Reprinted version in *The Faulkner Reader*, Copyright 1954 by William Faulkner (Random House, Inc.)]

something which did not exist before. So this award is only mine in trust.

It will not be difficult to find a dedication for the money part of it commensurate with the purpose and significance of its origin. But I would like to do the same with the acclaim, too, by using this moment as a pinnacle from which I might be listened to by the young men and women already dedicated to the same anguish and travail, among whom is already that one who will some day stand here where I am standing.

Our tragedy today is a general and universal physical fear so long sustained by now that we can even bear it. There are no longer problems of the spirit. There is only the question: When will I be blown up? Because of this, the young man or woman writing today has forgotten the problems of the human heart in conflict with itself, which alone can make good writing because only that is worth writing about, worth the agony and the sweat.

He must learn them again. He must teach himself that the basest of all things is to be afraid and, teaching himself that, forget it forever, leaving no room in his workshop for anything but the old verities and truths of the heart, the old universal truths lacking which any story is ephemeral and doomed: love and honor and pity and pride and compassion and sacrifice.

Until he does so, he labors under a curse. He writes not of love but of lust, of defeats in which nobody loses anything of value, of victories without hope and, worst of all, without pity or compassion. His griefs grieve on no universal bones, leaving no scars; he writes not of the heart but of the glands.

Until he relearns these things, he will write as though he stood among and watched the end of man. I decline to accept the end of man. It is easy enough to say that man is immortal simply because he will endure, that when the last ding-dong of doom has clanged and faded from the last worthless rock hanging tideless in the last red and dying evening, that even then there will still be one more sound, that of his puny, inexhaustible voice, still talking.

I refuse to accept this. I believe that man will not merely endure, he will prevail. He is immortal, not because he alone among creatures has an inexhaustible voice, but because he has a soul—a spirit capable of compassion and sacrifice and endurance. The poet's, the writer's, duty is to write about these things. It is his privilege to help man endure, by lifting his heart, by reminding him of the courage and honor and hope and pride and compassion and pity and sacrifice which have been the glory of his past. The poet's voice need not merely be the record of man, it can be one of the props, the pillars to help him endure and prevail.

DOUGLAS MACARTHUR
(1880–1964)

Address
Before Congress

April 19, 1951

Douglas MacArthur's career was consistently successful and vivid. A brilliant student at West Point, he quickly rose to high commands in the Army, became the youngest Chief of Staff in history, and after a dramatic role in World War II, governed occupied Japan. By the time of the Korean War, he was clearly fixed in the history and myth of his country. His openly stated policies as a military man, however, came into direct conflict with the declared American aims of a limited war in Korea, and President Truman was forced to relieve him of his command of the United Nations forces. Essentially the issue was the Constitutional one of civilian control of the military establishment. Popular reaction to the dismissal was heated, and rarely has any speaker appeared under more emotional circumstances than did MacArthur when he spoke before a Joint Session of Congress.

Few modern speeches have elicited stronger antithetical reactions. Experienced judges viewed it as literally inspired, an unquestionably great speech, while others equally experienced acidly damned it as meaningless or irresponsible or "corny." Of major significance, however, is the confusion of the critics on the major point of the speech: for good or ill, it is MacArthur on MacArthur. There is an appeal to himself as authority which places an enormous burden on his admittedly strong ethos and seduces him from logical development of issues. It is a glorious "farewell address" that is more personal than statesmanlike.

ANOTHER IMPORTANT SPEECH: "Farewell to the Cadets" (1962).

PUBLISHED VERSION: U.S., Congress, Joint, *Congressional Record*, 82nd Congress, 1st session, 1951, 97, pt. 3: 4123–25.

DISCOGRAPHY: Caedmon Records, TC 2035; playing time, 36:30.

Mr. President, Mr. Speaker, and Distinguished Members of the Congress. I stand on this rostrum with a sense of deep humility and great pride, humility in the wake of those great American architects of our history who have stood here before me, pride in the reflection that this forum of legislative debate represents human liberty in the purest form yet devised. Here are centered the hopes and aspirations and faith of the entire human race.

I do not stand here as advocate for any partisan cause, for the issues are fundamental and reach quite beyond the realm of partisan consideration. They must be resolved on the highest plane of national interest if our course is to prove sound and our future protected. I trust, therefore, that you will do me the justice of receiving that which I have to say as solely expressing the considered viewpoint of a fellow American. I address you, with neither rancor nor bitterness in the fading twilight of life, with but one purpose in mind: To serve my country.

The issues are global and so interlocked that to consider the problems of one sector, oblivious to those of another, is but to court disaster for the whole. While Asia is commonly referred to as the gateway to Europe, it is no less true that Europe is the gateway to Asia, and the broad influence of the one cannot fail to have its impact upon the other. There are those who claim our strength is inadequate to protect on both fronts, that we cannot divide our effort. I can think of no greater expression of defeatism. If a potential enemy can divide his strength on two fronts, it is for us to counter his effort. The Communist threat is a global one. Its successful advance in one sector threatens the destruction of every other sector. You cannot appease or otherwise surrender to Communism in Asia without simultaneously undermining our efforts to halt its advance in Europe.

Beyond pointing out these general truisms, I shall confine my discussion to the general areas of Asia. Before one may objectively assess the situation now existing there, he must comprehend something of Asia's past and the revolutionary changes which have—which have marked her course up to the present. Long exploited by the so-called colonial powers, with little opportunity to achieve any degree of social justice, individual dignity, or a higher standard of life, such as guided our own noble administration of the Philippines, the peoples of Asia found their opportunity in the war just past to throw off the shackles of colonialism and now see—see the dawn of new opportunity, a heretofore unfelt dignity, and the self-respect of political freedom. Mustering half of the earth's population, and 60 percent of its natural resources, these peoples are rapidly consolidating a new force, both moral and material, with which to raise the living standard and erect adaptations of the design of modern progress to their own distinct cultural environments. Whether one adheres to the concept of colonization or not, this is the direction of Asian progress, and it may not be stopped. It is a corollary to the shift of the world economic frontiers as the whole epicenter of world affairs rotates back toward the area whence it started.

In this situation, it becomes vital that our own country orient its policies in consonance with this basic evolutionary condition rather than pursue a course blind to the reality that the colonial era is now past and the Asian peoples covet the right to shape their own free destiny. What they seek now is friendly guidance, understanding, and support, not imperious direction, the dignity of equality, and not the shame of subjugation.

Their prewar standard of life, pitifully low, is infinitely lower now in the devastation left in war's wake. World ideologies play little part in Asian thinking and are little understood. What the people strive for is the opportunity for a little more food in their stomachs, a little better clothing on their backs, a little firmer roof over their heads, and the realization of the normal nationalist urge for political freedom.

10   These political-social conditions have but an indirect bearing upon our own national security but do form a backdrop to contemporary planning which must be thoughtfully considered if we are to avoid the pitfalls of unrealism.

Of more direct and immediate bearing upon our national security are the changes wrought in the strategic potential of the Pacific Ocean in the course of the past war.

Prior thereto the western strategic frontier of the United States lay on the littoral line of the Americas, with an exposed island salient extending out through Hawaii, Midway, and Guam to the Philippines. That salient
20   proved not an outpost of strength but an avenue of weakness along which the enemy could and did attack. The Pacific was a potential area of advance for any predatory force intent upon striking at the bordering land areas.

All this was changed by our Pacific victory. Our strategic frontier then shifted to embrace the entire Pacific Ocean, which became a vast moat to protect us as long as we held it. Indeed, it acts as a protective shield for all of the Americas and all free lands of the Pacific Ocean area. We control it to the shores of Asia by a chain of islands extending in an arc from the Aleutians to the Marianas, held by us and our free allies.

30   From this island chain we can dominate with sea and air power every Asiatic port from Vladivostok to Singapore—with sea and air power, every port, as I said, from Vladivostok to Singapore—and prevent any hostile movement into the Pacific. Any predatory attack from Asia must be an amphibious effort. No amphibious force can be successful without control of the sea lanes, and the air over those lanes, in its avenue of advance. With naval and air supremacy and modest ground elements to defend bases, any major attack from continental Asia toward us, or our friends of the Pacific, would be doomed to failure. Under such conditions, the Pacific no longer represents menacing avenues of approach for a prospec-
40   tive invader. It assumes, instead, the friendly aspect of a peaceful lake.

Our line of defense is a natural one and can be maintained with a minimum of military effort and expense. It envisions no attack against anyone, nor does it provide the bastions essential for offensive operations but, properly maintained, would be an invincible defense against aggression.

The holding of this littoral defense line in the western Pacific is entirely dependent upon holding all segments thereof, for any major breach of that line by an unfriendly power would render vulnerable to determined attack every other major segment. This is a military estimate as to which I have yet to find a military leader who will take exception.

For that reason, I have strongly recommended in the past, as a matter of military urgency, that under no circumstances must Formosa fall under Communist control. Such an eventuality would at once threaten the free- 10 dom of the Philippines and the loss of Japan and might well force our western frontier back to the coast of California, Oregon, and Washington.

To understand the changes which now appear upon the Chinese mainland, one must understand the changes in Chinese character and culture over the past fifty years. China up to fifty years ago was completely nonhomogeneous, being compartmented into groups divided against each other. The warmaking tendency was almost nonexistent, as they still followed the tenets of the Confucian ideal of pacifist culture.

At the turn of the century under the regime of Chan So Lin, efforts toward greater homogeneity produced the start of a nationalist urge. This 20 was further and more successfully developed under the leadership of Chiang Kai-shek but has been brought to its greatest fruition under the present regime to the point that it has now taken on the character of a united nationalism of increasingly dominant aggressive tendencies.

Through these past fifty years the Chinese people have thus become militarized in their concepts and in their ideals. They now constitute excellent soldiers, with competent staffs and commanders. This has produced a new and dominant power in Asia which, for its own purposes, is allied with Soviet Russia but which in its own concepts and methods has become aggressively imperialistic with a lust for expansion and increased power, 30 normal to this type of imperialism.

There is little of the ideological concept either one way or another in the Chinese makeup. The standard of living is so low and the capital accumulation has been so thoroughly dissipated by war that the masses are desperate and avid to follow any leadership which seems to promise the alleviation of local stringencies.

I have from the beginning believed that the Chinese Communists' support of the North Koreans was the dominant one. Their interests are, at present, parallel to those of the Soviet, but I believe that the aggressiveness recently displayed, not only in Korea but also in Indochina and Tibet 40 and pointing potentially toward the south, reflects predominantly the same lust for the expansion of power which has animated every would-be conqueror since the beginning of time.

The Japanese people, since the war, have undergone the greatest reformation recorded in modern history. With a commendable will, eagerness to learn, and marked capacity to understand, they have from the ashes left in war's wake erected in Japan an edifice dedicated to the primacy of individual liberty and personal dignity, and in the ensuing process there has been created a truly representative government committed to the advance of political morality, freedom of economic enterprise, and social justice.

Politically, economically, and socially, Japan is now abreast of many free nations of the earth and will not again fail the universal trust. That it
10   may be counted upon to wield a profoundly beneficial influence over the course of events in Asia is attested by the magnificent manner in which the Japanese people have met the recent challenge of war, unrest, and confusion surrounding them from the outside and checked Communism within their own frontiers, without the slightest slackening in their forward progress. I sent all four of our occupation divisions to the Korean battlefront without the slightest qualms as to the effect of the resulting power vacuum upon Japan. The results fully justified my faith. I know of no nation more serene, orderly, and industrious nor in which higher hopes can be entertained for future constructive service in the advance of the
20   human race.

Of our former ward—of our former ward, the Philippines, we can look forward in confidence that the existing unrest will be corrected and a strong and healthy nation will grow in the longer aftermath of war's terrible destructiveness. We must be patient and understanding and never fail them, as in our hour of need they did not fail us. A Christian nation, the Philippines stand as a mighty bulwark of Christianity in the Far East, and its capacity for high moral leadership in Asia is unlimited.

On Formosa, the government of the Republic of China has had the opportunity to refute by action much of the malicious gossip which so
30   undermined the strength of its leadership on the Chinese mainland. The Formosan people are receiving a just and enlightened administration with majority representation on the organs of government, and politically, economically, and socially, they appear to be advancing along sound and constructive lines.

With this brief insight into the surrounding areas, I now turn to the Korean conflict.

While I was not consulted prior to the President's decision to intervene in support of the Republic of Korea, that decision, from a military standpoint, proved a sound one. As we—as I say, proved a sound one,
40   as we hurled back the invader and decimated his forces. Our victory was complete, and our objectives within reach, when Red China intervened with numerically superior ground forces. This created a new war and an entirely new situation, a situation not contemplated when our

forces were committed against the North Korean invaders, a situation which called for new decisions in the diplomatic sphere to permit the realistic adjustment of military strategy. Such decisions have not been forthcoming. While no man in his right mind would advocate sending our ground forces into continental China, and such was never given a thought, the new situation did urgently demand a drastic revision of strategic planning if our political aim was to defeat this new enemy, as we had defeated the old.

Apart from the military need, as I saw it, to neutralize the sanctuary protection given the enemy north of the Yalu, I felt that military necessity in the conduct of the war made necessary, first, the intensification of our economic blockade against China; two, the imposition of a naval blockade against the China coast; three, removal of restrictions on air reconnaissance of China's coastal areas and of Manchuria; four, removal of restrictions on the forces of the Republic of China on Formosa, with logistical support to contribute to their effective operation against the Chinese mainland.

For entertaining these views, all professionally designed to support our forces committed to Korea and to bring hostilities to an end with the least possible delay and at a saving of countless American and Allied lives, I have been severely criticized in lay circles, principally abroad, despite my understanding that from a military standpoint the above views have been fully shared in past by practically every military leader concerned with the Korean campaign, including our own Joint Chiefs of Staff.

I called for reinforcements but was informed that reinforcements were not available. I made clear that if not permitted to destroy the enemy built-up bases north of the Yalu, if not permitted to utilize the friendly Chinese force of some 600,000 men on Formosa, if not permitted to blockade the China coast to prevent the Chinese Reds from getting succor from without, and if there were to be no hope of major reinforcements, the position of the command from the military standpoint forbade victory.

We could hold, in Korea, by constant maneuver and at an approximate area where our supply line advantages were in balance with the supply line disadvantages of the enemy, but we could hope at best for only an indecisive campaign with its terrible and constant attrition upon our forces if the enemy utilized its full military potential.

I have constantly called for the new political decisions essential to a solution.

Efforts have been made to distort my position. It has been said, in effect, that I was a warmonger. Nothing could be further from the truth. I know war as few other men now living know it, and nothing to me—and nothing to me is more revolting. I have long advocated its complete abolition, as its very destructiveness on both friend and foe has rendered it useless as a means of settling international disputes. Indeed, on the second day of September, 1945, just following the surrender of the Japanese nation on the battleship *Missouri*, I formally cautioned as follows:

Men, since the beginning of time, have sought peace. Various methods through the ages have been attempted to devise an international process to prevent or settle disputes between nations. From the very start workable methods were found insofar as individual citizens were concerned, but the mechanics of an instrumentality of larger international scope have never been successful. Military alliances, balances of power, leagues of nations, all in turn failed,
10 leaving the only path to be by way of the crucible of war. The utter destructiveness of war now blots out this alternative. We have had our last chance. If we will not devise some greater and more equitable system, Armageddon will be at our door. The problem basically is theological and involves a spiritual recrudescence and improvement of human character that will synchronize with our almost matchless advances in science, art, literature, and all material and cultural developments of the past two thousand years. It must be of the spirit if we are to save the flesh.

But once war is forced upon us, there is no other alternative than to apply every available means to bring it to a swift end. War's very object is
20 victory, not prolonged indecision. In war there is no substitute for victory.

There are some who, for varying reasons, would appease Red China. They are blind to history's clear lesson, for history teaches with unmistakable emphasis that appeasement but begets new and bloodier war. It points to no single instance where this end has justified that means, where appeasement has led to more than a sham peace. Like blackmail, it lays the basis for new and successively greater demands until, as in blackmail, violence becomes the only other alternative. Why, my soldiers asked of me, surrender military advantages to an enemy in the field? I could not
30 answer. Some may say to avoid spread of the conflict into an all-out war with China. Others, to avoid Soviet intervention. Neither explanation seems valid, for China is already engaging with the maximum power it can commit, and the Soviet will not necessarily mesh its actions with our moves. Like a cobra, any new enemy will more likely strike whenever it feels that the relativity in military or other potential is in its favor on a worldwide basis.

The tragedy of Korea is further heightened by the fact that its military action is confined to its territorial limits. It condemns that nation, which it is our purpose to save, to suffer the devastating impact of full
40 naval and air bombardment while the enemy's sanctuaries are fully protected from such attack and devastation. Of the nations of the world Korea alone, up to now, is the sole one which has risked its all against Communism. The magnificence of the courage and fortitude of the

Korean people defies description. They—they have chosen to risk death rather than slavery. Their last words to me were, "Don't scuttle the Pacific."

I have just left your fighting sons in Korea. They have met all tests there, and I can report to you without reservation they are splendid in every way. It was my constant effort to preserve them and end this savage conflict honorably and with the least loss of time and a minimum sacrifice of life. Its growing bloodshed has caused me the deepest anguish and anxiety. Those gallant men will remain often in my thoughts and in my prayers always.

I am closing my fifty-two years of military service. When I joined the Army, even before the turn of the century, it was the fulfillment of all of my boyish hopes and dreams. The world has turned over many times since I took the oath on the plain at West Point, and the hopes and dreams have long since vanished. But I still remember the refrain of one of the most popular barrack ballads of that day which proclaimed most proudly that "old soldiers never die, they just fade away." And, like the old soldier of that ballad, I now close my military career and just fade away, an old soldier who tried to do his duty as God gave him the light to see that duty. Good-by.

ADLAI E.
STEVENSON
(1900–1965)

Acceptance
of Nomination

July 26, 1952

Adlai E. Stevenson, then Governor of Illinois, accepted the Democrats' nomination in the 1952 Presidential campaign against Eisenhower. Most political observers have concluded that no one could have beaten the tremendously popular hero of World War II and that the country, wearied of war and rumors of war, wanted the reassurance of the warm and friendly general with the open smile. Although Stevenson lost in 1952 and again in 1956, in his campaigns he gained a national audience for what a critic has called "one of the most polished, literate, articulate men to ever run for the Presidency," and his speeches will endure for their wisdom, variety, and grace.

An avid reader, Stevenson was clearly a man who loved and needed language. He had significant experience as an editor at Princeton and, before his law practice, as a writer on his family's newspaper. Perhaps the real source of his speaking began with his rejection of the ghost writer and with his independence of speeches by committees. He argued that writing his own speeches was "a learning and synthesizing process" that deepened thought, polished expression, and freed delivery. Those speeches were his, stamped with his wit, and his thought, and his feeling.

Stevenson's Acceptance of Nomination is a speech of many purposes. After the hurly-burly of a national convention with its warring factions, unity must be established through praise of the party's history, major figures, and goals. The attacks of the Republicans must be challenged, especially those claiming that the Democrats have been so long in office that corruption is rife and "it's time for a change." Stevenson establishes himself as a party spokesman, but he also establishes both his humility and confidence. His deep respect for the office of the Presidency is clearly revealed, and while making no cheap promises about himself or his nation, he offers hope for a possible Golden Age if men of good will seek it. A campaign has begun.

OTHER IMPORTANT SPEECHES: "The True Nature of Patriotism" (1952), "The
    Quest for Peace and Tranquility" (1953), "The Political Relevance of
    Moral Principle" (1959), "Today's Most Fateful Fact" (1959), "Let Us
    Work While It Is Yet Day" (1964), and "Shades of Gray" (1965).
PUBLISHED VERSION: Adlai Stevenson, "I Accept Your Nomination and Your
    Program," *Vital Speeches*, August 15, 1952, pp. 645–46.
DISCOGRAPHY: Caedmon Record, TC 2035; playing time, 15:05.

Mr. President, Ladies and Gentlemen of the Convention, My Fellow Citizens. I accept your nomination and your program. I should have preferred to hear those words uttered by a stronger, a wiser, a better man than myself. But, after listening to the President's speech, I even feel better about myself. None of you, my friends, can wholly appreciate what is in my heart. I can only hope that you understand my words. They will be few.

I have not sought the honor you have done me. I could not seek it, because I aspired to another office, which was the full measure of my ambition, and one does not treat the highest office within the gift of the 10
people of Illinois as an alternative or as a consolation prize.

I would not seek your nomination for the Presidency, because the burdens of that office stagger the imagination. Its potential for good or evil, now and in the years of our lives, smothers exultation and converts vanity to prayer.

I have asked the Merciful Father—the Father of us all—to let this cup pass from me, but from such dread responsibility one does not shrink in fear, in self-interest, or in false humility. So, "If this cup may not pass from me, except I drink it, Thy will be done."

That my heart has been troubled, that I have not sought this nomina- 20
tion, that I could not seek it in good conscience, that I would not seek it in honest self-appraisal, is not to say that I value it the less. Rather it is that I revere the office of the Presidency of the United States.

And now, my friends, that you have made your decision, I will fight to win that office with—with all my heart and my soul. And, with your help, I have no doubt that we will win.

You have summoned me to the highest mission within the gift of any people. I could not be more proud. Better men than I were at hand for this mighty task, and I owe to you and to them every resource of mind and of strength that I possess to make your deed today a good one for 30
our country and for our party. I am confident too, that your selection for—of a candidate for Vice President will strengthen me and our party immeasurably in the hard, the implacable work that lies ahead of all of us.

I know you join me in gratitude and respect for the great Democrats

and the leaders of our generation whose names you have considered here
in this convention, whose vigor, whose character, whose devotion to the
Republic we love so well have won the respect of countless Americans and
have enriched our party. I shall need them, we shall need them, because I
have not changed in any respect since yesterday. Your nomination, awe-
some as I find it, has not enlarged my capacities, so I am profoundly grateful and emboldened by their comradeship and their fealty and I have been
deeply moved by their expressions of good will and of support. And I cannot, my friends, resist the urge to take the one opportunity that has been
10   afforded me to pay my humble respects to a very great and good American,
whom I am proud to call my kinsman, Alben Barkley of Kentucky.

Let me say, too, that I have been heartened by the conduct of this
convention. You have argued and disagreed, because as Democrats you
care and you care deeply. But you have disagreed and argued without calling each other liars and thieves, without despoiling our best traditions—you have not spoiled our best traditions in any naked struggles
for power.

And you have written a platform that neither equivocates, contra-
dicts, nor evades. You have restated our party's record, its principles and
20   its purposes, in language that none can mistake, and with a firm confidence in justice, freedom, and peace on earth that will raise the hearts and
the hopes of mankind for that distant day when no—no one rattles a saber
and no one drags a chain.

For all these things I am grateful to you. But I feel no exultation, no
sense of triumph. Our troubles are all ahead of us. Some will call us
appeasers; others will say that we are the war party. Some will say we are
reactionary; others will say that we stand for socialism. There will be inevitable—the inevitable cries of "throw the rascals out," "it's time for a
change," and so on and so on. We'll hear all those things and many more
30   besides. But we will hear nothing that we have not heard before. I'm not
too much concerned with partisan denunciation, with epithets and abuse,
because the workingman, the farmer, the thoughtful businessman, all know
that they are better off than ever before, and they all know that the greatest danger to free enterprise in this country died with the Great Depression under the hammer blows of the Democratic party.

Nor am I afraid that the precious two-party system is in danger. Certainly the Republican party looked brutally alive a couple of weeks ago—
and I mean both Republican parties.

Nor am I afraid that the Democratic party is old and fat and indo-
40   lent. After a hundred and fifty years, it has been old for a long time, and it
will never be indolent, as long as it looks forward and not back, as long as
it commands the allegiance of the young and the hopeful who dream the
dreams and see the visions of a better America and a better world.

You will hear many sincere and thoughtful people express concern about the continuation of one party in power for twenty years. I don't belittle this attitude. But change for the sake of change has no absolute merit in itself. If our greatest hazard—If our greatest hazard is preservation of the values of Western civilization, in our self-interest alone, if you please, it is the part—is it the part of wisdom to change for the sake of change to a party with a split personality, to a leader, whom we all respect, but who has been called upon to minister to a hopeless case of political schizophrenia?

If the fear is corruption in official position, do you believe with Charles Evans Hughes that guilt is personal and knows no party? Do you doubt the power of any political leader, if he has the will to do so, to set his own house in order without his neighbors having to burn it down?

What does concern me, in common with thinking partisans of both parties, is not just winning this election but how it is won, how well we can take advantage of this great quadrennial opportunity to debate issues sensibly and soberly. I hope and pray that we Democrats, win or lose, can campaign not as a crusade to exterminate the opposing party, as our opponents seem to prefer, but as a great opportunity to educate and elevate a people whose destiny is leadership, not alone of a rich and prosperous, contented country, as in the past, but of a world in ferment.

And, my friends even more important than winning the election is governing the nation. That is the test of a political party, the acid, final test. When the tumult and the shouting die, when the bands are gone and the lights are dimmed, there is the stark reality of responsibility in an hour of history haunted with those gaunt, grim specters of strife, dissension, and materialism at home and ruthless, inscrutable, and hostile power abroad.

The ordeal of the twentieth century, the bloodiest, most turbulent era of the whole Christian age, is far from over. Sacrifice, patience, understanding, and implacable purpose may be our lot for years to come. Let's face it. Let's talk sense to the American people. Let's tell them the truth, that there are no gains without pains, that there—that we are now on the eve of great decisions, not easy decisions, like resistance when you're attacked, but a long, patient, costly struggle which alone can assure triumph over the great enemies of man—war, poverty, and tyranny—and the assaults upon human dignity which are the most grievous consequences of each.

Let's tell them that the victory to be won in the twentieth century, this portal to the Golden Age, mocks the pretensions of individual acumen and ingenuity, for it is a citadel guarded by thick walls of ignorance and of mistrust which do not fall before the trumpets' blast or the politicians' imprecations or even a general's baton. They are, they are, my friends, walls that must be directly stormed by the hosts of courage, of morality, and of vision, standing shoulder to shoulder, unafraid of ugly truth, contemptuous of lies, half truths, circuses, and demagoguery.

The people are wise, wiser than the Republicans think. And the Democratic party is the people's party—not the labor party, not the farmers' party, not the employers' party—it is the party of no one because it is the party of everyone.

That, that, I—I think, is our ancient mission. Where we have deserted it, we have failed. With your help, there will be no desertion now. Better
10 we lose the election than mislead the people, and better we lose than misgovern the people. Help me to do the job in this autumn of conflict and of campaign. Help me to do the job in these years of darkness, of doubt, and of crisis which stretch beyond the horizon of tonight's happy vision, and we will justify our glorious past and the loyalty of silent millions who look to us for compassion, for understanding, and for honest purpose. Thus we will serve our great tradition greatly.

I ask of you all you have. I will give you all I have, even as he who came here tonight and honored me, as he has honored you, the Democratic party, by a lifetime of service and bravery that will find him an
20 imperishable page in the history of the Republic and of the Democratic party—President Harry S. Truman.

And finally, my friends, in this staggering task you have assigned me, I shall always try "to do justly, to love mercy, and to walk humbly with my God."

CARL SANDBURG

(1878–1967)

Abraham Lincoln

February 12, 1959

First known as a Midwestern poet, then as a collector of American folksongs, Carl Sandburg became increasingly identified with Abraham Lincoln after publication of his six-volume Lincoln biography, The Prairie Years (1926) and The War Years (1939). Admiring the spirit of Lincoln, his honesty, tenacity, and wit, Sandburg in this memorial speech wanted to project Lincoln rather than himself. The poet can be heard in the imagery and rhythms, the historian in the use of Lincoln's words and striking incidents, but these serve to thrust forward Lincoln, the complex man, the struggler, "hard as rock and soft as drifting fog."

Sandburg does more than pay simple tribute to a man already interwoven in American history and myth. It is Lincoln's character and principles, his sense of humanity and democracy, that are necessary to us now. By implication the speaker says that we must imitate Lincoln and be willing to struggle to work on the hard metal of reality, all the while knowing that reality may be unmalleable. It is in the struggle for liberty that hope lies.

OTHER IMPORTANT SPEECHES: "Chicago Stadium Speech" (1941) and "Commencement: The Need for Loneliness" (1941).

PUBLISHED VERSION: Carl Sandburg, "Abraham Lincoln," *Vital Speeches*, March 1, 1959, pp. 293–94.

DISCOGRAPHY: Caedmon Record, TC 2035; playing time, 20:45. [The recording of which this text is a transcription is of the speech as delivered over the radio after being presented to Congress.]

Before beginning this prepared address, I must make the remark that this introduction, this reception here calls for humility rather than pride. I am well aware of that.

Not often in the story of mankind does a man arrive on earth who is both steel and velvet, who is as hard as rock and soft as drifting fog, who

holds in his heart and mind the paradox of terrible storm and peace
unspeakable and perfect. Here and there across centuries come reports of
men alleged to have these contrasts, and the incomparable Abraham Lincoln, born one hundred and fifty years ago this day, is an approach if not a
perfect realization of this character. In the time of the April lilacs in the
year 1865, on his death, the casket with his body was carried north and
west a thousand miles, and the American people wept as never before.
Bells sobbed, cities wore crape, people stood in tears and with hats off as
the railroad burial car paused in the leading cities of seven states, ending
its journey at Springfield, Illinois, the home town. During the four years he
was President he at times, especially in the first three months, took to himself the powers of a dictator. He commanded the most powerful armies till
then assembled in modern warfare. He enforced conscription of soldiers
for the first time in American history. Under imperative necessity he abol-
ished the right of habeas corpus. He directed politically and spiritually wild,
massive, turbulent forces let loose in civil war, a war truly, as time has
shown, of brothers. He argued and pleaded for compensated emancipation
of the slaves. The slaves were property, they were on the tax books along
with horses and cattle, the valuation of each slave written next to his
name on the tax assessor's books. And failing to get action on compensated
emancipation, he took the only other course. As a Chief Executive having
war powers, he issued the paper by which he decleared the slaves to be free
under military necessity. In the end nearly four billion dollars worth of
property was taken away from those who were legal owners of it, property
confiscated, wiped out as by fire and turned to ashes, at his instigation and
executive direction. Chattel property recognized and lawful for three hundred years was expropriated, seized without payment.

In the month the war began, he told his secretary, John Hay, "My
policy is to have no policy." Three years later in a letter to a Kentucky
friend made public, he confessed plainly, "I have been controlled by
events." "I have been controlled by events." His words at Gettysburg were
sacred, yet strange with a color of the familiar. "We cannot consecrate, we
cannot hallow, this ground. The brave men, living and dead, who struggled
here, have consecrated it far beyond our poor power to add or detract." He
could have said "the brave Union men." Did he have any purpose in omitting the word "Union"? Was he keeping himself and his utterance clear of
the passion that would not be good to look at when the time came for
peace and reconciliation? Did he mean to leave an implication that there
were brave Union men and brave Confederate men, living and dead, who
struggled there? We do not know of a certainty. Was he thinking of the
Kentucky father whose two sons died in battle, one in Union blue, the
other in Confederate gray, the father inscribing on the stone over their
double grave, "God knows which was right"? We do not know. Lincoln's

changing policies from time to time aimed at saving the Union. In the end his armies won, and his nation became a world power immersed in international politics.

In August of 1864 he wrote a memorandum that he expected, in view of the national situation, he expected to lose the next November election. That month of August was so dark. But suddenly military victories brought the tide his way. The vote was 2,200,000 for him and 1,800,000 against him. Among his bitter opponents were such figures as Samuel F. B. Morse, inventor of the telegraph, and Cyrus M. McCormick, inventor of the farm reaper. In all its essential propositions the Southern Confederacy 10 had the moral support of powerful, respectable elements throughout the North, probably more than a million voters believing in the justice of the Southern cause in the North. While the war winds howled, he sat in the White House and insisted that the Mississippi was one river meant to belong to one country, that railroad connection from coast to coast must be pushed through and the Union Pacific Railroad made a reality. While the luck of war wavered and broke and came again, as generals failed and campaigns were lost, he held enough forces of the North together to raise new armies and supply them, until generals were found who made war as victorious war has always been made, with terror, frightfulness, destruc- 20 tion, and on both sides, North and South, valor and sacrifice beyond—past words of man to tell. In the mixed shame and blame of the immense wrongs of two crashing civilizations, often with nothing to say, he said nothing, slept not at all, and on occasions he was seen to weep in a way that made weeping appropriate, decent, even, you might say, majestic.

As he rode alone on horseback near Soldiers Home on the edge of Washington one night, his hat was shot off. A son he loved died as he watched at the bed in the White House. His wife was accused of betraying information to the enemy until denials from him were necessary. An Indiana man at the White House heard him say, "Voorhees, don't it 30 seem strange to you that I, who could never so much as cut off the head of a chicken, should be elected, or selected, into the midst of all this blood?" He tried to guide General Nathaniel Prentiss Banks, a Democrat, three times Governor of Massachusetts, into the governing of some seventeen of the forty-eight parishes of Louisiana controlled by the Union armies, an area holding a fourth of the slaves of Louisiana. He would like to see the state recognize the Emancipation Proclamation. "And while she is at it, I think it would not be objectionable for her to adopt some practical system by which the two races could gradually live themselves out of their old relation to each other, and both come out better prepared 40 for the new. Education for the young blacks should be included in the plan." And to Governor Michel Hahn, elected in 1864 by a majority of the eleven thousand white male voters who had taken the oath of allegiance to the Union, Lincoln wrote, "Now you are about to have a convention which, among other things, will probably define the elective franchise. I barely suggest for your private consideration, whether some of the colored people may not be let in, as for instance the very intelligent and especially those who have fought gallantly in our ranks."

Among the million words in the Lincoln utterance record, he interprets himself with a more keen precision than someone else offering to explain him. His simple opening of the House Divided speech in 1858 serves for today, "If we could first know where we are, and whither we are
10 tending, we could better judge what to do, and how to do it." To his Kentucky friend Joshua F. Speed he wrote in 1855, "Our progress in degeneracy appears to me to be pretty rapid. As a nation we began by declaring that 'all men are created equal, except Negroes,' When the 'know-nothings' get control, it will read 'all men are created equal except Negroes and foreigners and Catholics.' When it comes to this, I shall prefer emigrating to some country where they make no pretense of loving liberty."

And infinitely tender was his word from a White House balcony to a crowd on the White House lawn, "I have not willingly planted a thorn in
20 any man's bosom." "I have not willingly planted a thorn in any man's bosom." Or to a military governor, "I shall do nothing through malice, what I deal with is too vast for malice."

He wrote for Congress to read on December 1, 1862, "In the times like the present, men should utter nothing for which they would not willingly be responsible through time and eternity." Like an ancient psalmist he warned Congress, "Fellow citizens, we cannot escape history. We will be remembered in spite of ourselves. No personal significance or insignificance can spare one or another of us. The fiery trial through which we pass will light us down in honor or dishonor to the latest generation."
30 Wanting Congress to break and to forget past traditions, his words came keen and flashing, "The dogmas of the quiet past are inadequate for the stormy present. We must think anew, we must act anew, we must disenthrall ourselves."

These are the sort of words, we might say, that actuated the mind and will of the men who created and navigated that marvel of the sea, the *Nautilus*, and her voyage from Pearl Harbor and under the North Pole icecap.

The people, the people, of many other countries take Lincoln now for their own. He belongs to them. He stands for decency, honest dealing,
40 plain talk, and funny stories. "Look where he came from. Don't he know all us strugglers and wasn't he a kind of tough struggler all his life right up to the finish?" Something like that you can hear in any nearby neighborhood and across the seas. Millions there are who take Lincoln as a personal treasure. He had something they would like to see spread everywhere over

the world. Democracy? We can't find the words to say exactly what it is, but he had it. In his blood and bones he carried it. In the breath of his speeches and writings, it is there. Popular government? Republican institutions? Government where the people have the say-so, one way or another telling their elected leaders what they want? He had the idea, he embodied it, it's there in the lights and shadows of his personality, a mystery that can be lived but never fully spoken in words.

Our good friend, the poet and playwright Mark Van Doren, tells us now, "To me, Lincoln seems, in some ways, the most interesting man who ever lived, the most interesting man who ever lived. He was gentle but this gentleness was combined with a terrific toughness, an iron strength."

And how did Lincoln say he would like to be remembered? Something of it is in this present occasion, the atmosphere of this room. His beloved friend, Representative Owen Lovejoy of Princeton, Illinois, had died in May of 1864, and friends wrote to Lincoln and he replied that the pressure of duties kept him from joining them in efforts toward a marble monument to Lovejoy, the last sentence of Lincoln's letter saying, "Let him have the marble monument along with the well-assured and more enduring one in the hearts of those who love liberty, unselfishly, for all men."

Today we may say, perhaps, that the well-assured and most enduring memorial to Lincoln is invisibly there, today, tomorrow, and for a long, long time yet to come. It is there in the hearts of the lovers of liberty, men and women; this country has always had them in crises, men and women who understand that wherever there is freedom there have been those who fought, toiled, and sacrificed for it.

I thank you.

NIXON-KENNEDY

Opening Statements: The Fourth Debate

October 21, 1960

In September and October of 1960 a television audience numbering in the tens of millions experienced the "great debates" between Presidential nominees Vice President Richard M. Nixon and Senator John F. Kennedy. This inherently dramatic confrontation of political opponents has a long tradition in England and America and has been seen as a testing ground for a leader's capacity to analyze and express his own and his party's ideas on issues as well as to challenge the opposition's arguments. For the audience the suspense of impromptu speaking—what will happen? how heated may the speakers get?—brought many nonpolitical citizens into the realm of politics. The private and public discussions of the debates, both their issues and the expression of those issues, were at the very least healthy for a democracy. A particularly nice point is that voters who were inclined to listen to speakers of their own party only were forced to hear the opposition's arguments. The debates may not have been so rich an exploration of the issues as some critics demanded, but that charge reveals a naive confusion of the politician—or even statesman—with the philosopher. By any real standards, the debates were a splendid old form using a splendid new medium to present candidates to the people.

PUBLISHED VERSION: Sidney Kraus, ed., *The Great Debates: Background—Perspective —Effects*, pp. 411–16 (Bloomington: University of Indiana Press, 1962).

RICHARD M. NIXON (1913–   )

Historically the Vice Presidency had been more an honorary than a functional post in American government, but early in his Administration, Eisenhower determined that Richard Nixon should take a very active role in the executive branch. This innovation, generally applauded, identified Nixon closely with the policies and events of the two Eisenhower terms and justified Nixon's major theme in his campaign against Kennedy: I am the tested man, the candidate with experience. But the disadvantages were equally real. As Eisenhower observed, "To promise and pledge new effort, new programs, and new ideas without appearing to criticize the current party and Administration—that is indeed an exercise in tightrope walking."

As a Senator, Nixon had a reputation for tough, aggressive speaking that did not suit his position as Vice President. In the debates he was a careful, almost deliberate speaker. His major objective, other than the establishment of his authority through experience, is the development of the essential points of keeping the peace and of extending freedom. He repeats leading ideas, spells out transitions from one point to another, and summarizes regularly. With dignity he clearly and persuasively recalls the principles and the actions of the Republican Administration of that time and outlines their general future development.

OTHER IMPORTANT SPEECHES: "Expense Fund Speech" (1952) and "To the Russian People" (1959).

JOHN FITZGERALD KENNEDY (1917–1963)

By the time of the debates, John F. Kennedy had served for almost fourteen years as a Representative and Senator from Massachusetts, but compared with Richard M. Nixon, he was not a national figure politically. For him, then, the initial value of the television encounters was the raw exposure to a national audience. He was able to use these meetings to reveal himself as a vital and committed man, capable in thought and action.

In this debate, Kennedy sacrifices clear development for an energetic attack on many particular weaknesses in the Administration's policies and practices. In a classic rebuttal he immediately accepts and uses Nixon's argument. But then he turns it: "The question is: Are we moving in the direction of peace and security?" With short chopping sentences and questions, Kennedy vigorously demands, over and over, what is the actual situation now? What are we doing today? His quick-paced delivery suggests his eagerness to get at problems, and his readiness with examples reveals his awareness of world events. He dispels the caricature of the green boy and establishes himself as a knowledgeable, alert, and active man, able to meet the test of high office. Many commentators argue that his impressive performance in the debates was the deciding factor with the uncommitted voter in his extremely narrow victory over Nixon.

OTHER IMPORTANT SPEECHES: "The Strategy of Peace" (1963), "Before the United Nations" (1963), and "Cuba Quarantine" (1963).
DISCOGRAPHY: Caedmon Record, TC 2035; playing time, 16:04.

Mr. NIXON: Mr. Howe[1], Senator Kennedy, my fellow Americans. Since this campaign began I have had a very rare privilege. I have traveled to forty-eight of the fifty states, and in my travels I have learned what the people of the United States are thinking about. There is one issue that stands out above all the rest, one in which every American is concerned,

---

[1] Quincy Howe, the television news commentator, was the moderator of the debates.

regardless of what group he may be a member and regardless of where he may live. And that issue, very simply stated, is this: How can we keep the peace—keep it without surrender? How can we extend freedom—extend it without war?

Now in determining how we deal with this issue, we must find the answer to a very important but simple question: Who threatens the peace? Who threatens freedom in the world? There's only one threat to peace and one threat to freedom—that that is presented by the international Communist movement. And therefore if we are to have peace, if we
10 are to keep our own freedom and extend it to others without war, we must know how to deal with the Communists and their leaders. I know Mr. Khrushchev. I also have had the opportunity of knowing and meeting other Communist leaders in the world. I believe there are certain principles we must find in dealing with him and his colleagues, principles, if followed, that will keep the peace and that also can extend freedom. First, we have to learn from the past because we cannot afford to make the mistakes of the past. In the seven years before this Administration came into power in Washington, we found that 600 million people went behind the Iron Curtain. And at the end of that seven years we were engaged in a war in
20 Korea which cost over thirty thousand American lives. In the past seven years, in President Eisenhower's Administration, this situation has been reversed. We ended the Korean War. By strong, firm leadership we have kept out of other wars. And we have avoided surrender of principle or territory at the conference table. Now why were we successful, as our predecessors were not successful? I think there're several reasons. In the first place, they made a fatal error in misjudging the Communists, in trying to apply to them the same rules of conduct that you would apply to the leaders of the free world. One of the major errors they made was the one that led to the Korean War. In ruling out the defense of Korea, they invited
30 aggression in that area. They thought they were going to have peace; it brought war. We learned from their mistakes. And so, in our seven years, we find that we have been firm in our diplomacy. We have never made concessions without getting concessions in return. We have always been willing to go the extra mile to negotiate for disarmament or in any other area, but we have never been willing to do anything that, in effect, surrendered freedom any place in the world. That is why President Eisenhower was correct in not apologizing or expressing regrets to Mr. Khrushchev at the Paris Conference, as Senator Kennedy suggested he could have done. That is why Senator—President Eisenhower was also correct in his policy
40 in the Formosa Straits, where he declined, and refused to follow the recommendations, recommendations which Senator Kennedy voted for in 1955, again made in 1959, again repeated in his debates that you have heard, recommendations with regard to, again, slicing off a piece of free territory, and abandoning it, if—in effect, to the Communists. Why did

the President feel this was wrong and why was the President right and his critics wrong? Because, again, this showed a lack of understanding of dictators, a lack of understanding particularly of Communists, because every time you make such a concession, it does not lead to peace. It only encourages them to blackmail you, it encourages them to begin a war. And so I say that the record shows that we know how to keep the peace, to keep it without surrender.

Let us move now to the future. It is not enough to stand on this record, because we are dealing with the most ruthless, fanatical leaders that the world has ever seen. That is why I say that in this period of the sixties, 10 America must move forward in every area. First of all, although we are today, as Senator Kennedy has admitted, the strongest nation in the world militarily, we must increase our strength, increase it so that we will always have enough strength that regardless of what our potential opponents have, if they should launch a surprise attack, we will be able to destroy their warmaking capability. They must know, in other words, that it is national suicide if they begin anything. We need this kind of strength because we're the guardians of the peace.

In addition to military strength, we need to see that the economy of this country continues to grow. It has grown in the past seven years. It can 20 and will grow even more in the next four. And the reason that it must grow even more is because we have things to do at home and also because we're in a race for survival, a race in which it isn't enough to be ahead, it isn't enough simply to be complacent. We have to move ahead in order to stay ahead. And that is why, in this field, I have made recommendations which I am confident will move the American economy ahead, move it firmly and soundly, so that there will never be a time when the Soviet Union will be able to challenge our superiority in this field.

And so we need military strength, we need economic strength, we also need the right diplomatic policies. What are they? Again we turn to the 30 past. Firmness but no belligerence, and by no belligerence I mean that we do not answer insult by insult. When you are proud and confident of your strength, you do not get down to the level of Mr. Khrushchev and his colleagues. And that example that President Eisenhower has set, we will continue to follow.

But all this, by itself, is not enough. It is not enough for us simply to be the strongest nation militarily, the strongest economically, and also to have firm diplomacy. We must have a great goal. And that is not just to keep freedom for ourselves but to extend it to all the world, to extend to it all the world because that is America's destiny, to extend it to all the 40 world because the Communist aim is not to hold their own but to extend Communism. And you cannot fight a victory for Communism or a strategy of victory for Communism with the strategy simply of holding the line.

And so I say that we believe that our policies of military strength, of economic strength, of diplomatic firmness, first will keep the peace and keep it without surrender. We also believe that in the great field of ideals that we can lead America to the victory for freedom, victory in the newly developing countries, victory also in the captive countries, provided we have faith in ourselves and faith in our principles.

Mr. Howe: Now the opening statement of Senator Kennedy.

Mr. KENNEDY: Mr. Howe, Mr. Vice President. First uh—let me again try to correct the record on the matter of Quemoy and Matsu. I voted for
10   the Formosa resolution in 1955. I have sustained it since then. I've said that I agree with the Administration policy. Mr. Nixon earlier indicated that he would defend Quemoy and Matsu, even if the attack on these islands, two miles off the coast of China, were not part of a general attack on Formosa and the Pescadores. I indicated that I would defend those islands if the attack were directed against Pescadores and Formosa, which is part of the Eisenhower policy. I've supported that policy. In the last week, as a member of the Senate Foreign Relations Committee, I reread the testimony of General Twining, representing the Administration in 1959, and the Assistant Secretary of State before the Foreign Relations
20   Committee in 1958, and I have accurately described the Administration policy, and I support it wholeheartedly.

So that really isn't an issue in this campaign. It isn't an issue with Mr. Nixon, who now says that he also supports the Eisenhower policy. Nor is the question that all Americans want peace and security an issue in this campaign. The question is: Are we moving in the direction of peace and security? Is our relative strength growing? Is, as Mr. Nixon says, our prestige at an all-time high, as he said a week ago, and that of the Communists, at an all-time low? I don't believe it is. I don't believe that our relative strength is increasing. And I say that not as the Democratic standard-
30   bearer, but as a citizen of the United States who is concerned about the United States.

I look at Cuba, ninety miles off the coast of the United States. In 1957 I was in Havana, I talked to the American Ambassador there. He said that he was the second most powerful man in Cuba. And yet even though Ambassador Smith and Ambassador Gardner, both Republican ambassadors, both warned of Castro, the Marxist influences around Castro, the Communist influences around Castro, both of them have testified in the last six weeks that in spite of their warnings to the American government, nothing was done.
40   Our security depends upon Latin America. Can any American looking at the situation in Latin America feel contented with what's happening today, when a candidate for the presidency of Brazil feels it necessary to call, not on Washington during the campaign, but on Castro in Havana, in order to pick up the support of the Castro supporters in Brazil? At the

American Conference—Inter-American Conference this summer, when we
wanted them to join together in the denunciation of Castro and the
Cuban Communists, we couldn't even get the Inter-American group to
join together in denouncing Castro. It was rather a vague statement that
they finally made. Do you know today that the Com—the Russians broadcast ten times as many programs in Spanish to Latin America as we do?
Do you know we don't have a single program sponsored by our government to Cuba, to tell them our story, to tell them that we are their
friends, that we want them to be free again?

Africa is now the emerging area of the world. It contains 25 percent   10
of all the members of the General Assembly. We didn't even have a
Bureau of African Affairs until 1957. In the Africa south of the Sahara,
which is the major new section, we have less students from all of Africa in
that area studying under government auspices today than from the country
of Thailand. If there's one thing Africa needs it's technical assistance. And
yet last year we gave them less than 5 percent of all the technical assistance funds that we distributed around the world.

We relied in the Middle East on the Bagdad Pact, and yet when the
Iraqi Government was changed, the Bagdad Pact broke down. We relied
on the Eisenhower Doctrine for the Middle East, which passed the Senate.   20
There isn't one country in the Middle East that now endorses the Eisenhower Doctrine.

We look to Europe, uh—to Asia because the struggle is in the underdeveloped world. Which system, Communism or freedom, will triumph in
the next five or ten years? That's what should concern us, not the history
of ten, or fifteen, or twenty years ago. But are we doing enough in these
areas? What are freedom's chances in those areas? By 1965 or 1970, will
there be other Cubas in Latin America? Will Guinea and Ghana, which
have now voted with the Communists frequently as newly independent
countries of Africa—will there be others? Will the Congo go Communist?   30
Will other countries? Are we doing enough in that area? And what about
Asia? Is India going to win the economic struggle, or is China going to win
it? Who will dominate Asia in the next five or ten years? Communism?
The Chinese? Or will freedom?

The question which we have to decide as Americans, are we doing
enough today? Is our strength and prestige rising? Do people want to be
identified with us? Do they want to follow United States leadership? I
don't think they do, enough. And that's what concerns me.

In Africa—these countries that have newly joined the United
Nations. On the question of admission of Red China, only two countries   40
in all of Africa voted with us—Liberia and the Union of South Africa.
The rest either abstained or voted against us. More countries in Asia voted
against us on that question than voted with us.

I believe that this struggle is going to go on, and it may well be

decided in the next decade. I have seen Cuba go to the Communists. I
have seen Communist influence and Castro influence rise in Latin America. I have seen us ignore Africa. There are six countries in Africa that are
members of the United Nations. There isn't a single American diplomatic
representative in any of those six. When Guinea became independent, the
Soviet Ambassador showed up that very day. We didn't recognize them
for two months; the American Ambassador didn't show up for nearly eight
months.

I believe that the world is changing fast. And I don't think this
10 Administration has shown the foresight, has shown the knowledge, has
been identified with the great fight which these people are waging to be
free, to get a better standard of living, to live better. The average income
in some of those countries is twenty-five dollars a year. The Communists
say, "Come with us; look what we've done." And we've been in—on the
whole, uninterested. I think we're going to have to do better.

Mr. Nixon talks about our being the strongest country in the world. I
think we are today. But we were far stronger relative to the Communists
five years ago, and what is of great concern is that the balance of power is
in danger of moving with them. They made a breakthrough in missiles,
20 and by 1961, –2, and –3, they will be outnumbering us in missiles. I'm not
as confident as he is that we will be the strongest military power by 1963.

He talks about economic growth as a great indicator for freedom. I
agree with him. What we do in this country, the kind of society that we
build, that will tell whether freedom will be sustained around the world.
And yet, in the last nine months of this year, we've had a drop in our
economic growth rather than a gain. We've had the lowest rate of increase
of economic growth in the last nine months of any major industrialized
society in the world. I look up and see the Soviet flag on the moon.

The fact is that the State Department polls on our prestige and influ-
30 ence around the world have shown such a sharp drop that up till now the
State Department has been unwilling to release them. And yet they were
polled by the U.S.I.A.

The point of all this is, this is a struggle in which we're engaged. We
want peace. We want freedom. We want security. We want to be
stronger. We want freedom to gain. But I don't believe in these changing
and revolutionary times this Administration has known that the world is
changing, has identified itself with that change. I think the Communists
have been moving with vigor—Laos, Africa, Cuba—all around the world,
they're on the move. I think we have to revitalize our society. I think we
40 have to demonstrate to the people of the world that we're determined in
this free country of ours to be first—not first if, and not first but, and not
first when—but first. And when we are strong and when we are first, then
freedom gains. Then the prospects for peace increase. Then the prospects
for our security gain.

JOHN FITZGERALD KENNEDY
(1917–1963)

Inaugural Address

January 20, 1961

While being driven to the Inaugural Concert through the snow-filled Washington night, John F. Kennedy read the concert program, which included Jefferson's First Inaugural Address. He shifted and remarked to his wife, "Better than mine." If not better, Kennedy's Inaugural Address was different, in part because the world was different, in part because the man was different. Jefferson, after a divisive election, stressed national unity in a youthful country, while Kennedy, in spite of the extreme closeness of the popular vote, could presume he had national unity in a stable world power.

This "new generation of Americans" was not concerned with the national problems expressed in Roosevelt's First Inaugural Address but with America's foreign relations. So Kennedy outlined the thrust of those relations: It was to be unity with all. Pledges were given to old allies, new states, underdeveloped countries, neighbors, and the United Nations. "Those nations who would make themselves our adversary" were urged "to explore what problems unite us instead of belaboring those problems which divide us." The key to the speech was that the young President saw the problems of the world not as fearful obstacles that dispirit or frustrate but as worthy and exciting challenges that stimulate and invigorate. With confidence in the American people and in himself and with passionate commitment to noble ends, he called out "let us begin," and a nation responded.

PUBLISHED VERSION: "Inaugural Address: January 20, 1961." In *Inaugural Addresses of the Presidents of the United States from George Washington 1789 to John F. Kennedy 1961* (Washington: U.S. Government Printing Office, 1961).
DISCOGRAPHY: Caedmon Record, TC 2035; playing time, 14:03.

We observe today not a victory of party but a celebration of freedom, symbolizing an end as well as a beginning, signifying renewal as well as change, for I have sworn before you and Almighty God the same solemn oath our forebears prescribed nearly a century and three quarters ago. The world is very different now, for man holds in his mortal hands the power to abolish all forms of human poverty and all forms of human life. And yet the same revolutionary beliefs for which our forebears fought are still at issue around the globe—the belief that the rights of man come not from the generosity of the state but from the hand of God.

We dare not forget today that we are the heirs of that first revolution. Let the word go forth from this time and place to friend and foe alike that the torch has been passed to a new generation of Americans, born in this
10 century, tempered by war, disciplined by a hard and bitter peace, proud of our ancient heritage, and unwilling to witness or permit the slow undoing of those human rights to which this nation has always been committed, and to which we are committed today, at home and around the world.

Let every nation know, whether it wishes us well or ill, that we shall pay any price, bear any burden, meet any hardship, support any friend, oppose any foe, to assure the survival and the success of liberty.

This much we pledge and more.

To those old allies whose cultural and spiritual origins we share, we pledge the loyalty of faithful friends. United, there is little we cannot do
20 in a host of cooperative ventures. Divided, there is little we can do, for we dare not meet a powerful challenge at odds and split asunder.

To those new states whom we welcome to the ranks of the free, we pledge our word that one form of colonial control shall not have passed away merely to be replaced by a far more iron tyranny. We shall not always expect to find them supporting our view, but we shall always hope to find them strongly supporting their own freedom and to remember that, in the past, those who foolishly sought power by riding the back of the tiger ended up inside.

To those people in the huts and villages of half the globe struggling
30 to break the bonds of mass misery, we pledge our best efforts to help them help themselves, for whatever period is required, not because the Communists may be doing it, not because we seek their votes, but because it is right. If a free society cannot help the many who are poor, it cannot save the few who are rich.

To our sister republics south of our border, we offer a special pledge to convert our good words into good deeds in a new alliance for progress to assist free men and free governments in casting off the chains of poverty. But this peaceful revolution of hope cannot become the prey of hostile powers. Let all our neighbors know that we shall join with them to oppose
40 aggression or subversion anywhere in the Americas, and let every other power know that this hemisphere intends to remain the master of its own house.

To that world assembly of sovereign states, the United Nations, our last best hope in an age where the instruments of war have far outpaced the instruments of peace, we renew our pledge of support to prevent it from becoming merely a forum for invective, to strengthen its shield of the new and the weak, and to enlarge the area in which its writ may run.

Finally, to those nations who would make themselves our adversary, we offer not a pledge but a request that both sides begin anew the quest for peace before the dark powers of destruction unleashed by science engulf all humanity in planned or accidental self-destruction. We dare not tempt them with weakness, for only when our arms are sufficient beyond doubt can we be certain beyond doubt that they will never be employed. 10 But neither can two great and powerful groups of nations take comfort from our present course, both sides overburdened by the cost of modern weapons, both rightly alarmed by the steady spread of the deadly atom, yet both racing to alter that uncertain balance of terror that stays the hand of mankind's final war.

So let us begin anew, remembering on both sides that civility is not a sign of weakness and sincerity is always subject to proof. Let us never negotiate out of fear, but let us never fear to negotiate. Let both sides explore what problems unite us instead of belaboring those problems which divide us. Let both sides, for the first time, formulate serious and 20 precise proposals for the inspection and control of arms and bring the absolute power to destroy other nations under the absolute control of all nations. Let both sides seek to invoke the wonders of science instead of its terrors. Together let us explore the stars, conquer the deserts, eradicate disease, tap the ocean depths, and encourage the arts and commerce. Let both sides unite to heed in all corners of the earth the command of Isaiah to "undo the heavy burdens and let the oppressed go free." And if a beachhead of cooperation may push back the jungle of suspicion, let both sides join in creating a new endeavor, not a new balance of power but a new world of law, where the strong are just and the weak secure and the 30 peace preserved.

All this will not be finished in the first one hundred days, nor will it be finished in the first one thousand days, nor in the life of this Administration, nor even perhaps in our lifetime on this planet, but let us begin.

In your hands, my fellow citizens, more than mine, will rest the final success or failure of our course. Since this country was founded, each generation of Americans has been summoned to give testimony to its national loyalty. The graves of young Americans who answered the call to service surround the globe. Now the trumpet summons us again, not as a call to bear arms, though arms we need, not as a call to battle, though 40 embattled we are, but a call to bear the burden of a long twilight struggle, year in and year out, "rejoicing in hope, patient in tribulation," a struggle against the common enemies of man: tyranny, poverty, disease, and war itself. Can we forge against these enemies a grand and global alliance, north and south, east and west, that can assure a more fruitful life for all mankind? Will you join in that historic effort?

In the long history of the world, only a few generations have been granted the role of defending freedom in its hour of maximum danger. I do not shrink from this responsibility, I welcome it. I do not believe that any of us would exchange places with any other people or any other generation. The energy, the faith, the devotion which we bring to this endeavor will light our country and all who serve it, and the glow from that fire can truly light the world. And so, my fellow Americans, ask not what your country can do for you, ask what you can do for your country. My fellow citizens of the world, ask not what America will do for you, but what together we can do for the freedom of man.

Finally, whether you are citizens of America or citizens of the world, ask of us here the same high standards of strength and sacrifice which we ask of you. With a good conscience our only sure reward, with history the final judge of our deeds, let us go forth to lead the land we love, asking His blessing and His help, but knowing that here on earth God's work must truly be our own.

MARTIN LUTHER KING, JR.
(1929–1968)

I Have a Dream

August 28, 1963

For almost ten years the civil rights movement had been building, and one climax came on a hot summer day in Washington. Over 200,000, blacks and whites, marched to urge the passage of laws to ban discrimination and to fund programs for training and education. One of the most respected leaders was Martin Luther King, Jr., a young Southern Negro minister who practiced and preached the nonviolent resistance learned from Gandhi. As the wearing afternoon of songs and speeches drew to a close, it was he who stamped meaning on the day with his "dream deeply rooted in the American dream."

His great exhortation was structured on the chronology of American history: of the past he addressed the nation, of the present the Negro, and of the future himself and through himself all members of his partisan audience. This audience needed little evidence to establish the reality of oppression and hope—many lived it—so King simply listed instances of both his charges and his dreams. It was through direct and partial repetition of phrases that he set the powerful rhythms to carry those instances to his audience and to elicit their responses to his litany. And he brought his speech to a close with yet another allusion, another rhythm. Chief Justice Holmes, for one audience, rounded his speech with a quotation from classical literature; Reverend King ended his mightily with a line from a traditional Negro spiritual, "Free at last! Free at last! Thank God Almighty, we are free at last!" These words are his epitaph.

OTHER IMPORTANT SPEECHES: "Love, Law, and Civil Disobedience" (1961), "Drum Major Instinct" (1968), and "I've Been to the Mountain" (1968).

PUBLISHED VERSION: Martin Luther King, Jr., "I Have a Dream." *Representative American Speeches: 1963–1964*, edited by Lester Thonssen, pp. 44–48 (New York: H. W. Wilson, 1964).

DISCOGRAPHY: Caedmon Record to be issued; playing time, 16:07.

117

I am happy to join with you today in what will go down in history as the greatest demonstration for freedom in the history of our nation.

Five score years ago, a great American, in whose symbolic shadow we stand today, signed the Emancipation Proclamation. This momentous decree came as a great beacon light of hope to millions of Negro slaves, who had been seared in the flames of withering injustice. It came as a joyous daybreak to end the long night of their captivity.

But one hundred years later, the Negro still is not free. One hundred years later, the life of the Negro is still sadly crippled by the manacles of segregation and the chains of discrimination. One hundred years later, the Negro lives on a lonely island of poverty in the midst of a vast ocean of material prosperity. One hundred years later, the Negro still languished in the corners of American society and finds himself an exile in his own land.

So we've come here today to dramatize a shameful condition. In a sense we've come to our nation's capital to cash a check. When the architects of our Republic wrote the magnificent words of the Constitution and the Declaration of Independence, they were signing a promissory note to which every American was to fall heir. This note was a promise that all men—yes, black men as well as white men—would be guaranteed the unalienable rights of life, liberty, and the pursuit of happiness.

It is obvious today that America has defaulted on this promissory note insofar as her citizens of color are concerned. Instead of honoring this sacred obligation, America has given the Negro people a bad check, a check which has come back marked "insufficient funds." But we refuse to believe that the bank of justice is bankrupt. We refuse to believe that there are insufficient funds in the great vaults of opportunity of this nation. So we've come to cash this check—a check that will give us upon demand the riches of freedom and the security of justice.

We have also come to this hallowed spot to remind America of the fierce urgency of now. This is no time to engage in the luxury of cooling off or to take the tranquilizing drug of gradualism. Now is the time to make real the promises of democracy. Now is the time to rise from the dark and desolate valley of segregation to the sunlit path of racial justice. Now is the time to lift our nation from the quicksand of racial injustice to the solid rock of brotherhood. Now is the time to make justice a reality for all of God's children.

It would be fatal for the nation to overlook the urgency of the moment. This sweltering summer of the Negro's legitimate discontent will not pass until there is an invigorating autumn of freedom and equality. Nineteen sixty-three is not an end, but a beginning. Those who hope that the Negro needed to blow off steam and will now be content will have a rude awakening if the nation returns to business as usual. There will be neither rest nor tranquillity in America until the Negro is granted his citizenship rights. The whirlwinds of revolt will continue to shake the foundations of our nation until the bright day of justice emerges.

But that is something that I must say to my people who stand on the warm threshold which leads into the palace of justice. In the process of gaining our rightful place we must not be guilty of wrongful deeds. Let us not seek to satisfy our thirst for freedom by drinking from the cup of bitterness and hatred.

We must forever conduct our struggle on the high plane of dignity   10
and discipline. We must not allow our creative protest to degenerate into physical violence. Again and again we must rise to the majestic heights of meeting physical force with soul force. The marvelous new militancy which has engulfed the Negro community must not lead us to a distrust of all white people, for many of our white brothers, as evidenced by their presence here today, have come to realize that their destiny is tied up with our destiny. And they have come to realize that their freedom is inextricably bound to our freedom. We cannot walk alone.

As we walk, we must make the pledge that we shall always march ahead. We cannot turn back. There are those who asking the devotees of   20
civil rights, "When will you be satisfied?" We can never be satisfied as long as the Negro is the victim of the unspeakable horrors of police brutality. We can never be satisfied as long as our bodies, heavy with the fatigue of travel, cannot gain lodging in the motels of the highways and the hotels of the cities. We cannot be satisfied as long as the Negro's basic mobility is from a smaller ghetto to a larger one. We can never be satisfied as long as our children are stripped of their selfhood and robbed of their dignity by signs stating "For Whites Only." We cannot be satisfied as long as a Negro in Mississippi cannot vote and a Negro in New York believes he has nothing for which to vote. No, no ,we are not satisfied,   30
and we will not be satisfied until justice rolls down like waters and righteousness like a mighty stream.

I am not unmindful that some of you have come here out of great trials and tribulations. Some of you have come fresh from narrow jail cells. Some of you have come from areas where your crest—quest for freedom left you battered by the storms of persecution and staggered by the winds of police brutality. You have been the veterans of creative suffering. Continue to work with the faith that unearned suffering is redemptive.

Go back to Mississippi, go back to Alabama, go back to South Carolina, go back to Georgia, go back to Louisiana, go back to the slums and   40
ghettos of our Northern cities, knowing that somehow this situation can and will be changed. Let us not wallow in the valley of despair.

I say to you today, my friends, so even though we face the difficulties of today and tomorrow, I still have a dream. It is a dream deeply rooted in the American dream.

I have a dream that one day this nation will rise up and live out the true meaning of its creed: "We hold these truths to be self-evident; that all men are created equal."

I have a dream that one day on the red hills of Georgia the sons of former slaves and the sons of former slaveowners will be able to sit down together at the table of brotherhood.

I have a dream that one day even the state of Mississippi, a state swel-
10 tering with the heat of injustice, sweltering with the heat of oppression, will be transformed into an oasis of freedom and justice.

I have a dream that my four little children will one day live in a nation where they will not be judged by the color of their skin but by the content of their character.

I have a dream today.

I have a dream that one day, down in Alabama, with its vicious racists, with its governor having his lips dripping with the words of inter-position and nullification, one day right there in Alabama little black boys and black girls will be able to join hands with little white boys and white
20 girls as sisters and brothers.

I have a dream today.

I have a dream that one day every valley shall be exalted, every hill
• and mountain shall be made low, the rough places will be made plain and the crooked places will be made straight, and the glory of the Lord shall be revealed, and all flesh shall see it together.

This is our hope. This is the faith that I go back to the South with. With this faith we will be able to hew out of the mountain of despair a stone of hope. With this faith we will be able to transform the jangling discords of our nation into a beautiful symphony of brotherhood. With
30 this faith we will be able to work together, to pray together, to struggle together, to go to jail together, to stand up for freedom together, knowing that we will be free one day.

This will be the day . . . this will be the day when all of God's chil-dren will be able to sing with new meaning. "My country 'tis of thee, sweet land of liberty, of thee I sing. Land where my fathers died, land of the Pil-grims' pride, from every mountainside, let freedom ring," and if America is to be a great nation, this must become true.

So let freedom ring. From the prodigious hilltops of New Hampshire, let freedom ring. From the mighty mountains of New York, let freedom
40 ring, from the heightening Alleghenies of Pennsylvania!

Let freedom ring from the snowcapped Rockies of Colorado!

Let freedom ring from the curvaceous slopes of California!

But not only that.

Let freedom ring from Stone Mountain of Georgia!

Let freedom ring from Lookout Mountain of Tennessee!

Let freedom ring from every hill and mole hill of Mississippi.

From every mountainside, let freedom ring, and when this happens ... when we allow freedom to ring, when we let it ring from every village and every hamlet, from every state and every city, we will be able to speed up that day when all of God's children, black men and white men, Jews and Gentiles, Protestants and Catholics, will be able to join hands and sing in the words of the old Negro spiritual, "Free at last! Free at last! Thank God Almighty, we are free at last!" [10]

ADLAI E. STEVENSON
(1900–1965)

Eulogy:
John Fitzgerald
Kennedy

November 26, 1963

A long weekend in late November of 1963 became a strange point in time, a nightmare of disbelief and impotency. We heard a now mournful "Hail to the Chief" and watched the riderless black horse toss its head. The nation stopped and seemed as if it might never collect itself again for life.

But as with any death, life reasserted itself, and people had to be fed and clothed and sheltered. And important things had to be said to mark the violent passing of a leader.

Adlai Stevenson, appointed by the young President as Ambassador to the United Nations in 1961, delivered a eulogy before the General Assembly Plenary Meeting, an audience of the widest variety of cultures, histories, and policies. He praised the vitality and hope of John Fitzgerald Kennedy, mourning the loss of the President and the man. But he also introduced to a particular audience the ultimate stability of the American structure: though the President is dead, the Presidency continues. In his closing words he assigned the responsibility of the living: "We shall honor him in the best way that lies open to us—and in the way he would want it to be—by getting on with the everlasting search for peace and justice for which all mankind is praying."

OTHER IMPORTANT EULOGIES: "Eleanor Roosevelt" (1962) and "Winston Churchill" (1965).

PUBLISHED VERSION: Adlai Stevenson, "Tribute," *Representative American Speeches: 1963–1964*, edited by Lester Thonssen, pp. 31–33 (New York: H. W. Wilson, 1964).

DISCOGRAPHY: Caedmon Record, TC 2035; playing time, 10:04.

Mr. President, my dear colleagues. My privilege in this sad hour is to convey to you, Mr. President, to you, Mr. Secretary General, and to you, the assembled delegates of the world community, the profound gratitude of the people of my country for what has been done and for what has been said here today. Our grief is the more bearable because it is so widely and so genuinely shared, and for this we can only say, simply but from the depths of our full hearts, thank you.

President Kennedy was so contemporary a man, so involved in our world, so immersed in our times, so responsive to its challenges, so intense a participant in the great events and the great decisions of our day, that he seemed the very symbol of the vitality and the exuberance that is the essence of life itself.

Never once did he lose his way in the maze. Never once did he falter in the storm of spears. Never once was he intimidated. Like the ancient prophets, he loved the people enough to warn them of their errors, and the man who loves his country best will hold it to its highest standards. He made us proud to be Americans.

And so it is, that after four sorrowful days, we still can hardly grasp the macabre reality that the world has been robbed of this vibrant presence by an isolated act, conceived in the strange recesses of the human mind.

We shall not soon forget the late President's driving ambition for his own country, his concept of a permanently dynamic society, spreading abundance to the last corner of this land and extending justice, tolerance, and dignity to all of its citizens alike.

We shall not soon forget that, as the leader of a great nation, he met and mastered his responsibility to wield great power with great restraint. "Our national strength matters," he said, just a few weeks ago, "but the spirit which informs and controls our strength matters just as much."

We shall not soon forget that he held fast to the vision of a world in which the peace is secure, in which inevitable conflicts are reconciled by pacific means, in which nations devote their energies to the welfare of all their citizens, and in which the vast and colorful diversity of human society can flourish in a restless, competitive search for a better society.

We shall not soon forget that, by word and by deed, he gave proof of profound confidence in the present value and the future promise of this great organization, the United Nations.

And we shall never forget these ambitions, these visions, these convictions, that so inspired this remarkable young man and so quickened the quality and the tempo of our times in these fleeting past three years. And our grief is compounded by the bitter irony that he who gave his all to contain violence, lost his all—to violence.

Now he is gone. Today we mourn him. Tomorrow and tomorrow we shall miss him. And so we shall never know how different the world might have been had fate permitted this blazing talent to live and labor longer at man's unfinished agenda for peace and progress for all.

Yet for the rest of us, life goes on. Our agenda remains unfinished. Minutes after his spirit departed, Lyndon B. Johnson took his oath of allegiance to the permanent institutions of this country, institutions which outlast violence and outlive men. These hours of mourning are then but a pause in a process, not a break in purpose or in policy. President Johnson has directed me to affirm to this Assembly that there will be no Johnson policy toward the United Nations, any more than there was a Kennedy policy. There was, and is, only a United States policy, and that, too, outlasts violence and outlives men. As long ago as 1948, President Johnson told an American audience that "our long-term and sustained foreign policy must include full support of the United Nations." And now, on his behalf, and I repeat to you that my government will, as it has over the years, support every practical move to add to the capacity of the United Nations to keep the peace and to aid new nations to reach the stage of self-sustaining growth.

The foreign policy of this government will continue to be, as to the troubling issues of today and tomorrow, to work for agreement where agreement is possible and to negotiate with patience and persistence until agreement is possible. President Johnson is determined that the better feeling of these past few months shall not be lost; rather, that it must be increased. In that spirit we shall not falter on the stony path to peace.

Finally let me say that John Kennedy never believed that he or any man was indispensable. As several speakers have reminded us here this afternoon, of Dag Hammarskjold's death he said, "The problem is not the death of one man—the problem is the life of this organization." But he did believe passionately that peace and justice are indispensable. And he believed, as he told this Assembly in 1951 [sic], that "in the development of this organization lives the only true alternative to war."

So, my friends, we shall honor him in the best way that lies open to us, and the way he would want it to be, by getting on with the everlasting search for peace and justice for which all mankind is praying.

Thank you.

STUDIES

STUDIES OF SPEECH: TRUMAN, STEVENSON, AND KENNEDY

These four studies, as well as the first one in the Roosevelt section, indicate where speakers start: they believe in the importance of speaking and they dig. They use all resources open to them—their own knowledge, their files, all available authorities. Throughout these articles are many implications about the nature of the great speaker and his concept of audience. Of particular importance—as revealed especially in the Kennedy articles—is that "form" needs as much consideration as "matter," that an audience accepts particular ideas on a particular occasion put in a particular way that suits those ideas on that occasion.

1

What
Harry S. Truman
Told Us About
His Speaking

Eugene E. White

and

Clair R. Henderlider

One significant approach to the study of public address is through the biography of a speaker. In the following interview, Harry S. Truman informally answers questions on many aspects of his public speaking that help us to understand public speaking in general as well as the former President's speeches. He emphasizes the speaker's need for knowledge and sincerity and, in his own case especially, regular experience before an audience.

Our decision to seek an interview with former President Harry S. Truman grew out of our conviction that his views on speaking would be of interest to our profession, to historians and biographers, and to other Americans in various walks of life.

On May 23, 1953, we wrote to Mr. Truman, asking if he would see us. Our letter read in part

As college teachers we feel that determined efforts must be made to check academic theory with those techniques used by successful practitioners of public address. We hope that you will be willing to tell us something of your speech preparation, rehearsal, and delivery. We are particularly interested in your speechmaking during your whistle-stop trip of 1948, a tour uniquely effective in the history of American public address.

[Eugene E. White is Professor of Speech at Pennsylvania State University and Clair R. Henderlider is Associate Professor of Speech at Case Western Reserve University. This article originally appeared in the *Quarterly Journal of Speech*, XL (February 1954), 37–42, and is reprinted with the permission of the authors and the Speech Association of America.]

Mr. Truman replied,

I read your letter . . . with a lot of interest and I can appreciate your interest in public speaking. . . . If you are out in this part of the country, I'll be glad to see you and talk with you. I don't know whether I can give you any information that would be of interest to you, but I'll tell you the procedure which I followed.

Another exchange of letters resulted in agreement upon August 12, 1953, as the date for the interview to be held in his office in Kansas City, Missouri.

In the weeks preceding the meeting, we examined available literature which might offer clues to Mr. Truman's rhetorical practices. We also wrote to a number of our colleagues, asking for aid in planning the interview. Then we framed a list of questions designed to explore four basic areas: Mr. Truman's background and training in public speaking; his ideas on the essentials of effective speaking; his methods of preparation; and his techniques of rehearsal and delivery. We decided that these questions should serve only as a flexible framework around which to conduct the interview; our hope was to induce him to talk freely and at length about what he considered important in speechmaking.

We arrived at Mr. Truman's suite of offices on the eleventh floor of the Federal Reserve Bank Building a few minutes before the appointed time. We were greeted in the outer room by a receptionist, who told us that Mr. Truman would be ready to see us shortly. Promptly at 11:30 we were shown into the former President's private office. Mr. Truman, affable and gracious, shook hands with us and invited us to be seated. He was wearing a light-blue double-breasted suit, a white shirt and a grayish-blue tie. As we expected, in his lapel was his World War I service button. Tanned, and obviously enjoying excellent health and vitality, he seemed more imposing and impressive than we had expected. To put us at ease he inquired about our trip. His voice was brisk and friendly, free of the flat, twangy quality sometimes characteristic of his public speaking. As Mr. Truman turned the conversation to the dry spell Missouri was experiencing, we noted a stack of *Congressional Records* against a wall and a three-foot globe next to the window behind his desk. On his large desk we saw several books and magazines. Noticing that one of the magazines, *The William and Mary Quarterly*, had caught our eyes, Mr. Truman commented that his interest in early American history had led him to subscribe to the *Quarterly*. It was, he said, a fine, scholarly journal. Then, leaning back in his swivel chair, he rested his elbows on the chair arms, placed his finger tips together, and suggested that we feel free to ask any questions we desired about his speechmaking practices. During the next forty minutes he evidenced keen interest in our questions and answered directly and unhesitatingly. He spoke with friendly dignity, occasionally chuckling or laughing heartily. Here is a reconstructed report of our interview.

I. BACKGROUND AND TRAINING

Did public speaking come easily to you, or were you forced to work hard at it?

No, I wouldn't say that it came easily to me. I have never had any talent for public speaking. Whatever I have learned about speechmaking I have learned the hard way. My first speech was a complete failure. It took a lot of appearances after that before I felt at home on the platform and could put my ideas across the way I wanted.

Have you had any formal training in how to make a speech?

No, I have never read a textbook on public speaking, nor have I taken any course in that subject.

What about private coaching in preparing speeches and delivering them?

I have never had a speech coach. Of course, as President, I had such advisers as Charles Murphy, Charlie Ross, David Lloyd, and David Bell. Their function was to aid in gathering material and in putting speeches together. No one has trained me in how to deliver a speech.

May we then discount the story that early in 1948 you imported a radio personality from Ohio who suggested that you learn to adlib from a manuscript?

Like a lot of others, this story has no truth in it. I was adlibbing from a written speech even before I became County Judge in the 1920's.

Did anything happen prior to your entrance into public life which might have exerted an influence on your development as a speaker?

I don't think I can put my finger on anything of that nature, at least at this moment. I should mention, though, that I have always been a great reader. Before I was twelve I had read the Bible twice. Since then I've read it two more times. I carried home a lot of books from that little library in Independence. As a boy, I read Mark Twain, Shakespeare, George Eliot, Sir Walter Scott, and many others. I enjoyed them all. It was from my reading during this period that I acquired my love of history. I suppose few men in America today have accumulated a greater storehouse of irrelevant and inconsequential historical data than I have! Reading history is still one of my chief enjoyments. A good understanding of the history of government is a "must" for the public servant.

Did your early political experience influence your later development as a speaker?

I came up from the political grass roots. My early political experiences in Missouri taught me a lot about human nature. Among other things, I learned that a successful leader cannot afford to lose the common touch. To be a leader of an audience, or of a political party, for that matter, one must be accepted by that group as being one of its members. Like a successful politician, a good speaker must understand and like people before he can hope to influence them.

Did you do much speaking before you became President?

Yes, I got a lot of valuable experience in speaking. I didn't know it at the time, of course, but my campaigns for the Senate in 1934 and 1940 were excellent preparation for the Presidential campaign in 1948. In each Senatorial campaign I toured the state of Missouri talking "off-the-cuff" anywhere from six to sixteen times a day; at night over the radio or before a more formal gathering I would read from a typed copy. In the 1940 campaign I practiced a good many of my speeches by reading them into a recording machine. On the basis of what I heard I made adaptations in what I said and how I said it.

Is there a high point in your speaking career—one speech you consider most successful?

Speechmaking was, of course, an essential part of my duties as President. I believe it is still my most effective means of reaching the American people. Although I delivered hundreds of speeches prior to 1948, I never gained any reputation as a speaker until the campaign of that year. My most successful speech? I believe it was my acceptance address at the Democratic National Convention. That speech was something of a personal spiritual milestone. From that time on, I never doubted that we would win.

II. THE ESSENTIALS OF EFFECTIVE SPEAKING

How would you define the effective speaker?

I would say that the effective speaker is one who accomplishes what he sets out to do. To do that, he should know more about the subject than his audience. And he *must* believe what he is saying. These, in my opinion, are the two essentials. I can't emphasize too strongly the importance of getting the true facts; a man must know what he is talking about and know it well. As for sincerity, the public is quick to detect and reject the charlatan and the demagogue. It may be deceived for a brief period, but not for long.

In my opinion, mere talent without intellectual honesty and accurate information is not enough to make a successful speaker. I've never said anything in a speech that I did not firmly believe to be right.

Does the effective speaker possess any other important personal characteristics?

In addition to possessing personal integrity, which I've just mentioned, he should enjoy speaking. Otherwise, he will not be in the proper frame of mind to get his audience to do what he wants. A good speaker genuinely likes people; he respects his listeners.

What does the typical audience expect from a speaker?

People don't listen to a speaker just to admire his techniques or his manner; they go to learn. They want the meat of the speech—a direct statement of the facts and proof that the facts are correct—not oratorical trimmings. Of course, the political speaker must remember that the education of the average man is limited. Therefore, he must make his message as simple and clear as possible. Listeners have to feel a bond with the speaker; they aren't likely to if they believe he is a "high-hat" or "show-off." On the other hand, in working for simplicity one has to avoid "talking down" to an audience.

Would you care to mention any speaker, living or dead, as being especially worthy of emulation?

I believe an audience approves of Cicero's method, which was to state his case and then prove it. That is what I always tried to do. Charlie Ross and I used to translate Cicero's orations from the Latin. I guess I have read almost all of his speeches. They are models of clarity and simplicity. I wish I could do half as well.

III.   METHODS OF PREPARATION

To what extent do you personally prepare your major addresses?

Recently a prominent person in the government was asked why he stumbled in reading a particular speech. He replied that since he hadn't written the talk, he did not know what was in it. Can you imagine anyone giving a speech and not knowing what he was going to say on the next page? I have always taken great personal pains with every formal address. Each of my speeches goes through from three to ten drafts, and occasionally more. The San Francisco speech following my meeting with General MacArthur at Wake went through about twenty revisions.

What steps are involved in your preparation of a formal speech?

The procedure I followed as President was to suggest to my staff an outline of what I wanted to say. Never detailed, the outline consisted largely of a listing of the most important points. [Mr. Truman then permitted us to look at the preliminary outline and an early draft of his forthcoming Labor Day address in Detroit, his first major pronouncement since leaving the Presidency.] The staff then gathered the necessary data and drew up a rough draft. This and succeeding drafts were discussed in staff conference. After each of these discussions, I again studied the particular draft carefully and made additional changes. Even after the master copy was prepared I would frequently rework many pages. In the hope of making the message as clear and as simply worded as possible, I often made minor changes as late as an hour or so before delivery. Sometimes I would pencil an "off-the-cuff" remark into the margin just before going on the air.

During preparation are you conscious of organizing your speech into main divisions?

I haven't given much thought to the different divisions of a speech, but I do use an introduction, a main presentation, and an ending.

What do you attempt to accomplish in the introduction?

My introduction usually consists of some reference to the audience, to the circumstances surrounding the speech, or to the locality in which it is to be delivered. As you may remember, I always began the whistle-stop speeches in 1948 with a reference to the locale. In my speech notebook I carried a folder of data concerning each town—its history, its population, what was manufactured there, and so on. Before the train arrived at the station I would review the notes in the folder. That's something like the procedure Bryan followed in the campaign of 1896. However, I didn't need to rely upon the folder exclusively. I have a good memory, and it was no trouble to recall names, places, and incidents from former visits and from my reading.

I might add that the introduction is a good place to point up the importance of your subject. In the opening of my speech in December, 1950 [declaring a state of national emergency], I brought home as forcefully as I could the importance of the Korean struggle. I also like to state the essentials of my argument briefly in the introduction, so that the audience knows exactly what I am going to do in the remainder of the speech.

Do you have any favorite sequence or pattern for arranging your main points, such as saving the most important until the end, or using your strongest argument first?

No, I just present my arguments in what I believe is a logical sequence. I try to state them clearly and concisely, so that anyone can understand.

Do you deliberately select certain types of supporting materials because you have found them to be more effective? Do you avoid others?

I don't analyze what methods I am using to support my main contentions. I never decide that I must find a quotation to prove this point or a comparison to prove that point. I just use whatever materials seem to fit. Since I have never studied the niceties of speech composition, I cannot follow a set of rules or principles. Instead, I just go by a sense of "feel."

Do you make any effort to link your arguments to the basic drives which motivate people?

I know little about such techniques and have never consciously used them.

Perhaps we should rephrase that question. Do you think it wise to make the facts clear and meaningful to the listener by showing that they affect him vitally?

I would certainly agree that it is wise. All speakers attempt to do that. That's why speeches are given.

What do you attempt to accomplish in the conclusion?

In ending a speech, I summarize what I have already said, and try to leave my listeners in a positive state of mind. I never deliberately work toward an emotional climax. If you have the facts, you don't need to work on emotions. I am not constituted to use demagoguery. I believe in letting the facts themselves persuade the audience.

IV.   REHEARSAL AND DELIVERY

Do you rehearse your speeches? If so, what method do you use?

Before delivering a speech I like to read it aloud a time or two. As I mentioned before, when I was campaigning for the Senate I rehearsed speeches by means of a recording machine. I kept a wire recorder at the White House for the same purpose. In staff conferences on a forthcoming speech, I would sometimes read a draft aloud in pretty much the same manner I expected to use in the actual presentation.

For extempore speeches, such as the whistle-stop talks in the 1948 campaign, I needed little if any rehearsal. Campaign speeches are based on the party platform and on the party record. Of course, the person making such a speech knows both intimately. At the whistle-stops I didn't even take my speech notebook to the train platform. I spoke "off-the-cuff," without resorting to notes or manuscript.

How would you characterize your delivery?

I try to deliver my speeches simply and directly. I don't go in for theatrics. I do not believe that the American people expect their speakers to be entertainers. After all, there is plenty of entertainment on radio and television. The public wants the facts delivered in a sincere, straightforward manner.

Do you prefer to deliver a speech extemporaneously or to read it from manuscript?

If I had my choice, I would always speak extemporaneously. However, as President I was compelled to read most of my speeches. While I feel less strained than I used to, I'm still not completely at home when I have to read from a text. Like almost everyone else, I talk more effectively than I read. As I have said, sometimes I try to get away from the formality of a text by inserting adlibbed comments. Even in formal Presidential addresses I often strayed from the official copy.

Have you discovered any techniques for making manuscript reading easier and more effective?

Yes, I have the pages triple-spaced, with very wide margins at the sides and ample space at the top and bottom. Sentences and paragraphs are short—this makes it easier for me to read my ideas meaningfully. Three paragraphs are usually the maximum number for one page. I use regular type with conventional capitalization. (As President I frequently read news reports for the movie cameras. What I was going to say was placed on a board in capital letters. I found all those capitals a source of confusion.) The manuscript is placed in a black loose-leaf notebook.

For an appearance on television I prefer to use a manuscript rather than a teleprompter. I've tried the teleprompter and don't like it. I do not care to fool people. If I'm going to read, I want the copy on the desk where I can see what I'm doing and everybody else can, too.

Would you care to summarize your ideas on speechmaking?

I'll be glad to. The speaker must know what he wants to accomplish with his talk. Then he must get the facts. These must be put into a form which will prove his basic arguments and will be easily understood. The speaker should present his program simply and sincerely. Sincerity, honesty, and a straightforward manner are more important than special talent or polish.

Although the interview had extended into the former President's lunch period, he willingly agreed to a photograph of the three of us with the words: "Why not! I've had my picture taken a hundred thousand times; one more won't matter." Unfortunately, the flash bulb attachment on the camera refused to work. During the delay of several minutes, Mr. Truman showed us a rare volume of Kipling which he had recently received as a gift. The picture taken, he walked with us to the door. As he shook hands with us once again, he indicated his willingness to read our report of the meeting and wished us a safe and pleasant trip home.

Several weeks later we submitted to him our account of the interview. Here is his reaction as expressed in a letter dated October 27, 1953:

I am sorry to have been so long on this but, as you no doubt know, I've been on the run.

This is an excellent job of reporting. I've only made one suggestion on page six. [This suggestion was that we delete one sentence from our report, and we did so.]

Hope my experience will be of some use to you and your students.

Sincerely yours,

(signed)   HARRY S. TRUMAN

2

Public Address
in the Career of
Adlai E. Stevenson

Russel Windes, Jr.,
and James A. Robinson

The authors of this study also use a biographical approach but draw on many sources other than the direct interview. Furthermore, they investigate not only Stevenson's background and method of intensive preparation but also the public impact of his speaking, which they argue was his essential capacity for gaining national visibility.

I

Not since William Jennings Bryan won the leadership of the Democratic Party in 1896 with his famous "Cross of Gold" speech has public address contributed so much to establishing and maintaining a major party presidential candidate's national prominence as in the case of Adlai E. Stevenson. To be sure, in 1952, when Stevenson was chosen standard-bearer by his party's national convention, he possessed the political advantages which accrue to one who has been elected governor by an unprecedented majority in a state with a large vote in the Electoral College. But however great his successes and popularity in Illinois, Stevenson's national following was small in the summer of 1952. Compared with his Republican opponent, whose name had been a household word for a decade, Stevenson was virtually unknown. He had not been identified with any national movement as Wendell Willkie had been in 1940 nor with important legislation as Senator Robert A. Taft had been. No preconvention campaign to acquaint the public with his candidacy had been conducted, as had been done by James A. Farley in Franklin D. Roosevelt's behalf in 1931 and

[Russel Windes, Jr., is Professor of Speech at Queens College of the City University of New York, and James A. Robinson is Professor of Political Science at Northwestern University. This article originally appeared in the *Quarterly Journal of Speech*, XLII (October 1956), 225–33, and is reprinted with the permission of the authors and the Speech Association of America.]

1932, by Thomas E. Dewey in 1944 and 1948, and by Estes Kefauver, Taft, and Dwight D. Eisenhower in 1952. Consequently, when the Democratic Convention adjourned on July 26, 1952, Stevenson had but three precious months in which to communicate his name and his cause to his countrymen.

It is true that during the spring of 1952 Stevenson had attracted considerable attention by his continued refusal to seek the Presidency. For the most part, however, what the public knew about him prior to his nomination depended on which, if any, of the spate of articles *by* and *about* him they had read in several national magazines between January and June of 1952.[1] In addition, he had appeared on "Meet the Press," the television and radio program, the day following President Truman's announcement that he would not again be a candidate for reelection,[2] and he had made a series of speeches in New York, on the West Coast, and in Dallas during April and May. These speeches had fired his party's imagination and undoubtedly led party leaders to a stronger consideration of the man from Illinois. For most Americans, however, an image of him had to be formed primarily through his campaign speeches in the fall of 1952.

In those speeches, which have been described by one standard historical reference as "eloquent and forthright . . . among the most distinguished oratorical efforts in United States political history,"[3] Stevenson was able to raise himself from the comparative obscurity of the governorship of Illinois to great national popularity. The election result, for which his speeches deserve a large share of the credit or blame, was that even in defeat he won more votes than any defeated candidate in history, and only Franklin D. Roosevelt in 1936 and Dwight D. Eisenhower in 1952 received larger endorsements. The demand for copies of his speeches was so great that an edition of fifty of his major addresses was published.[4] RCA Victor issued a long-playing record album of selections from many of his campaign

---

[1] The following articles by Governor Stevenson appeared in the first six months of 1952: "Organized Crime and Law Enforcement: Problem for the People," *American Bar Association Journal*, xxxviii (January 1952), 26–29; "Who Runs the Gambling Machines?" *Atlantic Monthly*, clxxxix (February 1952), 35–38; "Korea in Perspective," *Foreign Affairs*, xxx (April 1952), 349–60; "Quizzing Stevenson: An Interview," *U.S. News and World Report*, xxxii (April 25, 1952), 50–56; "The States: Bulwark Against 'Big Government,' " *Look*, xvi (June 3, 1952); "Lincoln as a Political Leader," *Abraham Lincoln Quarterly*, vii (June 1952), 79–86; "Stevenson and the Independent Cat," *Harper's*, cciv (June 1952), 65. The articles in the *American Bar Association Journal*, *Atlantic*, and the *Abraham Lincoln Quarterly* were adapted from material originally used in speeches.

[2] For text of this program, see Noel F. Busch, *Adlai E. Stevenson of Illinois* (New York: Farrar, Straus and Young, 1952), pp. 207–22.

[3] Richard B. Morris, ed. *Encyclopedia of American History* (New York: Harper and Bros., 1953), p. 718.

[4] *Major Campaign Speeches of Adlai E. Stevenson 1952* (New York: Random House, 1953).

speeches.[5] There were suggestions that he make regular weekly television commentaries on public questions. In short, his campaign speeches were received with popular acclaim rarely accorded political addresses.

After the election Stevenson held no public office. His term as Governor of Illinois expired in January, 1953. If he were to continue a political career, he would have to do so without benefit of a platform or official position from which to act and speak. During the next four years, the electorate would have to judge him primarily by what he would say, not by what he would do. Once more he would be dependent to an uncommon degree on his speeches as the major avenue for creating the public's image of his personality and philosophy.

Six months of world travel provided material for eight articles in *Look*,[6] for a major radio address upon his return from abroad, and for the Godkin Lectures at Harvard in the spring of 1954. Throughout the congressional campaign of 1954 he spoke for Democratic candidates and sought to help pay off his party's debts incurred by his campaign of 1952. Wherever he went in the fall of 1954 his speaking attracted large crowds. After the mid-term elections, and for a period lasting not quite a year, he practiced law in Chicago, participated in a seminar at the Northwestern University Law School, made business trips to Africa and Latin America, and only occasionally returned to the platform for a political speech, a non-partisan lecture, or a commencement address.

From the day of his defeat on November 4, 1952, until November 15, 1955, when he formally announced his candidacy for renomination, Stevenson made 111 speeches and published 28 articles, from which he edited two books.[7] Where is there another man in the history of American politics whose public image has been created and sustained so largely by his public addresses?

II

In an effort to learn how Stevenson and his advisers view the role of speeches in politics, we conferred with several members of the Stevenson staff and then with Stevenson himself. What follows is a summary of those talks. The first part of our summary covers Stevenson's early background and training as a public speaker. The second part relates to his own

[5] James Fleming, editor and narrator, "Adlai Stevenson Speaks" (New York: RCA Victor Records, 1953).

[6] *Look*, xvii, issues of May 19, June 3, June 17, July 14, August 11, August 25, September 9, and September 23, 1953.

[7] The Godkin Lectures were published under the title, *Call to Greatness* (New York: Harper and Bros., 1954). Thirty-two other speeches, lectures, and articles were reprinted in *What I Think* (New York: Harper and Bros., 1956).

conception of the purposes, importance, and problems of campaign speaking. The third part offers a description of the organization which provides material for him and the method through which his speeches are prepared.

III

Neither as a student at prep school or college did Stevenson have any courses or training in public speaking. When in high school at Bloomington, Illinois, in 1915, he upheld the negative in one debate on the proposition, "Resolved, That the United States Should Free the Philippines." He lost, but today he says, "I don't think I really regretted losing, for I couldn't find it in my heart not to free them." He thinks that perhaps the major reason why he did not debate at Princeton was not that he lacked interest, but that in his time (1918–1922) there was little debate and speaking among undergraduates at the University, not even in the old American Whig and the Cliosophic Societies.

In his senior year at Princeton Stevenson edited the *Daily Princetonian*, and he interrupted his law studies later to work on his family newspaper, the Bloomington *Pantagraph*, for more than a year. He believes the practice of writing and revising required of him during his early journalistic career made an important contribution to the style of his speech composition.

The first major opportunity for him to develop his forensic talents, however, came with his election to the presidency of the Chicago Council on Foreign Relations in the 1930's. At that time the Council was sponsoring prominent speakers from here and abroad in an effort to awaken the Midwest to the gathering storm overseas. Stevenson's job was to introduce visiting dignitaries. Of his feelings towards that job he says: "I was scared to death when I spoke. I still am for that matter." But by what he describes as "hard work and deliberate and diligent discipline" he gradually improved as a public speaker. Indeed, many members of the Council took his introductions to be charmingly spontaneous, when the fact was they had been worked on assiduously.

We asked Stevenson whether he memorized his speeches, and he replied: "I've never been able to memorize word for word. I found I could do much better concentrating on a succession of ideas." Did he wish that he had had more academic training in speech in his early career and did he think public speaking had a place in a liberal education? He replied that, although he had not thought seriously about this question before, he could wish that there had been an easier way to learn public speaking than he had found. He added that, while some people might think public speaking to be more of a procedural than a substantive study, he felt that, if it

increases self-confidence and helps with the communication and understanding of ideas, it would very well be an important addition to a liberal
education.

Stevenson recalls several other kinds of early experiences which he
thinks have contributed to his interest in public matters and the way he
thinks about and analyzes public questions. "For as long as I can remember," he says, "I have been preoccupied with public affairs—probably at the
expense of private affairs—I mean business and professional obligations."
His parents took him abroad at the age of twelve. He traveled a good deal
in Europe as a youngster, and he also saw a considerable part of his own
country during his boyhood. To satiate his "geographic curiosity" he
became an avid reader of travel stories and books and magazines on travel.
In addition he lived in a highly political-minded family. Both his grandfa-
thers were active in Illinois politics. One was Vice-President of the United
States, and the other was an important newspaper editor. Stevenson
describes his father as a "politician at heart, though most of the time not a
practicing one." Between his father's staunchly Democratic view and his
mother's strong Republicanism he was "caught in a constant cross-ruffing
of political controversy." As the result of his family political connections
his "horizons were enlarged almost from birth by meeting famous people."
He remembers especially the vivid impression made on him when he went
with his father to visit Woodrow Wilson in 1912 before Wilson's election
to the Presidency; and he repeated to us a story he had told before in campaign speeches about the time William Jennings Bryan visited in his grand-
father's house:

Bryan had a gargantuan appetite and a reputation for being a mean
trencherman. I decided I was a mean trencherman, too, and would match him
for every piece of chicken he could eat. I did! And then we went out to the
Chautauqua where Bryan spoke and I fell asleep on the front row, much to the
discomfiture of my mother.

Stevenson's early reading was omnifarious. Until adolescence he read
almost wholly in the classics, especially in Greek mythology. When he
went to Wyoming at the age of fifteen, he became so interested in the
West that he began reading all of the "Western books" he could find. "I
think I must have read everything Zane Grey wrote. You might say my
reading followed the flag. Wherever I went I read about the area and the
people I was visiting."

Until fifteen years ago Stevenson continued to read considerably.
Since then his reading has been almost wholly "parochial," that is, confined to the law, politics, and international affairs. He does not find that his
parochial reading has impaired his sources of political information, but he
often feels "hungry and ill-fed" because he cannot read much of what he

would like to read. "This I regret very much; it is perhaps the heaviest price I have had to pay for this so-called prominence."

We raised the question whether Stevenson had read any of the classic works on rhetoric, including Aristotle, Cicero, Quintilian, and John Quincy Adams. He said that he had read Aristotle, Cicero in the Latin, and a "smattering" of Adams' lectures on oratory and rhetoric, but he would not say that he had read them as a "thoughtful, critical scholar" and modestly claims to be "rhetorically illiterate."

Stevenson has always been interested in political addresses. The greatest speech he can recall having heard was given by Newton D. Baker at the Democratic National Convention in 1924. Baker presented a minority report on the League of Nations plank in the party platform. The resolutions committee had made only an equivocal endorsement of the League, and Baker, in proposing an unqualified endorsement, made an eloquent appeal on behalf of the international organization and the ideas of Woodrow Wilson. "It was," Stevenson recalled, "the most moving speech I think I have ever heard."[8]

Stevenson heard Wilson seldom but has read many of his speeches and books. Franklin D. Roosevelt, of course, he heard many times, and he particularly remembers Roosevelt's "Quarantine" speech in Chicago in 1937. "I suppose I was so deeply impressed because of the drama of the historical moment mixed with oratory of the speaker," he recalls.

IV

While he considers winning votes the first object of most political speaking, Stevenson's basic purpose as a speaker is to inform, for he believes that, if he can inform the public, he has found the best means of winning votes. He believes that, however successful demagogy may be in the short run, it is morally intolerable and should never be resorted to by the political speaker. "It never succeeds in the long run, and the people who resort to such means soon find that out. The best way to win votes is through reason. People are educable on the issues." When asked whether he believed that a speaker could create conviction by facts and reasoning, Stevenson replied: "If I didn't believe that, I couldn't believe in the democratic process. So my basic purpose in speaking is to inform."

There has been occasional criticism of Stevenson for spending too much time working on his speeches. We asked why speeches mean so

[8] For the text of this speech, see "Address of Newton D. Baker of Ohio, in Support of the Minority Report Submitting the Amendment to the League of Nations Plank," *Official Report of the Proceedings of the Democratic National Convention, 1924* (Indianapolis: Bookwalter, Ball, Greathouse Printing Company, 1924), pp. 259–270.

much to him and why he thinks them so important to his career. His first reason was that he believes he owes it to the people to communicate as effectively as he can if he is to fulfill his responsibility to democracy. "I think a candidate should work on his own speeches, because that is the best way to acquire the information and the understanding of the issues of the campaign. It is a learning and synthesizing process." Secondly, Stevenson derives much "personal satisfaction" from working on a speech, although he acknowledges that perhaps he cannot see as many people as he would like in a campaign because of the time devoted to speech writing.

When asked for his reaction to the criticism that his speeches lack "the common touch," Stevenson merely sat back in his chair, laughed, and shook his head. He takes with good humor the criticism of his use of humor and with a smile described his reaction to this point as, one of "sullen indignation." He said that he does not believe a public figure has to be "solemn and serious about everything." Nor does he believe that he himself "talks over people's heads." The problem, as he sees it, is one of informing the public. If the people have adequate information about public questions, then politicians can't talk over their heads. Summarizing this point, Stevenson said: "There are people who talk over my head, scientists for example. I haven't the background and information to understand them. But if I can give the people the information, I don't see that I am talking over their heads."

Stevenson is not only aware of other people's criticism of his speeches, but he has some of his own. His self-criticism is usually about matters of emphasis, about the use of certain illustrations, and about delivery, voice, and timing. He is often concerned over his failure to mention someone or something in a speech. Describing his intense self-evaluation after every speech, he says, "I am always depressed." Yet he adds:

> I shouldn't say that I am never satisfied, but I am always wishing I had done better. I think a speaker really makes four speeches: the speech he thinks about ahead of time; the speech he writes; the speech he gives; and the speech he gives on the way home.

He considers the speech he gave on his return from his world trip in 1953 to be his most important speech between the 1952 and the 1956 campaigns; and he ranks next in order during this period his speech on "massive retaliation" and "McCarthyism" in Miami in the spring of 1954, and his national radio address on the Formosan Crisis in April, 1955.[9] We asked him what he regards as the most satisfying speeches of his 1956 preconven-

---

[9] John Bartlow Martin, "Adlai Girds for Battle," *Saturday Evening Post*, ccxxviii (October 22, 1955), 115–118. The dates of these speeches are September 15, 1953, March 7, 1954, and April 11, 1955. For the texts, see *What I Think*, pp. 193–199, 64–71, and 215–224.

tion campaign. He mentioned his convocation address at the University of Minnesota, his speech on the hydrogen bomb before the American Society of Newspaper Editors, his address on the Bill of Rights at a Stevenson-for-President dinner in New York, and a television talk given the night before the primary election in California.[10]

From these questions about Stevenson's conception of the role and importance of campaign speeches, we turned to inquiries about some special campaign speaking problems. For example, we asked, "Should the same speech be made to a television audience as to a party gathering?" This is a problem which has plagued the Stevenson campaign staff for some time, as well as the staff of other candidates. Stevenson himself refers to this problem as "most baffling." It is a problem of communicating to two different audiences in two different situations and in two different moods. A party rally ordinarily is strongly partisan and excited, with the tendency to see things in black and white, and is perhaps little interested in the finer distinctions of reason. The television audience, on the other hand, is much less partisan and in the mood for quite different appeals. Indeed, the appeals to a purely partisan gathering might alienate rather than win large segments of the television audience.

In the past Stevenson has resolved this conflict at times by making a different speech for each occasion, one addressed to the "unseen" audience and the other to the party rally. This, of course, is a taxing solution. The only alternative to it seems to be to direct the speech primarily to the television audience on the theory that it is much larger and that presumably the partisans are already won. Stevenson confesses that there seems to be no satisfactory answer as yet to this problem of political communication.

Another special problem of campaign speaking is that of "whistle-stopping." Stevenson regards the whistle-stop as an important opportunity for closer identification of the candidate with the voters, but the identification is not usually a forensic one. That is, what the candidate says is not so important as what the whistle-stop gives him in the way of an opportunity to meet with people in a particular area. Thus he can learn from local officials precisely what issues are troubling local areas.

At most whistle-stops in 1952 Stevenson confined himself to a few minutes of remarks. He insisted, however, upon making speeches at two or three whistle-stops each day and upon attempting in each to say something substantial. For example, he and his staff recall the whistle-stop speech at Reading, Pennsylvania, on October 30, 1952, in which he developed some new ideas about the role of business in American life.[11] "There is always the temptation to do something more than simply satisfy the amenities of the situation," Stevenson says. This urge to say something new several

---

[10] The dates of these speeches are March 2, April 21, April 25, and June 4, 1956.
[11] For the text of this speech, see *Major Campaign Speeches*, pp. 292–296.

times a day rather than merely to repeat a speech already given perhaps explains why his campaign train was so often behind schedule in 1952.

We asked Stevenson about the role of speeches in presidential preference primaries. After the Minnesota election the press reported that he was making a more "personal" campaign in Florida and California. He and his staff, however, did not regard their campaigns in Florida and California as a radical departure from their strategy in Minnesota. There were fewer speeches each day in Florida and California, and this made it possible for Stevenson to talk a little longer and more deliberately to each audience. He could move into a meeting more casually and more informally and wait around afterward to talk with the people. This he had not been able to do in Minnesota. As a result of the revised strategy, he was given more opportunity to hear from the people instead of having the people merely hear from him. It might be recalled that the "personal" campaign is the kind of campaign that Stevenson had conducted when he was a candidate for Governor of Illinois in 1948. It could hardly be said, therefore, that "beating his opponent at his own game" in Florida and California in 1956 was anything new for him.

V

Before a speech is written, Stevenson and his advisers discuss the nature of the occasion, the place where the speech is to be delivered, the kind of audience likely to attend, whether radio or television will carry it, and what issues are of current interest and importance.

"The issues," says Stevenson, "almost determine themselves." There are fundamental, basic issues that always persist—those of war and peace, of the relationship of the citizen to his government, of public morality, and of public welfare. The complexity of these issues confronts the political speaker with one of his gravest problems: how to treat the issues fairly and thoroughly without oversimplification and distortion within the short time allotted to each speech. It is tempting for the politician to speak of an issue in broad general terms and to ignore the details in which most people are not interested. Yet Stevenson notes that many thoughtful and well-informed constituents are mainly concerned with details, because "they recognize that the great issues are never finally or completely resolved, and the best that can be done is to work on the details."

In addition to national issues, there are issues peculiar to local areas, as well as to particular parts of the population. These local or regional issues deserve discussion but ought not to obscure the larger ones. "Ideally," Stevenson believes, "a campaign should be based on issues and speaking in an attempt to put those issues clearly before the people. That is what I have tried to do, and that is what I will always try to do."

Presidential candidates have more opportunities to speak than they can accept, and the decision to speak in one place rather than another is based on an analysis of the political situation. Where, for example, is a statement on civil rights most needed and most appropriate? Where can time best be spent in terms of winning votes? Such questions as these are usually considered and worked at long before the composition and delivery of the resulting speech, for the itineraries of candidates are normally drawn up several weeks in advance.

When these decisions have been made, Stevenson prepares his speech in one of two ways. One method consists in writing a first draft in which he indicates the major theme he wishes to stress, some arguments he intends to make, and the kinds of supporting material he wants to include. This is discussed with those who advise him on issues. Someone will give this draft a "fact check," i.e., will see whether matters of detail, such as statistics, are accurate. Finally Stevenson writes the introduction and the conclusion. This is the method which he applies to almost all major speeches, especially to those dealing with such important issues as foreign policy, civil rights, civil liberties, agriculture, education, social security, conservation, and the national economy.

Stevenson much prefers this method to the second, in which he calls on an assistant or perhaps a friend not on the staff to submit a memorandum. From this he may borrow ideas, phrases, and perhaps whole sentences. But he always edits rigorously, adapting the memorandum to his own style, adding literary allusions and supporting material, and attaching an appropriate introduction and conclusion. His introductions are habitually apt—a reference to local history, a humorous anecdote or incident which occurred some place in the campaign, a mention of a previous visit, or a mention of some family connection in the area. He revises constantly, changing language and sentence structure even after advance copies of the speech have been released to the press. While waiting to speak he may be seen marking his manuscript. Examination of almost any of his manuscripts would reveal penciled corrections of words, sentences, and punctuation, as well as additions, deletions, marginal notes, and underlining for emphasis.

In 1952 Stevenson devoted three to four hours each day to speechwriting. In the 1956 preconvention campaign he did not find it necessary to spend so much time on his speeches, because he had the benefit of a research staff which had been organized and working for more than a year. In his first try for the Presidency, Stevenson had only the five weeks between his nomination in late July and Labor Day to organize a campaign staff. On his second try, he opened a research office several weeks before he announced his candidacy. This grew from a modest beginning into a large, crowded office containing a massive collection of data on virtually every issue likely to emerge in the presidential campaign. Several major daily newspapers, including the New York *Times*, the New York *Herald Tribune*, *Wall Street Journal*, the St. Louis *Post-Dispatch*, and the Chicago papers are clipped. Almost every magazine covering national and international politics is culled for information likely to be of use at some stage of the campaign. Special memoranda are prepared summarizing the essential facts and issues on major public questions. Such data are organized and filed according to topics running from agriculture to veterans.

Files are also kept on the public statements and record of leading political personalities. A catalogue containing Stevenson's statements on any subject on which he has ever spoken has been assembled. Standard reference works are at hand, including reports of congressional hearings, the *Congressional Record*, the *Congressional Quarterly*, and the New York *Times Index*. State histories are available to provide material on the political and economic interests of local areas, and a full-time staff of librarians and secretaries, together with volunteers recruited from among graduate students at the University of Chicago and Northwestern University, keep the files up to date.

VI

Good language and good speaking by themselves do not qualify a man for high office. The case for or against Stevenson must turn on issues other than that of his public addresses. Yet it cannot be gainsaid that effective speaking is an ingredient, an important ingredient, for winning an election and sustaining support. Without eloquence Lincoln and Franklin D. Roosevelt would perhaps not have been Presidents at all, and certainly they would have been very different Presidents. Stevenson's speeches have been vital to his career, and their quality assures him a high place in the history of American public address. As John Mason Brown has written, "Stevenson has already made his invaluable contribution to American politics, regardless of his ultimate fate politically."[12] Or to put it another way, his importance in our time is beyond dispute; the open question is whether his present importance will be lasting.

[12] John Mason Brown, *Through These Men* (New York: Harper and Bros., 1956), p. 140.

This article illuminates the richness of Kennedy's Inaugural Address by noting his regular use of language, allusion, paradox, alliteration, and other traditional literary devices. It is important to insist that such devices need not be consciously observed by an audience. They strike often only at the rim of consciousness, and though no one blow may be overwhelming, their cumulative effect is powerful.

3

President Kennedy's Inaugural Address

Burnham Carter, Jr.

After John Fitzgerald Kennedy had delivered his Inaugural Address on January 20, 1961, many hailed it as "a great speech" (*Life*) or as "distinguished for its style and brevity as well as for its meaty content" (*The New York Times*). A few commentators denigrated it as mere "mood music" for a new administration (*The Reporter*). In the last year I have asked several groups of students to study it as a piece of rhetoric. On each occasion the class has enjoyed working with a piece of contemporary prose by a man of eminence, and they are pleased to discover so much to discuss about Mr. Kennedy's word choice, figurative language, phrase-making, and variety of appeals.

Alliteration offers an easy start: "Civility is not a sign of weakness, and sincerity is always subject to proof" is a fine instance, although the smoothness of the phrasing will lead some to overlook the host of *s*'s. When the President says he hopes to enlarge the area in which the UN's "writ may run," many will not see the economy and force of this example until they try a paraphrase, such as "until its decisions may have the force of law." Along the same lines, an alert reader will enjoy an internal rhyme like "the *steady spread* of the *deadly* atom."

In considering connotations, one notices right away that Mr. Kennedy uses the word *pledge* seven times in a row (the last two with slight varia-

[Burnham Carter, Jr., is Professor of English and Dean of Briarcliff College. This article originally appeared in *College Composition and Communication*, xiv (1963), 36–40, and is reprinted with the permission of the author and the National Council of Teachers of English.]

tions, to avoid monotony). *Promise* would never do here, for "promises, promises, always promises" has become a cant phrase for us. The reasons for his choice are clear when we remember the happy contexts in which we use *pledge*: swearing allegiance to the flag, making a gift to the church or other charity, drinking a friend's health, and even in the marriage ceremony ("and thereto I plight thee my troth"). The final use of this key word shows a nice distinction. To Soviet Russia Mr. Kennedy offers "not a *pledge* but a *request*," for one's enemy does not deserve the same promise of support as do one's allies. *Request* will suffice. Lest he seem petulant, he dignifies the U.S.S.R. as "those nations who would make themselves our *adversary*," a designation that recalls the high seriousness of Milton's virtue that "sallies out and seeks her *adversary*," or the word's use in the Sermon on the Mount and elsewhere in Scripture.

The address is full of richly connotative words. Consider the force of "*unleashed* powers of destruction" as opposed, say, to *released*, or the refurbishing of the tired phrases *balance of power* and *iron curtain* with fresh variants, "balance of *terror*" and "iron *tyranny*." With such changes the President calls upon an echo in the reader's mind yet avoids the cliché.

It is as a phrasemaker that Mr. Kennedy has made his strongest mark in both his formal and informal speeches. The two best known epigrams in the Inaugural Address are "Let us never negotiate out of fear, but let us never fear to negotiate" and "Ask not what your country can do for you, but what you can do for your country." These inversions sound deceptively easy and inevitable, as do all such concise and pointed expressions. The writer uses few and simple words; he changes the order or alters the wording only slightly; and the result is memorable because it is short, witty, and precise. In his September 25th speech to the UN, the President employs a similar reversal when he asserts, "Mankind must put an end to war, or war will put an end to mankind."

Mr. Kennedy is fond of paradox; witness the following two examples: "Only when our arms are sufficient beyond doubt can we be certain beyond doubt that they will never be employed" (from the Inaugural Address), and terror will always fail as a policy weapon because "men are not afraid to die for a life worth living" (from the UN address). The first of these points up the inescapable irony of any massive defensive effort. The triple walls of Carcassonne were a major reason why it was rarely attacked and, after 1240, never taken; similarly the United States is to spend billions for defense to make sure, hopefully, that none of it will ever be used. How absurd, and yet how true—that is the calculated effect of paradox. The second example relies on the ancient and honorable concept of dying in order that another might live better, of giving up one's life to "save" it. In each instance the writer must produce a statement that is self-contradictory on the surface but in a larger sense correct.

Wit of this sort is risky. It demands attention, and listeners to political speeches are notoriously slack. It depends on the reader's catching on to the allusion, irony, or contradiction quickly, and often the writer receives only incomplete comprehension, as Dean Swift learned with *A Modest Proposal*. In his Inaugural Address Mr. Kennedy requests that new nations remember that "in the past, those who foolishly sought power by riding the tiger end up inside." Whether the allusion is to a folk saying of the sort Mr. Khrushchev favors, or to the old limerick of the lady from Niger,[1] Mr. Kennedy's witty analogy may miss the listeners who have never heard of it or annoy others who distrust all cleverness. Those who know the allusion or have a taste for the wry epigram, however, will enjoy this touch of the sardonic. That the President himself savors a bit of sarcasm is evident from the following dinner party parody he gave of his own famous address.

We observe tonight not a celebration of freedom but a victory of party, for we have sworn to pay off the same party debt our forebears ran up nearly a year and three months ago. Our deficit will not be paid off in the next hundred days, nor will it be paid off in the first one thousand days, nor in the life of this Administration. Nor, perhaps, even in our lifetime on this planet. But let us begin—remembering that generosity is not a sign of weakness and that ambassadors are always subject to Senate confirmation. For if the Democratic party cannot be helped by the many who are poor, it cannot be saved by the few who are rich. So let us begin. (*The New York Times* Magazine, Feb. 25, 1962, p. 70.)

Not all of Mr. Kennedy's care for phrasing is for elegance. Much of it is for clarity and emphasis, especially the repetitions, which are of course intentional and not (like many of our own) the result of inattention or an impoverished vocabulary. The President uses them to give order and balance to a series of thoughts, as in the five paragraphs beginning "To *those* old allies . . . , to *those* new states," etc. Such repetition of a minor word in the construction allows the listener to rest as he follows the steps in the speaker's program. Later Mr. Kennedy's four repetitions of "let both sides" stress the mutual responsibility of the U.S.A. and the U.S.S.R., and at the same time organize his proposals so that the millions in his audience can follow him easily.

Parallelism and antithesis are major devices in the President's style. He describes the new generation of Americans as "born in this country, tempered by war, disciplined by a hard and bitter peace, proud of our

---

[1] There once was a lady from Niger
Who smiled as she rode on a tiger.
They came back from the ride
With the lady inside
And the smile on the face of the tiger.

ancient heritage." Studied parallelism should hardly become an earmark of every writer's style—such a return to euphuism would be appalling—but it is important for him to recognize it when he sees it and to be able to use it himself when the occasion demands. The same is true for Mr. Kennedy's fondness for antithesis. His opening sentence, "We observe today *not a* victory of party *but a* celebration of freedom," employs the same careful contrast as "I came to bury Caesar, not to praise him." Throughout the Inaugural Address one finds *not because, not because, but because,* or "*not as a call* to bear arms . . . , *not as a call* to battle . . . , *but a call* to bear the burden." In part this device is definition of an idea by elimination, but it also offers a welcome simplicity of argument. "If a free society cannot help the many who are poor, it cannot save the few who are rich," regardless of its position, is a good example of a phrasing that is tidy, balanced, and easy on the ear. A sentence that seems to say so much in so little is always likely to be persuasive. Mr. Kennedy's poet laureate, Robert Frost, has a similar penchant for gnomic utterances, as in "We dance around in a ring and suppose, / But the secret sits in the middle and knows," or "I never dared be radical when young / For fear it would make me conservative when old." As a final example of Mr. Kennedy's balanced style, the conclusion of his address to the UN is notable:

Together we shall save our planet or together we shall perish in its flames. Save it we can and save it we must, and then shall we earn the eternal thanks of mankind and, as peacemakers, the eternal blessings of God.

Here the repetition in the first sentence allows the contrast of *save* versus *perish* to shine forth, just as the repetition of *save it we* stresses the double obligation of *can* and *must*. Seldom do most of us think to reverse the order of subject and verb, as the President effectively does here.

President Kennedy relies on metaphor throughout his address. "The bonds of mass misery . . . , the chains of poverty . . . , a beachhead of cooperation [pushing back] the jungles of suspicion." We need to ask, "Is this comparison correct?" and then "How effective do I find it?" In his third paragraph Mr. Kennedy says that "the torch has been passed to a new generation of Americans." As a symbol of freedom, of any light we use to hold back the dark, be it physical or spiritual, *torch* has a traditional value. To some it may even be a cliché, however honored by the wind and weather of time, like the Statue of Liberty. Perhaps the listener will recall Olympic runners bringing the divine flame from Mt. Olympus to the meeting of the competitors. *Torch* is surely correct enough here, for the parallel is clear; whether or not it is wholly successful depends on the degree of literary sophistication of the audience.

A similar reliance on a traditional symbol occurs in the President's peroration, when he announces that "now the trumpet summons us again," for bugles have been used in times of crisis since the days of Charlemagne or even Joshua. A more direct metaphor occurs later in the reference to the four "common enemies of mankind: tyranny, poverty, disease, and war itself." With the trumpet having already established a Biblical context, it is not much of a leap to associate these four adversaries with a similar quartet, the four horsemen of the Apocalypse: conquest, slaughter, famine, and death. Unfortunately, mention of "the four horsemen" in a Midwestern classroom is liable to produce only "Miller, Crowley, Layden, and Stuhldreher," the lethal backfield of Notre Dame in the twenties.

Lastly, the various appeals of the Inaugural Address are designed to call upon all the ideals of the listener. The opening paragraph urges a new unity, a closing of ranks after the campaign, by reference to the common tradition of Presidents taking office in the last 171 years. Mr. Kennedy speaks of "our forebears ... nearly a century and three quarters ago," just as Mr. Lincoln cited "our forefathers ... four score and seven years ago." Unity established, the President speaks of Americans as *tempered, disciplined,* and *proud,* as men willing to *pay any price, bear any burden, meet any hardship, support any friend, oppose any foe.* Such an appeal to stoicism and courage insures an optimistic attitude toward the obligations which he will list next. Finally, for over two thirds of the speech Mr. Kennedy speaks only of *we,* from the opening words, "We observe today," to "But let us begin." Only when his sense of our unified strength has been well established does he switch to "in *your* hands" and "will *you* join in that historic effort?" By way of encouragement he speaks briefly of his own attitude: "I do not shrink from this responsibility—I welcome it." Then quickly he returns to "the devotion which *we* bring to this endeavor," and the final, overriding emphasis is on *our* reward, *our* deeds and *our* work.

The last paragraph of the Inaugural Address illustrates almost all the rhetorical techniques noted so far: the alliteration, the simple yet precise wording, the inverted sentences, the intentional repetitions, the sense of community and tradition. All are here, plus another, as yet unmentioned, element. The subject matter of this address is foreign policy, but the aim is not only to reassure other nations of our plans but to encourage Americans to implement them. Many a speaker makes his cause a crusade, for "if God be on our side, who can be against us?" A religious motif runs through this speech, from the reference to "Almighty God" and "the hand of God" to the quotations from Isaiah 58:6 and Romans 12:12, the allusion to Armageddon in "mankind's final war," that trumpet call, and "the faith, the devotion" stressed in the final paragraphs and especially in the last sentence:

With a good conscience our only sure reward, with history the final judge of our deeds, let us go forth to lead the land we love, asking His blessing and His help, but knowing that here on earth God's work must truly be our own.

Few will miss the echo here of Lincoln's "With malice toward none, with charity toward all," and the phrase "God's work must truly be our own" has a Puritan ring. Such company is highly honorific.

As these religious and historical allusions are ticked off, a danger arises that threatens the integrity of the entire speech. The familiarity of a religious or idealistic appeal may lead to the superficial conclusion that a successful speech is pure semantics. The easily cynical will sneer that political speeches are all "hokum," "political propaganda," or "Fourth of July oratory." A careful analysis of this address, however, ought not to persuade the writer that now he has the inside story, that now, like Mr. Barnum, he can fool some of the people some of the time. Instead, he should see in this address a craftsman at work, but not let his sophomoric glee at discovering how words are used lead him to scoff at the idealism present, however familiar its form. Such a reader should be asked to look at his own last piece of writing. Can he, like Mr. Kennedy, vary his sentence length from 80 words to 4, yet average a mature 26? Can he successfully echo his opening stand in his conclusion, as the President does with "Let us go forth"? And would he be willing to submit a statement of his beliefs to the scrutiny of the entire world? Few of us risk as much in a lifetime of speaking and writing as does the President in a single day.

The 1961 Inaugural Address offers an appealing entry into the world of word choice, sentence construction, and emotional appeals. And as we watch a young, successful, and highly literate man like Mr. Kennedy work successfully to convince others, perhaps we will become more concerned with our own ability to express ourselves. The Inaugural Address forms a good exercise in close reading, and the student will find in it more to write about than he has time for. A cynical few will demur at parts of the speech as old bromides, but by far the majority will conclude, as Dr. Johnson did with Gray's *Elegy*, that there we meet "images which find a mirror in every mind, and sentiments to which every bosom returns an echo."

4

John Kennedy in the Tradition of Inaugural Speeches

Donald L. Wolfarth

Many studies of public address attempt to place a speech in a clear historical context so that we can understand the speech through the problems that demanded its delivery. This article takes a similar approach by trying to place Kennedy's Inaugural Address in the rhetorical context of a speech type, the Presidential inaugural. Through statistics and summaries of typical ideas, the author demonstrates that in part Kennedy's address satisfied his audience because it was "quite consistent with the broad outline of inaugural tradition." The data presented in this study, however, should serve as a basis for a more extensive analysis of the speech itself.

On March 4, 1817, President Monroe delivered his inaugural address as part of the first outdoor inauguration of an American president. On January 20, 1961, the thirty-fifth president, John F. Kennedy, faced east from the Capitol toward the grounds that have known inaugural crowds since the days of Monroe and presented our most recent presidential inaugural address. One news magazine later observed that the new president "followed the tradition of all Presidents at such ceremonies."[1]

Although the inaugural address is custom, it has no legal basis. The first section of Article II of the United States Constitution provides, merely, that "Before he [the president-elect] enter on the Execution of his Office, he shall take the following Oath or Affirmation:—'I do solemnly swear (or affirm) that I will faithfully execute the office of President of the United States, and will to the best of my Ability, preserve, protect and defend the Constitution of the United States." Observing the Constitutional provisions, Henry S. Commager concludes that the inaugural address itself is but "a product of custom and tradition."[2]

Just what are the customs and traditions which surround this first major address of each new president? It is the purpose of this paper to out-

[Donald L. Wolfarth is Professor of Speech at Wisconsin State University—Eau Claire. This article originally appeared in the *Quarterly Journal of Speech*, XLVII (April 1961), 124–32, and is reprinted with the permission of the author and the Speech Association of America.]
[1] *U.S. News and World Report*, L (January 30, 1961), 35.
[2] Henry S. Commager, "To Preserve, Protect and Defend," *Senior Scholastic*, LIII (January 19, 1949), 11.

line the principal lines of rhetorical tradition found in the inaugural addresses of American presidents and to inspect the address of John F. Kennedy in the light of this tradition.[3]

What is the traditional length of an inaugural address? There are 1300 words in Washington's first inaugural and no successor has gauged his first inaugural more closely to that of Washington than did Kennedy with 1355 words. Only five presidents have had shorter first inaugurals than Washington. The longest address was the 8578-word speech of William Henry Harrison which has been variously reported as lasting "an hour"[4] and extending "an hour and forty minutes."[5]

The average length of a first inaugural address is 2848 words. Seventeen of the thirty-one first inaugurals have been shorter than this. The twentieth century has heard both the shortest first inaugural (T. Roosevelt's 983 words) and the second longest (Taft's 5425 words). Franklin Roosevelt broke the chain of longer first inaugurals running from Harding through Hoover, and all subsequent speeches, both first and second inaugurals, have been significantly below the average for first inaugurals.

The average length of a second inaugural address is only 1545 words. Washington's second inaugural is only 134 words long and is by far the shortest. The 4466-word second inaugural of Monroe is twice as long as any other second inaugural. Twentieth-century second inaugurals have averaged 1565 words.

Table I presents a listing of the word length of all inaugural addresses. The number in parentheses following each word total indicates the word-length rank order ("1" means the longest address; "31," the shortest first inaugural). Although there have been thirty-five presidents, four—Tyler, Fillmore, Johnson, and Arthur—succeeded from the vice presidency and did not deliver presidential inaugurals. Second inaugurals are ranked separately, "1" through "13." The statistically average inaugural address, including both first and second inaugurals, contains 2463 words.

Is there a relation between political party and the length of an inaugural address? A comparison of the word length of the first ten inaugurals spoken by Democrats (Jackson through Truman) with the first ten inaugurals delivered by Republicans (Lincoln through Coolidge) discloses that the Democrats averaged 703 words per speech less than the Republicans.

---

[3] Textual authenticity must always be a concern of speech analysis. In this interest, line-by-line collation was made of collections of inaugural addresses, of addresses found in published works by various presidents, the *Congressional Record*, Richardson's *Messages and Papers of the Presidents*, newspaper accounts, and phonograph and tape recordings. The best single source was the 1952 *Inaugural Addresses of the Presidents of the United States* (House Document 540, the 82nd Congress). Used for this research was the GPO edition plus tape recordings of the more recent inaugural addresses, including Kennedy's.
[4] Joseph B. Bishop, *Presidential Nominations and Elections* (New York, 1916), p. 210.
[5] "Custom," *New Yorker*, January 22, 1949, p. 17.

In a further comparison of the word length of the ten most recent first inaugurals by Democrats (Kennedy to Van Buren) with the ten most recent first inaugurals by Republicans (Eisenhower to Hayes), Democrats averaged 821 words per speech less than the Republicans. In only one comparison, that of the first ten inaugurals, is this tendency reversed. In this instance Democrats averaged a mere 28 words per speech *more* than the Republicans. But the most convincing case of all for Democratic brevity is found by comparing the ten most recent speeches of each party, including both first and second inaugurals. This comparison of inaugurals from Cleveland to Kennedy with those of Benjamin Harrison to Eisenhower reveals an average word length per speech for Democrats of 1604 and for Republicans of 3235. Here the Democrats averaged 1631 words per speech less than the Republicans. And Kennedy has supplied an emphatic example of this trend.

What does an inspection of the inaugural sentence reveal? Inaugural sentences range in length from two to 730 words. As a concluding sentence for his review of the events leading to the Spanish-American War, McKinley said, "It came" (II:21).[6] In a sentence of poetic beauty and syntactical sagacity, John Adams turned from praise of his predecessor to a declaration of principles of "preference":

On this subject it might become me better to be silent or to speak with diffidence; but as something may be expected, the occasion, I hope, will be admitted as an apology if I venture to say that if a preference, upon principle, of a free republican government, formed upon long and serious reflection, after a diligent and impartial inquiry after truth; if an attachment to the Constitution of the United States, and a conscientious determination to support it until it shall be altered by the judgments and wishes of the people, expressed in the mode prescribed in it; if a respectful attention to the constitutions of the individual States and a constant caution and delicacy toward the State governments; if an equal and impartial regard to the rights, interest, honor, and happiness of all the States in the Union, without preference or regard to a northern or southern, an eastern or western, position, their various political opinions on unessential points of their personal attachments; if a love of virtuous men of all parties and denominations; if a love of science and letters and a wish to patronize every rational effort to encourage schools, colleges, universities, academies, and every institution for propagating knowledge, virtue, and religion among all classes of the people, not only for their benign influence on the happiness of life in all its stages and classes, and of society in all its forms, but as

---

[6] The McKinley quotation is from his second inaugural address, sentence number 21. Hereafter the source of inaugural address quotations is identified in parentheses following their appearance, such as "(Lincoln I:15)" meaning Lincoln's first inaugural, sentence 15. Where the president is identified in the text, the shortened form "(II:20)," indicating the president's second inaugural, sentence 20, is used. When the president quoted is identified in the text and has only one inaugural address, a reference such as "(25)," meaning sentence number 25, will complete the identification of the source.

the only means of preserving our Constitution from its natural enemies, the spirit of sophistry, the spirit of the party, the spirit of intrigue, the profligacy of corruption, and the pestilence of foreign influence, which is the angel of destruction to elective governments; if a love of equal laws, of justice, and humanity toward the aboriginal nations of America, and a disposition to meliorate their condition by inclining them to be more friendly to them; if an inflexible determination to maintain peace and inviolable faith with all nations, and that system of neutrality and impartiality among the belligerent powers of Europe which has been adopted by this Government and so solemnly sanctioned by both Houses of Congress and applauded by the legislatures of the States and the public opinion, until it shall be otherwise ordained by Congress; if a personal esteem for the French nation, formed in a residence of seven years chiefly among them, and a sincere desire to preserve the friendship which has been so much for the honor and interest of both nations; if, while the conscious honor and integrity of the people of America and the internal sentiment of their own power and energies must be preserved, an earnest endeavor to investigate every just cause and remove every colorable pretense of complaint; if an intention to pursue by amicable negotiation a reparation for the injuries that have been committed on the commerce of our fellow-citizens by whatever nation, and if success can not be obtained, to lay the facts before the Legislature, that they may consider what further measures the honor and interest of the Government and its constituents demand; if a resolution to do justice as far as may depend upon me, at all times and to all nations, and maintain peace, friendship, and benevolence with all the world; if an unshaken confidence in the honor, spirit, and resources of the American people, on which I have so often hazarded my all and never been deceived; if elevated ideas of the high destinies of this country and of my own duties toward it, founded on a knowledge of the moral principles and intellectual improvements of the people deeply engraven on my mind in early life, and not obscured but exalted by experience and age; and, with humble reverence, I feel it to be my duty to add, if a veneration for the religion of a people who profess and call themselves Christians, and a fixed resolution to consider a decent respect for Christianity among the best recommendations for the public service, can enable me in any degree to comply with your wishes, it shall be my strenuous endeavor that this sagacious injunction of the two Houses shall not be without effect (35).

This sentence of Adams abundantly illustrates what can be called the inaugural "chock-full" sentence. Particularly in vogue among the earlier presidents, the "chock-full" sentence is usually long and contains from five to fifteen different specific subject assertions. Adams' sentence opened this tradition and contained eleven specific subject assertions. Four years later, Jefferson used a similar sentence comprised of fifteen specific subject assertions (I:29). Madison's "chock-full" sentence was one of 375 words which made assertions about fourteen different specific subjects (I:16).

Such sentences often contain the bulk of the president's policy statements. In the inaugurals of J. Q. Adams, Taylor, and in the second inaugural of Grant one may find additional examples of the "chock-full" sentence. The first inaugural of Wilson revived the tradition; the President began his sentence with these words, "We have itemized with some degree of particularity the things that ought to be altered and here are some of the chief items: A tariff . . ." (I:42). Sentence 191 in the Coolidge inaugural is of this type. Two such sentences are found in the inaugural address of Hoover. Sentence 141 enumerates what he terms "important further mandates from the recent election." A few lines later one finds a 123-word sentence which signals the final example of this characteristic of inaugural sentence style. President Kennedy did not revive this waning tradition.

Table I indicates the sentence total of each inaugural with the rank order of the speech in relation to the total number of sentences in other inaugural addresses. Also represented is the word-length of the average sentence for each inaugural. Revealed is a rather marked stylistic change during the long course of inaugural addresses. The longest average sentences tend to reflect an earlier period. Average sentence length has dropped from a high of 62 words per sentence in the inaugural of John Adams to the low average sentence length of 18 words in the second inaugural of Eisenhower. The shortening of the inaugural sentence has been quite gradual and had been remarkably constant until January 20, 1961. Reversed in just fourteen minutes was a 44-year trend. Kennedy's average sentence length of 26 words puts him in stylistic league with Wilson.

The statistically average first inaugural has 94 sentences, each averaging 34 words in length. The average second inaugural has 58 sentences, each averaging 29 words in length. Since nearly one half of all second inaugurals are products of the twentieth century, the shorter average second inaugural sentence is readily explained.[7] The statistical average of all inaugural addresses yields an average of 84 sentences per speech, with each sentence composed of 33 words.

Inaugural salutations boast both a primary and a secondary tradition. Kennedy followed them both when he began, "Vice President Johnson, Mr. Speaker, Mr. Chief Justice, President Eisenhower, Vice President Nixon, President Truman, Reverend Clergy, Fellow Citizens." Franklin Roosevelt initiated the secondary tradition of recognizing specific members of the audience. In 1945 Roosevelt began in this way: "Mr. Chief Justice, Mr. Vice President, my friends." Truman followed the pattern. In 1957 Eisenhower continued the tradition with significant augmentation: "Mr. Chairman, Mr. Vice President, Mr. Chief Justice, Mr. Speaker, members of my family and friends, my countrymen, and friends of my country, wherever they may be."

To be consistent with primary tradition, the President must include the salutation "Fellow Citizens." This custom began in 1789 when Wash-

[7] For the purpose of this study and statistical facility, Franklin Roosevelt's second, third, and fourth inaugurals were classified as second inaugurals.

ington addressed the "Fellow-Citizens of the Senate and of the House of Representatives." To begin a speech abounding in unity appeals, Jefferson employed, "Friends and Fellow-Citizens." Consistency prevailed until Pierce used the original "My Countrymen." Buchanan reverted to "Fellow-Citizens." In 1861 Lincoln significantly used the salutation, "Fellow-Citizens of the United States"; to precede his second inaugural, Lincoln created "Fellow-Countrymen." Perhaps Grant was influenced by Lincoln's example; in 1869 Grant began with the words, "Citizens of the United States."

"Fellow-Citizens" preceded all inaugural addresses from 1873 to Cleveland's 1893 innovation, "My fellow citizens." McKinley followed the Cleveland example by using "Fellow-Citizens" in 1897 and "My Fellow-Citizens" in 1901. Taft once and Wilson twice used the popular "My Fellow Citizens." Harding reached back to the example of Pierce and used the salutation, "My Countrymen." Republicans Coolidge and Hoover continued with "My Countrymen."

The inaugural address of John F. Kennedy contains what might be called an internal and international salutation. When he said, "My fellow citizens of the world: Ask not what America will do for you, but what together we can do for the freedom of man" (50), was it an inaugural innovation, merely stylistic emphasis, or the exercise of ambiguity?

If indeed the sentence were addressed to all but American citizens, it stands as a uniquely direct international salutation. However, in view of the Eisenhower inaugurals, the Kennedy internal salutation may appear as but stylistic variation. In 1953, Eisenhower said, "We wish our friends the world over to know this above all: we face . . ." (69). And in his 1957 address Eisenhower declared, "In Europe, we ask that enlightened and inspired leaders . . ." (90). The suggestion of ambiguity arises when we consider that American citizens are as much "citizens of the world" as any to be found. In fact it was Franklin Roosevelt, on January 20, 1945, who observed, "We have learned to be citizens of the world, members of the human community" (17). Based on the evidence of context and vocal inflection, it would seem that Kennedy's audience experienced an expression new to the inaugural salutation tradition.

Once into their address, with what issues do the presidents deal? Space does not permit a detailed answer but some verifiable conclusions are clear. What the presidents say about specific issues traditionally tends to center around what to them were the principal issues of their day. Domestic issues play a much larger role in the nineteenth-century inaugurals, and inaugural attention to international affairs rises sharply in the twentieth century.

The issues most frequently treated from Washington to Truman were those concerning interpretations of our form of government. Such concepts as democracy, function and powers of the general government, executive function and power, relations with state governments, citizen equality, freedom and justice were treated by many presidents. Not all presidents have treated these issues, but such issues have consumed the length of more issue-bearing inaugural sentences than any other.

International interpretations, such as assertions about war and peace, freedom, justice, international brotherhood, references to foreign peoples, their problems and ideologies rank just behind domestic governmental interpretations as popular issues for inaugural addresses. Madison spoke about "the injustice and violence of the belligerent powers" (I:11). Kennedy requested "that both sides begin anew the quest for peace" (23).

Although it hasn't appeared in an inaugural address since 1937, the third most common issue from Jefferson to Franklin Roosevelt was the concept of frugality and efficiency in governmental operations. Despite the fact that not a dissenting inaugural assertion was ever recorded about this issue, Coolidge marshaled twenty-one sentences in support of economy in government. Said he: "I favor the policy of economy, not because I wish to save money, but because I wish to save people" (120).

Ranked fourth as an issue for inaugural attention are assertions which reveal how the President feels the United States should relate herself to other nations. Most of our presidents from John Adams to Kennedy have declared themselves for friendly cooperation. Adams advocated an "inviolable faith with all nations" (35). Kennedy pledged to our old allies "the loyalty of faithful friends" (10). Some presidents, especially those of the twentieth century, have also included a tougher line. In 1953 Eisenhower spoke of "the futility of appeasement; we shall never try to placate an aggressor" (I:78). Kennedy said, "And let every other power know that this hemisphere intends to remain the master of its own house" (21).

Specific domestic and foreign issues holding frequency rankings from five through ten are these: national finance, the tariff, comments about the Constitution, remarks about domestic lands and territories, references to our military establishment and, in tenth place, international economic relations. The only specific domestic issue raised by Kennedy concerned our military establishment: "For only when our arms are sufficient beyond doubt can we be certain beyond doubt that they will never be employed" (25).

How much of an inaugural address is apt to deal with domestic issues and how much with international affairs? In Table II, all inaugural content is shown for "Domestic Issues" and for "International Relations." Also included in the table is a grouping of items under "American Tradition," comment upon America or Americans, and the drawing upon American history. A fourth column in the table, called "Other," accounts for such content as non-specific expository remarks, unity appeals, divine invocations, ambiguous sentences, and other non-specific references.

TABLE I NUMBER OF WORDS AND SENTENCES IN INAUGURAL ADDRESSES

1st Inaugurals	Words	(Rank)	Sentences	(Rank)	Word-Length of Average Sentence	(Rank)
Washington	1300	(26)	23	(29)	57	(2)
John Adams	2311	(18)	37	(26)	62	(1)
Jefferson	2123	(20)	41	(24)	52	(4)
Madison	1170	(27)	21	(31)	56	(3)
Monroe	3322	(11)	123	(10)	27	(21)
J. Q. Adams	2944	(14)	76	(18)	39	(10)
Jackson	1116	(29)	25	(28)	45	(6)
Van Buren	3884	(7)	98	(15)	40	(8)
Wm. Harrison	8578	(1)	214	(1)	40	(9)
Polk	4904	(3)	152	(6)	32	(14)
Taylor	1096	(30)	22	(30)	50	(5)
Pierce	3319	(12)	104	(14)	32	(15)
Buchanan	2772	(15)	89	(16)	31	(16)
Lincoln	3588	(9)	135	(8)	27	(22)
Grant	1139	(28)	40	(25)	28	(20)
Hayes	2472	(16)	59	(20)	42	(7)
Garfield	2949	(13)	111	(13)	27	(23)
Cleveland ('85)	1688	(24)	44	(23)	38	(11)
B. Harrison	4588	(4)	157	(5)	29	(19)
Cleveland ('93)	2020	(21)	58	(21)	35	(12)
McKinley	3966	(6)	130	(9)	31	(17)
T. Roosevelt	983	(31)	33	(27)	30	(18)
Taft	5425	(2)	159	(4)	34	(13)

162

Wilson	1699	(23)	68	(19)	25	(25)
Harding	3325	(10)	148	(7)	22	(27)
Coolidge	4054	(5)	196	(2)	21	(29)
Hoover	3704	(8)	164	(3)	23	(26)
F. Roosevelt	1883	(22)	85	(17)	22	(28)
Truman	2171	(19)	116	(12)	19	(31)
Eisenhower	2442	(17)	119	(11)	21	(30)
Kennedy	1355	(25)	52	(22)	26	(24)
Totals:	88290		2899			
Averages:	2848		94		34	
2nd Inaugurals						
Washington	134	(13)	4	(13)	34	(4)
Jefferson	2159	(3)	45	(7)	48	(1)
Madison	1142	(10)	33	(9)	35	(3)
Monroe	4466	(1)	131	(1)	34	(5)
Jackson	1167	(9)	30	(10)	39	(2)
Lincoln	588	(11)	26	(11)	23	(8)
Grant	1332	(8)	44	(8)	30	(6)
McKinley	2215	(2)	100	(2)	22	(10)
Wilson	1526	(6)	59	(6)	26	(7)
F. Roosevelt II	1800	(4)	96	(3)	19	(12)
F. Roosevelt III	1342	(7)	68	(5)	20	(11)
F. Roosevelt IV	557	(12)	24	(12)	23	(9)
Eisenhower	1651	(5)	92	(4)	18	(13)
Totals	20079		752			
Averages	1545		58		29	
Averages 1st and 2nd Inaugurals	2463		84		33	

Table II suggests a consistent increase in first inaugural address assertions about international affairs. Washington was silent on the subject of
foreign affairs. In 1953, 36% of Eisenhower's first inaugural assertions were
about international issues. Kennedy confirmed this trend with the figure of
44%. It should be noted that the pattern of increase for international
issues parallels a rather even decrease in content about domestic affairs.
Kennedy's figure of 4% for domestic issues provides an unusually sharp
de-emphasis.

Just under 50%. of Washington's first inaugural contained non-
specific praise, blame, or comment on America or Americans. This topic
has continued to be a popular avenue of inaugural expression. In 1961,
"the torch has been passed to a new generation of Americans ..." (Ken-
nedy:7).

All inaugural addresses contain sentences which are not assertions
about specific subjects. Certain transitional remarks are among the content
described in the category "Other." Sentence 9 in the Kennedy inaugural
illustrates a typical transitional remark: "This much we pledge—and more."
The figure of 37% of Kennedy's content which falls in the "Other"
column is not greatly different from percentage figures based on other
shorter inaugural addresses.

Perhaps in no instance is the inaugural tradition stronger than in
effecting a climactic close. Certain patterns are quite discernible. A president who follows the style of the majority will conclude his inaugural
address with a divine invocation. Washington set the pace in this regard
with an effusive quality that has never been surpassed:

Having thus imparted to you my sentiments as they have been awakened by
the occasion which brings us together, I shall take my present leave; but not
without resorting once more to the benign Parent of the Human Race in
humble supplication that, since He has been pleased to favor the American
people with opportunities for deliberating in perfect tranquility, and disposi-
tions for deciding with unparalleled unanimity on a form of government for
the security of their union and the advancement of their happiness, so His
divine blessing may be equally conspicuous in the enlarged views, the temper-
ate consultations, and the wise measures on which the success of the Government must depend (I:23).

Eisenhower employed this sentence to close his first inaugural address:
"This is the work that awaits us all, to be done with bravery, with charity,
and with prayer to Almighty God" (I:119). Twenty-one presidents have
concluded with a divine invocation.

Seven other presidents closed by augmenting the divine invocation
with an appeal for unity. In 1801 Jefferson said: "Relying, then, on the
patronage of your good will, I advance with obedience to the work, ready
to retire from it whenever you become sensible how much better choice it
is in your power to make. And may that Infinite Power which rules the des-

TABLE II CHRONOLOGY OF INAUGURAL CONTENT IN FOUR CATEGORIES

	Domestic Issues Percentage	International Relations Percentage	American Tradition Percentage	Other Percentage
First Inaugural Addresses				
Washington through Polk	42	3	32	23
Taylor through Cleveland ('93)	47	6	20	27
McKinley through Eisenhower	31	19	22	28
Averages Pre-Kennedy	40	9	25	26
Kennedy	4	44	15	37
Averages All 1st Inaugurals	38	11	24	27
Second Inaugural Addresses				
Washington through Monroe	22	14	33	31
Jackson through McKinley	23	14	25	38
Wilson through Eisenhower	16	25	26	33
Averages 2nd Inaugurals	19	19	28	34
Averages 1st and 2nd Inaugurals	34	13	25	28

tinies of the universe lead our councils to what is best, and give them a favorable issue for your peace and prosperity" (I:40–1).

Four inaugural addresses conclude with praise for America. The final sentences of the Coolidge inaugural fully illustrate this: "America seeks no earthly empire built on blood and force. No ambition, no temptation, lures her to thought of foreign dominions. The legions which she sends forth are armed, not with the sword, but with the cross. The higher state to which she seeks the allegiance of all mankind is not of human, but of divine origin. She cherishes no purpose save to merit the favor of Almighty God" (192–6).

"Exhortation" is the classification which may be given to sentences wherein the speaker incites the audience to virtuous thought or action. Five presidents concluded their inaugurals in this manner. The final sentence of Lincoln's first inaugural is an impressive example. In 1917 Wilson used these words: "The shadows that now lie dark upon our path will soon be dispelled, and we shall walk with the light all about us if we be but true to ourselves—to ourselves as we have wished to be known in the counsels of the world and in the thought of all those who love liberty and justice and the right exalted" (II:59).

President Kennedy combined effectively the elements of exhortation with a divine invocation: "With a good conscience our only sure reward, with history the final judge of our deeds, let us go forth to lead the land we love, asking His blessing and His help, but knowing that here on Earth God's work must truly be our own" (52).

In summary, what conclusions can be drawn from a comparison of the Kennedy address with inaugural tradition? Only by its brevity did the speech make a significant departure from traditional first inaugural addresses. In this respect, as well as by issue selection, the address more closely follows the tradition of a *second* inaugural address. With some exceptions, presidents have typically been more domestic-minded in first inaugurals and have given more attention to international issues in a second inaugural address.[8]

The address of Kennedy ranks above the average inaugural in emotional color. Few inaugurals carry as high a percentage of sentences of exhortation. Even fewer have used an illustration as picturesque as the admonition that "those who foolishly sought power by riding the back of the tiger ended up inside" (15).

During fourteen minutes of an announced "celebration of freedom," Americans received the inaugural address of John F. Kennedy—a speech quite consistent with the broad outline of inaugural tradition.

[8] The best and most recent example of second inaugural focus on international issues is Eisenhower's 1957 address, which bears the title, "The Price of Peace."

STUDIES OF A SPEAKER: FRANKLIN DELANO ROOSEVELT

These five studies, all of which focus on a single speaker, give us a chance to examine his thought and art from a variety of angles, as well as to appreciate the variety of approaches we may take to speech analysis. No one study is complete in itself, and even as a group, there are gaps concerning the source of Roosevelt's ideas, the opposition's philosophy, and both the audience for and reaction to particular speeches. The many suggestions in these studies on the spirit of the times, however, help us to place the larger human appeals of Roosevelt's speeches in the context of America during his Presidency.

The Presidency has grown increasingly complex and, as with any busy public figure, the speech adviser has become an essential staff member. In this study the author attempts to trace what might be called the careful and controlled evolution of Roosevelt's speeches, to follow a group of them from the initial draft through consultations with experts until a final version emerges. His major conclusion is a refutation of the charge that Roosevelt's speeches were "ghost-written"; they were, in essence, his own, made more so by his ready ad-libbing.

5

The Preparation of Franklin D. Roosevelt's Speeches

Earnest Brandenburg

Franklin D. Roosevelt "has [already] become a towering figure in U.S. mythology."[1] Less than half a decade after his death, his position as one of this nation's outstanding political leaders seems certain. Since his eminence is commonly recognized as stemming in large part from his speaking ability,[2] a consideration of the methods of preparing Franklin Roosevelt's speeches would seem of interest and value.

1

Widely varying opinions are held as to whether or not Mr. Roosevelt wrote his own speeches. Accusations were common that he was content

[The late Earnest Brandenburg was the President of Drury College, Springfield, Missouri. This article originally appeared in the *Quarterly Journal of Speech*, xxxv (April 1949), 214–21, and is reprinted with permission of the author and the Speech Association of America.]
[1] Hamilton Basso, "The Roosevelt Legend," *Life*, November 3, 1947, pp. 23, 126.
[2] Karl Schriftgieser, *The Amazing Roosevelt Family, 1613–1942* (New York, 1942), p. 347; Lew Sarett and William Trufant Foster, *Basic Principles of Speech* (New York, 1936), p. 561; Archibald Campbell Knowles, *A Rendezvous with Destiny* (Philadelphia, 1946), pp. 55–56; Mabel Platz, *The History of Public Speaking* (New York, 1935), p. 282; O. G. Villard, "Evolution of President Roosevelt," *Contemporary Review*, 145 (1934), 522–30; Albert Shaw, "One year of President Roosevelt," *Review of Reviews* 89 (March 1934), 11–15.

simply to let others prepare the addresses he delivered. The mordant H. L. Mencken, when asked what he thought of the wide praise accorded Roosevelt for his ability as a speaker, replied, "I think it's hooey. I don't believe Roosevelt writes his fireside speeches."[3] Another critic bluntly stated: "He had never done much writing. He was one of those many public men who were willing to have their speeches written for them."[4] On the other hand, unequivocal statements have frequently been made that Roosevelt did "write his own speeches."[5]

Which of these views one accepts depends upon his particular definition of the word *write*, for the general procedure of preparing Roosevelt's speeches has been explained both by the late President himself and by several of his advisers who worked with him at various times. In the 1937 collection of his *Public Papers and Addresses*, Roosevelt explains in detail "the preparation of campaign speeches as well as speeches on other occasions." He freely admits:

I have called on many different people for advice and assistance. . . . On various subjects I have received drafts and memoranda from different people, varying from short suggestions as to a sentence here and there to long memoranda of factual material, and in some cases complete addresses.

In addition to such suggestions, I make it a practice to keep a "speech material file." Whenever anything catches my eye, either in the course of reading articles, memoranda, or books, which I think will be of value in the preparation of a speech, I ask her [Miss Marguerite A. Le Hand, Personal Secretary] to put it away in the speech material file.

In preparing a speech I usually take the various office drafts and suggestions which have been submitted to me and also the material which has been accumulated in the speech file on various subjects, read them carefully, lay them aside, and then dictate my own draft, usually to Miss Tully. Naturally, the final speech will contain some of the thoughts and even some of the sentences which appeared in some of the drafts or suggestions submitted.

I suppose it is human that two or three of the many persons with whom I have consulted in the preparation of speeches should seek to give the impression that they have been responsible for the writing of the speeches, and that one or two of them should claim authorship or should state that some other individual was the author. Such assertions, however, are not accurate.

On some of my speeches I have prepared as many as five or six successive drafts myself after reading drafts and suggestions submitted by other people; and I have changed drafts from time to time after consulting with other people either personally or by telephone.[6]

[3] "Mencken Derides Roosevelt Voice," *New York Times*, 21 October 1937.
[4] John T. Flynn, *Country Squire in the White House* (New York, 1940), p. 57.
[5] Knowles, 13; Frank Kingdon and Rex Stout, *That Man in the White House* (New York, 1944), p. 128.
[6] Franklin D. Roosevelt, *The Public Papers and Addresses of Franklin D. Roosevelt* (New York, 1938), 6, 391–92.

This explanation of his general method has been confirmed by those close to the President. Frances Perkins, who served in Roosevelt's cabinet during the entire time he was President, relates that his advisers and associates were eager to do their best in helping the President, and that Roosevelt, in turn, was happy to receive suggestions.[7] Robert Sherwood has explained:

When he wanted to give a speech for some important purpose, whether it was connected with a special occasion or not, he would discuss it first at length with Hopkins, Rosenman, and me, telling us what particular points he wanted to make, what sort of audience he wished primarily to reach and what the maximum word limit was to be. He would dictate pages and pages, approaching his main topic, sometimes hitting it squarely on the nose with terrific impact, sometimes rambling so far away from it that he couldn't get back, in which case he would say, "Well—something along those lines—you boys can fix it up."[8]

Eleanor Roosevelt called her husband's speech preparation a "regular routine."

First of all he decided on the subject with which he was going to deal, then he called in the Government officials charged with the responsibility for the work on this particular subject: for instance, if it was to be a fiscal speech, the Treasury Department and the Federal Reserve Board were consulted; if agriculture, the Department of Agriculture and allied agencies, and so on.

After he had all the facts, he usually sat down with two or three people and explained his ideas of what he wished said. They made a first draft and brought it back to him. He then went over it, and sometimes there were as many as six or eight or ten drafts of the same speech. . . . In between each rewriting my husband went over it again. . . .

When a speech was finally written, my husband always practically knew every word that was in it by heart, as he had gone over it so often. It was the final expression of his original thoughts.[9]

Those who worked with Roosevelt respected the fact that it was he who would and did make the final decisions. He often utilized vast resources to obtain knowledge or furnish ideas, but "the final thought and the final form of expression [were] his own."[10] Even after discontinuing work on the President's speeches and maintaining some bitterness toward Roosevelt, Raymond Moley agreed that the President was the one whose ideas and phraseology were predominant in his addresses. Moley advised a friend:

[7] Frances Perkins, *The Roosevelt I Knew* (New York, 1946), p. 113.

[8] Robert E. Sherwood, *Roosevelt and Hopkins: An Intimate History* (New York, 1948), pp. 371–72.

[9] Eleanor Roosevelt, "If You Ask Me," *Ladies' Home Journal*, 65 (October, 1948), p. 45.

[10] Charles W. B. Hurd, "The President's Job," *Current History* 43 (1935), 233–38. "The Silent Orator," *Time*, January 19, 1948, pp. 51, 25; Perkins, p. 113.

He and I have argued endlessly over what the substance of a speech should be. But once he reached a decision, I've never slipped anything over on him.*. . . Remember, when you get to work on speeches, that you're a clerk, not a statesman.[11]

2

I have made a detailed study of seventeen addresses on international affairs delivered by Mr. Roosevelt between September 3, 1939, and December 7, 1941.[12] A brief review of facts uncovered concerning the drafting of those speeches will serve to clarify the late President's general methods of speech preparation. Miss Grace Tully, who personally typed most of the drafts for the seventeen addresses analyzed, provided much general information about the procedure and the persons involved in helping Roosevelt prepare those speeches.[13] For each of his addresses, Roosevelt called upon the tremendous resources available to him. Drafts of suggested speeches, or of portions of a possible speech, typically came from some dozen different people, members of the Cabinet, or those in position to be of special assistance.

During the period between September 3, 1939, and December 7, 1941, the President himself normally dictated to Miss Tully the first draft of a speech from his general knowledge or from materials which he had had submitted concerning certain issues. Frequently, some of his close advisers, such as Judge Samuel I. Rosenman, Harry L. Hopkins, Cordell Hull, or Robert Sherwood, were present and would intersperse comments or make suggestions.

After a first draft had been completed, copies of it were circulated to those designated by Roosevelt. For example, Secretary Hull read the speeches having to do with foreign policy. After Henry L. Stimson became a member of the Cabinet, June 20, 1940, he was called upon for suggestions concerning foreign policy. If an issue involving the military was to be included, General Marshall and Admirals Leahy and King were asked for opinions. The various comments and suggestions were then reviewed by Roosevelt or his immediate speech assistants—Rosenman, Hopkins and Sherwood—and the President would dictate another draft. Or, a new draft might be prepared by one or more of the President's advisers working from marginal notes written into the previous draft by Mr. Roosevelt. The next draft would again be circulated.

[11] Raymond Moley, *After Seven Years* (New York, 1939), p. 343.
[12] Earnest Brandenburg, "An Analysis and Criticism of Franklin D. Roosevelt's Speeches on International Affairs Delivered Between September 3, 1939 and December 7, 1941" (State University of Iowa, 1948), Ph.D. dissertation.
[13] Interview in Washington, D.C., August 27, 1947.

Most Cabinet members saw some draft of the speech before it was finally delivered. Cordell Hull, or the Acting Secretary of State, usually saw one or more of the drafts of every one of the speeches of this period. With the receipt of comments and suggestions, and usually in the presence of one or more of his close advisers, Roosevelt dictated a new version of the address. He dictated (holding before him the previous draft which he had marked up in considerable detail) by striking out and substituting words, sentences, or entire sections. Each speech had some three to ten complete revisions. Available at the Roosevelt Library at Hyde Park, New York, are drafts which have been numbered for each of the addresses as follows:

Sept. 3, 1939: Drafts 1, 2, and the Original Reading Copy.[14]
Sept. 21, 1939: Draft 2 and the Original Reading Copy.
Jan. 3, 1940: Drafts 1, 2, and the Original Reading Copy.
April 15, 1940: One draft, unnumbered, and the Original Reading Copy.
May 10, 1940: No available drafts.
May 16, 1940: Drafts 1, 2, and the Original Reading Copy.
May 26, 1940: Drafts 1, 2, and the Original Reading Copy.
June 10, 1940: No available drafts.
July 19, 1940: Drafts 1, 2, 3, and the Original Reading Copy.
Sept. 2, 1940: Drafts 1, 2, and the Original Reading Copy.
Dec. 29, 1940: Drafts 1, 4, 5, 6, 7, and the Original Reading Copy.
Jan. 6, 1941: Drafts 1, 2, 3, 4, 5, 6, 7, and the Original Reading Copy.
Jan. 20, 1941: Drafts, 1, 2, 3, 4, 5, 6, and the Original Reading Copy.
March 15, 1941: Drafts 1, 2, 4, 5, and the Original Reading Copy.
May 27, 1941: Drafts 1, 2, 3, 4, 5, 6, 8, 9, and the Original Reading Copy.
Sept. 11, 1941: Drafts 1, 2, 3, and the Original Reading Copy.
Oct. 27, 1941: Drafts 1, 2, 3, 6, and the Original Reading Copy.

Roosevelt's interest in the opinions of his advisers, as well as the many conferences he held as he worked on his addresses, is well indicated by the *New York Times* account of his activities while he was making final preparations for his address of September 11, 1941:

On his way from Hyde Park his train stopped at the 138th Street station in New York and picked up Harry L. Hopkins, who brought him a report from all government departments and, it was understood, from Prime Minister Churchill on recent developments.

The two, together with Judge Samuel I. Rosenman, who assists the Chief Executive with some speeches and is regarded as a defense organization expert, were closeted together all the way from New York to Washington. . . .

[14] Original Reading Copy is the designation the President gave to the *final* copy—the actual manuscript from which he spoke. The term is employed here to maintain the identifications of manuscripts available at the Roosevelt Library, Hyde Park, New York.

The President was greeted at the Union Station here by Secretary Hull, who went aboard the Executive's car for a brief chat before they drove to the White House, where they were joined by Secretaries Stimson and Knox.[15]

Roosevelt's former personal stenographer (Miss Tully) had aided in the preparation of all the addresses analyzed, and she attempted to recall exactly which of the advisers around Roosevelt during those years had been most active in helping with each address. She had only her memory to rely upon, but she was reasonably certain that the persons whose names appear below assisted with the addresses given on the date indicated:

Sept. 3, 1939: Messrs. Hull, Welles, Norman Davis.

Sept. 21, 1939: Judge Rosenman, Messrs. Hopkins, Hull, Welles, Senator Barkley.

Jan. 3, 1940: All Cabinet members, Judge Rosenman, Mr. Hopkins.

April 15, 1940: Messrs. Welles, Hull.

May 10, 1940: Messrs. Welles, Hull.

May 16, 1940: General Marshall, Admiral Leahy, Admiral King, Judge Rosenman, Mr. Hopkins.

May 26, 1940: Judge Rosenman, Mr. Hopkins.

June 10, 1940: Messrs. Hull, Welles.

July 19, 1940: Messrs. Thomas G. Corcoran, Benjamin Cohen, Judge Rosenman.

Sept. 2, 1940: Judge Rosenman (at Hyde Park), Mr. Ickes (on train to Tennessee).

Dec. 29, 1940: Messrs. Robert Sherwood, Hopkins, Hull, and Judge Rosenman.

Jan. 6, 1941: All Cabinet members, Judge Rosenman, Messrs. Hopkins, William Knudsen, Sherwood.

Jan. 20, 1941: Judge Rosenman, Messrs. Hopkins, Sherwood.

March 15, 1941: Messrs. Hopkins, Sherwood, Edward R. Stettinius, Jr., General James H. Burns.

May 27, 1941: Messrs. Welles, Hull, Sherwood.

Sept. 11, 1941: Judge Rosenman, Messrs. Hopkins, Hull, Stimson, Knox.

Oct. 27, 1941: Messrs. Sherwood, Knox, Hull, Stimson, Welles.

She emphasized the fact that Roosevelt's State of the Union addresses (delivered January 3, 1940, and January 6, 1941) were the product of at least ten days' careful work, and had received comment and suggestions from all Cabinet members.

Miss Tully was understandably reluctant to designate specific portions of the texts as having been contributed by certain individuals. Robert Sherwood, who joined Roosevelt's inner circle of speech advisers and collabora-

---

[15] Frank L. Kluckhorn, "Roosevelt Likely to Announce Navy Will Protect U.S. Shipments on Seas," *New York Times*, September 11, 1941.

tors during the campaign of 1940, has explained that he is able to identify a few

specific passages or ideas that were suggested by Hopkins, Rosenman or me or by others outside the White House, but the collaboration between the three of us and the President was so close and so constant that we generally ended up unable to say specifically who had been primarily responsible for any given sentence or phrase.[16]

Miss Tully did remark that the frequent succession of short sentences was "completely Roosevelt." She remembered that the idea of quoting exact flying distances from possible Axis attacking positions to strategic points in the Western Hemisphere was Roosevelt's own idea. He had guessed at the distances and then had Daniel Callahan (of the Department of Justice) check and substitute the correct figures. Miss Tully also found at least one passage she was certain appeared in the final speech almost exactly as originally written by the playwright, Robert Sherwood. When informed of Miss Tully's statement, and asked if he could confirm her memory about that passage, Mr. Sherwood wrote:

I worked throughout the long preparation of that speech [delivered May 27, 1941]—in fact, I was living in the White House at the time—but I can quite honestly say that I have no idea who made the major contribution to the paragraph you quote. I should guess that it represented a composite of the various minds then at work, but the final sentence about "our children . . . goosestepping in search of new gods," sounds to me as if it had been written entirely by President Roosevelt himself.[17]

3

I have found no indications that Franklin Roosevelt spent any time thinking about the organization to be followed in any address. Rather, he dictated (or wrote) a first draft, with no particular concern about the over-all structure. As a result, perhaps, no characteristic organizational patterns are to be noted in his addresses. Typically, he discussed some three to ten different topics in a speech, with each unit complete in itself. Miss Tully

[16] From a letter, dated October 1, 1948, signed by Robert Sherwood, addressed from The Playwrights Co., 630 Fifth Avenue, New York, N.Y.

[17] Mr. Sherwood's statement is quoted from the same letter as the preceding footnote. The passage in question is the following from the address of May 27, 1941: "Even our right of worship would be threatened. The Nazi world does not recognize any God except Hitler; for the Nazis are as ruthless as the Communists in the denial of God. What place has religion which preaches the dignity of the human being, of the majesty of the human soul, in a world where moral standards are measured by treachery and bribery and fifth columnists? Will our children, too, wander off, goose-stepping in search of new gods?"

reported that Judge Rosenman was the person most responsible for organization. The President trusted the Judge's ability to rearrange the speeches by changing sections from one part of an address to another.

Available at the Roosevelt Library in Hyde Park are three sheets of yellow paper upon which Franklin Roosevelt had written in pencil what was obviously the first draft of his third inaugural address, delivered January 20, 1941. Seven successive drafts of this speech have been preserved, so we know it went through at least that many stages. Yet the first half of the final speech followed closely the pattern of ideas originally written by the President, and many striking phrases appear almost exactly the same in the first and the last versions. In the President's handwriting, for example, appeared the following:

Always it is worth while in the midst of swift happenings to pause for a moment to take stock of our thoughts. If we do not we risk a pitfall or a wrong turning.

Eight years ago a danger hung over our land; we were in the midst of it; we knew its shock and its actual immediate bearing upon our daily lives as individuals and as a nation. We sensed its causes, and we were in agreement that quick action, unwonted action, bold action, was not merely desirable but urgently requisite.

Note the following excerpts from the address of January 20, 1941, as actually delivered by Roosevelt:

To us there has come a time, in the midst of swift happenings, to pause for a moment and take stock—to recall what our place in history has been, and to rediscover what we are and what we may be. If we do not, we risk the real peril of isolation, the real peril of inaction. ...

Eight years ago, when the life of this Republic seemed frozen by a fatalistic terror, we proved that this is not true. We were in the midst of shock, but we acted, we acted quickly, boldly, decisively.

This typical instance gives further credence to the testimony of the President and others that Roosevelt laid down the broad outlines of his addresses and was personally responsible for many of the striking phrases he used.

Materials were frequently forwarded to Roosevelt which had been prepared as a speech or a possible portion of a speech. For example, the Hyde Park Library has, with the collections of the various drafts of the December 29, 1940, address, a fourteen-page manuscript written by Dorothy Thompson and forwarded to the President for use if he desired. Mrs. Eleanor Roosevelt had sent the manuscript to the President, since it bore this note:

For the President:
F.D.R.

Dorothy Thompson says she offers this humbly as suggestions, for what she longs to hear you say.

E.R.

Miss Thompson's suggestions, dated December 13, 1940, dealt with the general problem of America's peril with a world at war and the necessity of supplying aid to the Allies, a subject which the President did consider in his next address, delivered December 29, 1940. There were no apparent transfers from her manuscript to his, however, in terms either of ideas or of phraseology.

On the other hand, almost all of the specific facts Roosevelt used in his speech of September 11, 1941, in which he argued for "freedom of the seas" and announced that the American navy would, henceforth, shoot German war vessels "on sight," were included in a five-and-one-half page "Memo" from Cordell Hull.[18]

Robert Sherwood, however, quotes at some length from Harry Hopkins' notes to show that Roosevelt did request and use Hull's ideas, but only to the extent that he agreed with them. Hopkins had recorded:

The President liked the statement Hull was making verbally [at a conference on Sept. 5th of Roosevelt with Hopkins and Hull to discuss the address of Sept. 11, 1941] and asked him to dictate what he had just said and send it to the White House late that afternoon.

The draft from Hull arrived and instead of being the vigorous, determined memorandum that had been represented in his verbal talk with the President, it was a pretty weak document, although it built up a fairly strong case for the necessity for some action. But there was no recommendation of any action.

The President, of course, said at once that Hull's draft was totally inadequate. . . . We made another draft. . . .

I later learned from the President that Hull made a very strong argument, urging the President to take out of the speech the real guts in it [reference to shooting first]. The speech itself indicates that this was not done.[19]

On the last page of the typed copy from which Roosevelt talked when he delivered his address of July 19, 1940, appear these words in his own handwriting, "I put in a number of extemporaneous interpolations." Similarly, on the last page of the Original Reading Copy of the March 15, 1941, address, Roosevelt wrote under his signature, "Original Reading Copy, but there was much adlibbing!" Those comments were not exaggera-

---

[18] Dated September 6, 1941, the memorandum was in the form of a telegram signed by "Hull." Available at the Roosevelt Library at Hyde Park, N.Y.
[19] Sherwood, *Roosevelt and Hopkins*, pp. 371–72.

tions, and they might well have been made for almost any of his addresses.

The first two or three minutes of his address of September 2, 1940, illustrate Roosevelt's typical *platform* revisions. The italicized portions were added to the text during delivery; the sections in parentheses were omitted by the President from his prepared manuscript:

> *Secretary Ickes, Governor Hoey, Governor Cooper and our neighbor, Governor Maybank of South Carolina, and my friends from all the states:*
>
> *I have listened with attention and great interest to the thousands of varieties of plants and trees and fishes and animals that Governor Cooper told us about, but he failed to mention the hundreds of thousands of species of human animals that come to the park.*
>
> Here in the Great Smokies, we (meet today) *have come together* to dedicate these mountains, and streams and forests, *the thousands of them,* to the service of the *millions of* American people. We are living under governments (which) *that* are proving their devotion to national parks. The Governors of North Carolina and of Tennessee have greatly helped us, and the Secretary of the Interior is so active that he has today ready for dedication *a number of other great National* (two more) parks—*like* Kings Canyon in California and the Olympic National Park in the State of Washington, *the Isle Park up in Michigan and, over here, the Great Cavern of Tennessee,* and soon, I hope, *he will have another one for us to dedicate* (a third), the Big Bend Park *away down* in Texas, *close to the Mexican line.*

4

Roosevelt showed his ability to adapt his phrasing and thoughts with instant facility. In delivering his address of September 21, 1939, the President, instead of saying as he planned, "When and if repeal of the embargo is accomplished," introduced, following the word *if,* the additional sentence, "I do not like even to mention the word *if,* I would rather say when—when."

In his address of May 26, 1940, the President followed a rhetorical question with some unpremeditated explanation. After the sentence, "What did we get for this money?" he added, "Money, incidentally, not included in the new defense appropriations, only money hitherto appropriated."

Besides deliberately introducing ideas and comments as he was speaking, he also adapted his words to fit the unexpected. In his address of January 20, 1941, for example, he had planned the sentence, "If we do not, we risk the real peril of inaction." Instead of saying *inaction,* he mis-read the word as *isolation,* but then immediately followed with the words, "the real peril of inaction." The sentence as actually delivered was: "If we do not, we risk the real peril of isolation, the real peril of inaction." Roosevelt's own pride in his ability to do this sort of thing is indicated by the note in his handwriting on the Original Reading Copy of this address. He underlined the word *inaction* and wrote, "I misread this word as 'isolation'—then added 'and inaction.' All of which improved it! FDR."

Mr. Roosevelt frequently placed long dashes in his manuscript, apparently where applause was expected. When applause from his immediate audience unexpectedly interrupted his train of words, the President skillfully adapted to the situation by introducing some additional bit of explanation. In the State of the Union address of January, 1940, the President had stated: "The only important increase in any part of the budget is the estimate for national defense. Practically all other important items show a reduction." Applause broke out. Roosevelt had intended to express, then, his request for additional taxes "to meet the emergency spending for national defense." He met the unexpected applause, however, with the rejoinder: "But you know you can't eat your cake and have it, too." The applause which followed this impromptu remark lasted more than twice as long as that which preceded it, and Roosevelt then continued as he had intended.

In his "defense message" of May 16, 1940, the President planned to say: "I ask for immediate appropriation of $896,000,000 divided approximately as follows:" But as he stated the amount of money, Congress, to whom he was speaking at a joint session of the two houses, broke into applause. He then made the comment: "And may I say that I hope there will be speed in giving the appropriations," which drew even greater applause. After that, Roosevelt continued: "That sum of $896,000,000 of appropriations I would divide approximately as follows:"

Copies of Roosevelt's speeches were released to the press before they were actually delivered, a common practice to enable newspapers to make their deadlines. Although the President did *extemporize* considerably, he also wrote into his own copy before delivering a particular address some deviations from the text released to the press. Examples occur in almost every speech. Sometimes the President wrote in a change, but preferred in delivery the presentation he had previously approved, or changed the wording in still another way.

5

To summarize: In the preparation of his speeches during the period studied Franklin D. Roosevelt relied on a number of his advisers (most notably, Judge Samuel I. Rosenman, Robert E. Sherwood, Harry Hopkins, and Cordell Hull) both for materials and for suggested ways of expressing ideas. Various persons voluntarily forwarded ideas to the President for consideration in his addresses, and he frequently requested specific information. Roosevelt decided the final phraseology. The ultimate product of combined efforts invariably yielded addresses identifiable as peculiarly *Rooseveltian.*

Each of his important addresses went through a number of revisions and was the product of long, careful work both from the President and several of his advisers. Available resources of government, fact-finding agencies, opinions of Cabinet members, expert advice from military men—were all called upon for specific details and for general plans. Roosevelt made many changes in his speeches as he was speaking. He was particularly adept at handling unexpected situations as they arose. Some supposedly impromptu changes, however, had actually been written into his own manuscript. The investigation of Franklin Roosevelt's methods of preparing seventeen of his addresses on international affairs reveals that the late President was the primary source of the ideas, the arguments, and the language of those speeches.

6

Franklin D. Roosevelt's Voice and Pronunciation

Earnest S. Brandenburg
and Waldo W. Braden

This technical study poses some basic problems: The authors must first establish the fact and cause of a sound, difficult tasks in themselves, but then they must attempt to analyze that sound's possible impact on a given audience. Once their findings are reasonably established, however, they have the additional problem of translating their specialists' language into intelligible prose for the nonspecialist. Particular attention should be paid to their adjectives, since they exemplify the difficulty of finding meaningful, objective terms for describing a voice.

During his twelve years as President of the United States, Franklin D. Roosevelt was heard by more persons more frequently and more intimately than any other President in history.[1] The advent of extensive radio networks expanded by millions his potential audience. His radio talks became an established American institution. His extensive travel brought him before other millions, for during his years in Washington he made 399 trips by rail, totaling 544,868 miles.[2] On these cross-country jaunts he made hundreds of rear platform appearances as well as many major addresses. Those who could not hear him face to face could always see him in newsreels, in which he averaged thirty appearances each year.[3]

Because of the frequency of his appearances in person, on the screen, and over the air, Roosevelt became a familiar figure. Americans had the warm feeling that they personally knew their president.

Obviously Franklin D. Roosevelt's delivery—his pleasing voice quality, his highly expressive intonations and inflections, his mastery of the

[The late Earnest S. Brandenburg was the President of Drury College, and Waldo W. Braden is Professor of Speech and Chairman of the Department at Louisiana State University. This article originally appeared in the *Quarterly Journal of Speech*, xxxviii (February 1952), 23–30, and is reprinted with the permission of the authors and the Speech Association of America.]
[1] The writers are much indebted to Claude M. Wise of Louisiana State University for his helpful and expert criticism, especially of the section on pronunciation.
[2] John Gunther, *Roosevelt in Retrospect* (New York, 1950), p. 139.
[3] *Ibid.*, p. 102. The Franklin D. Roosevelt Library has 275,000 feet of film, much of it devoted to F.D.R.

conversational mode, and his direct speaking manner—contributed significantly to his effectiveness. His detractors often asserted that his delivery was the sole source of his effectiveness. Though such claims are refuted by the presence in public life of many less successful persons with as good or better voices and vocal control, this reluctant testimony gives an important clue to Roosevelt the orator. An analysis of specific aspects of his delivery should therefore provide data of interest and significance to students of public address. This paper will concern itself only with Franklin D. Roosevelt's voice and his pronunciation.

VOICE

The late President's voice quality was widely praised. For example, Professors Sarett and Foster explain in their speech text, "The cues in Franklin D. Roosevelt's voice—the voice alone—inspired confidence [in his inaugural address in 1933]. . . . If Herbert Hoover had spoken the same words into the microphone . . . the stock market would have fallen another notch and public confidence with it."[4] Roosevelt's voice frequently was given such labels as "fresh," "brilliant," "pleasant," "rich," and "melodious." According to Professor Robert T. Oliver, Roosevelt had "the best modulated radio voice in public life."[5] John Carlile, production director of the Columbia Broadcasting System, called his voice "one of the finest on the radio."[6] The radio director of the University of Chicago characterized him as the "glamor boy of radio," with a voice "like honey syrup oozing through the steel filter that jackets the microphone."[7] Even his bitter critic, John T. Flynn, freely admits the "general verdict . . . that Roosevelt possessed a golden voice and a seductive and challenging radio technique."[8] Perhaps no other aspect of F.D.R.'s speaking evoked such unanimity of opinion as the superior quality of his speaking voice. Eleanor Roosevelt circulated her mother-in-law's statement that Franklin had inherited his "good radio voice" not from the Roosevelts but from the Delanos.[9]

Laura Crowell's analysis of F.D.R.'s 1936 campaign led her to sound a significant warning against attempts to isolate Roosevelt's voice without reference to his personality and his ideas.

[4] Lew Sarett and William Trufant Foster, Basic Principles of Speech (New York, 1936), pp. 193–194.
[5] Robert T. Oliver, "The Speech That Established Roosevelt's Reputation," QJS, xxxi (October 1945), 274.
[6] "Personality on the Air," New York Times, March 20, 1932, Section 8, p. 14.
[7] Sherman H. Dryer, "Air Power," Colliers, cvi (September 14, 1940), 18.
[8] John T. Flynn, The Roosevelt Myth (New York, 1948), p. 283.
[9] "I told my mother-in-law yesterday that I thought my husband had inherited his good radio voice from her, and with her usual family spirit she replied: 'My husband had a very good voice, but Franklin's voice is like all the Delanos'!" Eleanor Roosevelt, "My Day," Copyright, May 21, 1937.

The conclusion that Roosevelt's voice was the one cause of his effectiveness in speaking, as many have casually asserted, must be reassessed. It is true that his unusual flexibility of voice and his excellence of vocal timbre gave particularly full representation of his reactions to ideas, listeners, and the total situation; what must not be overlooked is that this representation was of a person vibrant and engaging, a person vividly real to his audience. His hearers felt the warmth of regard for all persons expressed through the medium of his voice, but many, without analysis, attributed the warmth to his voice alone and neglected its more fundamental basis in personality.[10]

Although it is obviously impossible completely to divorce one aspect of a speaker's delivery from all others (or to divorce his delivery from his language or from his proofs),[11] final judgments need to be based both upon over-all general impressions and upon the careful analysis of specific elements. The study of Franklin D. Roosevelt's vocal quality, pitch, speaking rate, and use of loudness as separate factors should contribute to the rhetorician's ultimate understanding of his voice.

Roosevelt's habitual pitch, that is, the pitch that he used most frequently, is difficult to ascertain; his voice quality is equally difficult to describe in exact terms. For the purposes of this paper exact description seems unnecessary. Generally his voice was thought of as tenor.[12] In fact, as a youth he was a member of the tenor section of the Groton Glee Club. During most of his speaking, his voice was clear and resonant, or as one observer said, "vibrant with enthusiasm,"[13] but occasionally his sinus trouble[14] gave him a slightly nasal quality.[15]

What was popularly regarded as Roosevelt's pronunciation was often much more than pronunciation, for it included the inseparable concomi-

[10] Laura Crowell, "Franklin D. Roosevelt's Audience Persuasion in the 1936 Campaign," *Speech Monographs*, xvii (March 1950), 63–64.

[11] According to Harold P. Zelko, for example, "rhythmic structure is not a random technique of Franklin Roosevelt's. It is . . . designed as a basis for a better style and for helping to achieve a rhythm and cadence in delivery." Harold P. Zelko, "Franklin D. Roosevelt's Rhythm in Rhetorical Style," *QJS*, xxviii (April 1942), 138. [Reprinted in this text, pp. 191–94.]

[12] One Roosevelt student says that his "tenor voice proved to be one of his greatest assets." Lowery LeRoy Cowperthwaite, "A Criticism of the Speaking of Franklin D. Roosevelt in the Presidential Campaign of 1932," Unpub. diss. (State University of Iowa, 1950), p. 307.

[13] Orrin E. Dunlap, Jr., "A Study of Voices," *New York Times*, September 6, 1936, Sec. 9, p. 10.

[14] It is interesting to note that in selecting his personal physician, he chose Ross T. McIntire, an eye, nose, and throat specialist. Vice-Admiral McIntire says, "Sinus flare-ups were my chief worry, for the President's one susceptibility was to colds." *White House Physician* (New York, 1946), pp. 56–68.

[15] In the Roosevelt literature it is difficult to find anyone who was not favorably impressed by Roosevelt's voice quality and his skillful use of vocal techniques. For a more detailed analysis of the Roosevelt literature on this point, see Earnest Brandenburg, "An Analysis and Criticism of Franklin D. Roosevelt's Speeches on International Affairs Delivered Between September 3, 1939 and December 7, 1941" (State University of Iowa, 1948), Ph.D. dissertation, p. 646.

tant—intonation. When persons caricatured Roosevelt's speech, they invariably repeated expressions such as "My Friends," "I hate war," "My Fellow Americans," or perhaps the entire sentence, "I have said not once, but many times, that I have seen war and that I hate war. I say that again and again."[16] These expressions were hallmarks of his speech in the minds of millions. The characteristics imitated included his intonations and inflections as well as his pronunciations of certain words such a *war* [wɔə] and *again* [agern].

The tenor voice, never monotonous, was capable of either wide and startling or slight and subtle changes in pitch, but Roosevelt did not place extreme reliance on pitch changes. Occasionally, like many who do much public speaking, he ended a sentence with an upward inflection when a downward inflection would have been more meaningful. This effect seemed to occur at the ends of sentences for which he apparently expected and invited applause,[17] or where, although he had reached the end of a statement, his immediate, central idea was continued into the next sentence.[18]

Roosevelt's speaking rate was comparatively slow. Most studies report extremes for individual speeches between 95 and 125 words per minute, with a mean rate over several speeches of about 105 to 110 words per minute. Persons who assisted in the preparation of his speeches considered 100 words per minute[19] a normal rate for him—a rate unquestionably slower than that of most superior speakers. F.D.R. varied his rate in accordance with the size of his immediate audience. Just as speech authorities recommend, he spoke more slowly when face to face with many listeners than when speaking before small audiences such as he had at the White House for his Fireside Chats.

He was able consciously to vary his speaking rate to meet the rigid requirements of radio schedules. He often marked off his final reading copies[20] into five-minute sections,[21] and he seldom had trouble making his speaking rate conform to changes necessitated by applause or by his own impromptu insertions.

[16] From the Fireside Chat delivered September 3, 1939.
[17] For example, the following sentence ended on an upward inflection and, quite obviously, Roosevelt expected and asked for applause by the inflection of his voice: "And the strength of the British fleet in the Atlantic has been a friendly strength: it is still a friendly strength." Address of January 6, 1941.
[18] For example, "I regret that the Congress passed that act. I regret equally that I signed that act, . . . but that is not the issue. The step I recommend is to put this country back on a solid footing of real and traditional neutrality." Address of September 21, 1939.
[19] Robert E. Sherwood, *Roosevelt and Hopkins* (New York, 1948), p. 217. Grace Tully, *F.D.R., My Boss* (New York, 1949), p. 98.
[20] The addresses delivered on the following dates, for example, had five-minute time intervals marked in ink or pencil: May 26, 1940; December 29, 1940; May 27, 1941; September 11, 1941.
[21] For example, 9:35, 9:40, 9:45, etc.

Roosevelt frequently divided his sentences into short phrases of four to six words, relieved by occasional long phrases or entire sentences with no pauses, introduced for variety. The cadence of his speech ofttimes was measured and deliberate; words in important passages received equal stress, and pauses between words and sentences gave dramatic emphasis.[22] He was particularly effective in pointing up parallel structure by repeating patterns of intonation and inflection.

In general, important passages were delivered more slowly and with more pauses than less important passages. Vowels in the stressed syllables of emphasized words and significant words were prolonged.[23] According to one critic, his slow speaking rate caused Roosevelt "to prolong slightly" his vowel sounds and in turn made his speech more euphonious and more pleasant to the ear than it would otherwise have been.[24]

Although he has been praised for using wide variations in loudness,[25] seldom, if ever, was Roosevelt's speech staccato and never did he sound hurried. According to the reports of those handling radio control boards while he was speaking, F.D.R. did not reach the extremes of loudness or weakness in volume.[26] He did frequently employ variations in loudness to emphasize important words and thoughts,[27] although he was rarely guilty of violent outbursts or conversely of periods of imperceptibility.[28] Syllables and words as well he emphasized by combining prolongation of the vowel sounds with increased loudness.[29] Roosevelt's practice of underlining words in the final reading manuscript as a reminder to speak them more loudly when he delivered the address indicates that these variations in loudness were often consciously planned and produced.

[22] Note, for example, the pauses he made where diagonal lines are inserted: "Our acts must be guided by one/single/hard-headed/thought/—keeping America/out/of this war." Address of September 21, 1939.

[23] "No soporific lullabies that a wide ocean protects us from him—can long have any effect on the *hard*-headed, *far*-sighted, and *real*istic American people." Address of September 11, 1941.

[24] Joanna Givan, "A Consideration of the Qualities Which Contribute to the Effectiveness of the Speeches of Franklin Delano Roosevelt," M.A. Thesis (College of the Pacific, 1944), p. 68.

[25] "His tremolos, his staccatos, his crescendos and fortissimos are masterpieces." Erich Brandeis, *Franklin D. Roosevelt the Man* (New York, 1936), p. 6.

[26] Dryer, *op. cit.*

[27] "That is why every member of the executive branch of the government and every member of the Congress faces *great responsibility—great accountability*." Address of January 6, 1941.

[28] Charles H. Voelker's "phonetic study" of Roosevelt's annual address to Congress on January 3, 1936, offers some contrary evidence. "His use of loudness emphasis sometimes causes words to become too staccato. It shortens his prolongation of vowels so as to be characteristic of a much younger speaker. This gives an impression of choppiness. This is especially evident in words starting with plosives, such as [p] [b] [g]. Final [l] is sometimes omitted. Final [s] is sometimes lowered in pitch so as to become a mere passing of breath. Polysyllabic words at times become monosyllabic." Charles H. Voelker, "A Phonetic Study of Roosevelt," *QJS*, xxii (October 1936), 366.

[29] For example: "Such aid is not an act of war, even if a dictator should *uni*laterally proclaim it so." Address of January 6, 1941.

Franklin Roosevelt had the happy faculty of adapting his conversational mode of delivery to a variety of circumstances. Grave passages became measured and deliberate. Sentences of less consequence were delivered more rapidly with less ponderousness. In a rear platform appearance he could be extremely conversational and informal while he jokingly introduced his "little boy Jimmy," or replied to an impromptu question from a bystander. When the moment demanded, he could resort to the sustained, uplifted tone of the great leader. At the political rally he became direct and informal, engaged in raillery, sarcasm, scorn, and earnest pleading—whatever the immediate moment demanded. Over the radio he gave his listeners the feeling of direct conversation and gracious familiarity. The analyzer of one of his addresses explains, for example, "The voice came into their own homes from the familiar radio grill . . . in friendly, social tones—neighborly, yet with a patrician assurance of born leadership."[30] Since he never resorted to bombast, Roosevent was able readily to adapt his speaking to the microphone. His power to extend his personality, to convince, and to win radio listeners was due in important measure to his ability to adapt his vocal control to a variety of occasions.

What conclusions can we reach concerning Franklin Roosevelt's voice? Its quality proved a significant advantage, for it was pleasant and distinctive. Skillful variations, although never extreme, in pitch, rate, and loudness helped communicate specific ideas and emotions. We note that he talked at an unusually slow rate and that he was typically identified as a tenor. Unquestionably, Franklin Roosevelt's superior voice was one of his important assets as a speaker.

PRONUNCIATION

In spite of the popular assertion that he had a "Groton-Harvard" accent, Franklin D. Roosevelt spoke like other members of the educated class of New York City and its environs. Technically, he used what phoneticians call eastern dialect.[31] His articulation was characteristically distinct and clear. "Roosevelt's excellent articulation and pronunciation undoubtedly

---

[30] Oliver, op. cit.

[31] This judgment is not unanimously accepted. For example, "Careful listening to the electrical transcriptions available for the 1932 campaign leads this investigator to conclude that, with certain notable exceptions which appear to be typically Eastern-American, the speaker's general pronunciation and articulation approach the standard for General American speech." Cowperthwaite, op. cit., pp. 296–297.

"No one could say he comes from the South, the East or the West. . . . He is an example of what our speech can and should be—the speech of an educated and cultured man." Lee Emerson Bassett, Professor of Public Speaking at Stanford University, before the convention of the National Association of Teachers of Speech in Chicago, New York Times, December 28, 1933.

enhanced his vocal effectiveness in the 1932 campaign."[32] "Practically all
the sounds in the words he [used were] . . . pronounced. There [were] . . .
very few examples of the elisions characteristic of rapid speech."[33]

The most conspicuous characteristic of his eastern dialect was his
treatment of the preconsonantal, final (before a pause), and intervocalic *r*.
With practically complete consistency, his *r* was silent after [ɑ], [ɜ], and
[ə] followed by a consonant. Thus *hard* [hɑːd], *heard* [hɜd], *world* [wɜld],
fostered [fɔstəd], *sisters* [sɪstəz]. With the same consistency, *r* was silent
after [ɑ], [ɜ], and [ə] finally before a pause. Thus, *star* [stɑ], *concur* [kən-
'kɜ], *father* [fɑðə]. After [ɔ], preconsonantally or finally before a pause, *r*
was either silent or pronounced [ə]. Thus, *world order* [wɜld 'ɔdə], *armed
force* [ɑmd fɔəs], *war* [wɔ], *I hate war* [aɪ heɪt wɔə]. After all other vowels
(including most diphthongs), preconsonantally or finally before a pause,
r was pronounced [ə]. Thus *years* [jrəz], *fear* [fɪə], *where* [ʍɛə], *to serve
their country* [tə sɜv ðɜə 'kʌntrɪ], *fair weather* [fæə 'wɛðə], *care* [kæə], *more
men* [moə mɛn], *door* [doə], *poor time* [pʊə taɪm], *sure* [ʃʊə], *fire then* [faɪə
ðɛn], *tire* [taɪə], *our peace* [aʊə pis], *our* [aʊə].

All this runs true to the eastern pattern. But Roosevelt's consistency
wavered a little in the [aʊ] in *our* and in possibly a few other words, where
the occasional light pronunciation of the *r* suggested the general American
pattern. Thus, *our way* [aʊr weɪ], *our wisdom* [aʊr 'wɪzdəm], *our people*
[aʊr 'pipl]. Probably this inconsistency with the diphthong [aʊ] caused
some commentators to speak of the general American characteristics in
Roosevelt's speech. But this slight deviation is actually much less conspicuous than similar ones in the speech of many easterners, who often stray
momentarily from what is regarded as the strict regional pattern. Roosevelt's wide travel and his broad associations would make for some leaning
toward general American speech.

In respect to the intervocalic *r*, Roosevelt held with nearly perfect
consistency to the eastern pattern. If the intervocalic *r* occurred within a
single word, he never failed to pronounce it, saying *very* ['vɛrɪ] and *carry*
[kærɪ]. If the intervocalic *r* occurred at the end of a word which was immediately, i.e., without pause, followed by a word beginning with a vowel,

[32] Cowperthwaite, *op. cit.*, p. 298.
[33] Voelker, *op. cit.*

James C. Bender gives an explanation for the observations made by Cowperthwaite
and Bassett in the following statement: "Mr. Roosevelt . . . follows the intonations
and phonetic patterns of the so-called Eastern or New England dialect. This general
observation needs qualification. Like most people with good hearing capacity, the
President's speech is influenced by his environment, and the President's environment
has been varied. That is why his speech includes a number of deviations from the
Eastern dialect." James C. Bender, "Two Men: A Radio Analysis," *New York Times*,
September 17, 1944, Section 6, p. 36.

he pronounced it. He said, for example, *war is* [wɔr ɪz], *their arms* [ðɛr ɑmz].[34]

A pause will inhibit a linking *r* in eastern speech as in *we shall try next year* [jɪə]. *After that* . . . Here the pause between *year* and *after* precludes the link. Roosevelt's pauses were sometimes very brief; therefore the researcher, playing a recorded speech, sometimes expects a link which does not materialize. A second playing will usually reveal that the pause, even if brief, is overt.

Roosevelt was inconsistent in his use of [ju] in words in which *u, eu,* and *ew* followed [t], [d], and [n]. He said [djutɪ] and [djurəbl], but he used both [ju] and [u] in the word *new*; sometimes it was [nju] and at other times it was [nu]. In his Lend Lease message of January 6, 1941, he spoke of a *new congress, new needs, new circumstance* [nju kɑŋgrəs], [nju nidz], and [nju səkəmstænts]. On another occasion, he spoke of the [nu ɔdə]. The word *neutral* in the famous speech delivered at the outbreak of World War II, September 3, 1939, gave the President some difficulty. In three sentences he used three pronunciations: [njutrəl], [nɪutrəl], and [nutrəl]. Nevertheless, apparently he leaned toward [ju], which is the choice of many easterners.

Roosevelt used [ʍ], not [w], in such words as *where, whether,* and *when.* Furthermore, he did not use the so-called "broad" *a.* He might say *ask* [æsk] or *vast* [væst], or he might say [ask] or [last] or [pasɪŋ]. Both of these pronunciations, as well as [ɑ], are accepted in eastern dialect. The tendency to use the [a] may have been developed during the period of Groton and Harvard, since [a] in "broad" *a* words is exceedingly common in New England but seldom found in the New York area. In no sense was his pronunciation extremely broad eastern dialect.

In general, Roosevelt's pronunciation was crisp and distinct. He consistently enunciated vigorously. He always sounded his final consonants, and he never substituted [n] for [ŋ] as in *writin'* [raɪtn] for *writing* [raɪtŋ]. This brief paper cannot cover every element of his pronunciation in every possible combination. The sounds selected for emphasis (r, ju, ʍ, and a) seem to us to have been the most conspicuous and, therefore, the most significant to an understanding of F.D.R.'s pronunciation.

Roosevelt brought to countless Americans their first, and unquestionably their most impressive, knowledge of how easterners talk. The exact effect of his dialect in terms of winning or losing support is not a matter of general agreement. His dialect has been assumed by some to have been an advantage, by others a handicap. Perhaps Roosevelt's "cultivated eastern" pronunciation actually inspired confidence from the "one-third ill-housed,

[34] This intervocalic *r*, or linking *r*, may have confused some hearers who did not recognize it for what it was, a standard feature of eastern speech. The linking *r* should not suggest general American speech when found in context with preconsonantal and final *r*'s which are silent or pronounced [ə] as indicated earlier.

ill-clothed, and ill-fed" whom he constantly championed; perhaps the "downtrodden" were the more inclined to accept his words because they identified him not only as a man highly sympathetic to their cause but also as one whose background and experiences were "superior" to their own and who, therefore, deserved their support.

Professor Donald C. Bryant of Washington University tells of an interesting experience he had during the 1936 campaign. In a radio broadcast from Albany, he explained that Roosevelt's pronunciation most nearly conformed to that of New England and the East generally, while Landon's more closely resembled that of up-state New York, i.e., what is termed general American. Bryant added that general American was the dialect of about 85 percent of the people of the United States. One newspaper construed Professor Bryant's words to mean that Landon spoke the homespun language of 85 percent of the people, concluded that the voters would probably prefer a man who used language like their own and intimated that such a man was much more likely to think the way the people do.[35]

Because Roosevelt's speeches almost invariably merited praise for clear, incisive articulation,[36] because he seemed clear and natural, his pronunciation received acclaim, in spite of minor inconsistencies. The American listeners, most of whom were not prepared to analyze the President's dialect, were usually so impressed by his friendly, direct manner that they forgot what seemed like idiosyncrasies. Furthermore, the frequency with which he spoke made his speech familiar.

SUMMARY

The overall appraisal of Roosevelt the speaker is perhaps complicated by his outstanding delivery. No judgment of the effectiveness of his ideas or

[35] An interesting accusation was made by Alfred M. Landon. He disclaimed any pretense to oratorical ability himself, because: "There is a certain deceit in oratory in that it may appeal to the emotions more than to reason. The important thing to me in what I had to say was the idea I would convey and what I stood for. The Presidency is primarily an executive office, not a broadcasting station.

"Mr. Roosevelt's adaptability appeared one night when I heard him say 'war' with the New York accent, which made it 'waw' to Westerners, and then change to 'war-r' with a sturdy 'r' the next time he used the word." Alfred M. Landon, "Landon Recounts Unequal Battle," New York Times, August 22, 1938.

[36] Few of his listeners were aware of the "problem" of his false tooth. "He had a separation between two of his lower front teeth and a single-tooth removable bridge had been fitted for it. He didn't particularly like to wear it, and carried it most of the time in a tiny heart-shaped silver box. With the tooth out, however, he whistled slightly on certain words and this extra sound effect was most noticeable on the radio.

"He forgot it on more than one occasion and quite often there was a mad last-minute dash by somebody from the Oval Room to his bedroom to rescue the little silver box from his bedside table." Grace Tully, F.D.R., My Boss (New York, 1949), p. 100.

his language can ignore his superior speaking voice, his attractive appearance, or his captivating speaking personality. Superlative delivery became so much a known and expected part of his speaking that when circumstances combined to prevent optimum use of his voice and speaking manner, listeners were quick to sense the difference.[37]

Obviously the advent of radio and the wide use of the public address system at the time Roosevelt was reaching national political prominence were tremendous aids to him. Speakers before the microphone might be forced to restrain their movements and their gestures, but this restriction meant no loss of effectiveness for F.D.R. Radio forced upon all speakers the restrained movement necessitated by Roosevelt's physical condition. F.D.R.'s handsome, expressive face and his powerful torso were ideally suited to enhance his speaking before a microphone in the presence of an audience. His voice, which did not have the tremendous carrying power demanded of great speakers in preceding generations, was ideally suited to radio because it did have a pleasant, distinctive quality, and because it was exceptionally direct and conversational.

Franklin Roosevelt's delivery possessed no characteristics which detracted from his effectiveness. His voice quality, pitch, speaking rate, and use of loudness all served to enhance the ideas he was presenting, without calling attention to themselves. Although his eastern dialect was sometimes noticed, it rarely brought forth a negative response. His enunciation was always clear, and he was always understood. Roosevelt's excellent voice and his clear, incisive articulation contributed materially to his delivery and thus to his total effectiveness as a speaker.

[37] Judge Rosenman has supplied this significant information of such a speech: "Several unfortunate circumstances combined to make this [address at Puget Sound Navy Yard, Bremerton, Washington, August 12, 1944] one of the poorest speeches Roosevelt ever delivered. He spoke from the forecastle deck of a destroyer, and a stiff wind was blowing throughout the speech. There was a marked slant to the deck. The slant and the wind meant that, to maintain his balance, he had to depend more heavily than usual on his braces. In recent months the President had lost some weight, which meant that his braces did not fit him. Under the best of conditions, his position was none too secure and the steel braces hurt when worn for any length of time. Under the conditions at Bremerton, the President's feeling of insecurity was increased.

"The speech itself, although rambling in nature, ordinarily might have been an acceptable, chatty account of the President's journeys and experiences on his recent trip. However, the pain of the braces, the feeling of insecurity, and the other adverse circumstances combined to make the President's delivery hesitant, halting and ineffective.

"The reaction of the audience—which the President was always quick to sense during the delivery of a speech—was so unfavorable that it only served to make the President's delivery worse.

"The reaction of the entire country to this speech was very bad. Even some of the President's best friends and most loyal supporters began to whisper to each other that they were afraid the old master had lost his touch, that his days of campaigning must be over and that he would be a sorry spectacle in the coming campaign against the young, virile Governor of New York." The Public Papers and Addresses of Franklin D. Roosevelt, 1944–1945, ed. Samuel I. Rosenman (New York, 1950), pp. 227–228.

In this short article on Roosevelt's regular use of parallelism and repetition, the author cites many examples of these stylistic devices, and they seem self-evidently effective. But the possible causes of that effectiveness are never really faced. Since verbal, structural, and metrical repetitions play so large a role in poems and songs as well as speeches, a careful analysis of the reasons for such repetition would make a needed extension of this study.

7

Franklin D. Roosevelt's Rhythm in Rhetorical Style

Harold P. Zelko

Much has been said in praise of Franklin Roosevelt's ability to deliver a speech, his splendid vocal quality, his personal charm. It can be said that this praise crosses political boundaries and is rather generally agreed upon regardless of the critic. But when we look to the content of Mr. Roosevelt's speeches we naturally do not find this degree of accord in passing judgment on his rhetoric. Perhaps rhetorical scholars hesitate to confess that an unbiased, truly objective evaluation can be made at the present time of Mr. Roosevelt's rhetoric.

With some wariness, therefore, I have chosen to comment on what appears to be a rather unusual characteristic of the rhetorical style of this speaker. I speak of the rare rhythm[1] that is attained in the structural development of sentences and ideas throughout the speeches. This is evident in a number of ways, such as the use of parallel sentence structure in a sequence of sentences, identical reiteration of words and phrases, parallel introduction of a sequence of ideas.

[Harold P. Zelko is Professor of Speech at Pennsylvania State University. This article originally appeared in the *Quarterly Journal of Speech*, xxviii (April 1942), 138–41, and is reprinted with the permission of the author and the Speech Association of America.]

[1] I have in mind rhythm in composition, not in delivery. The former naturally leads to the latter, but this article does not concern itself with Mr. Roosevelt's delivery. Charles H. Voelker, in an article on "A Phonetic Study of Roosevelt," *Quarterly Journal of Speech*, xxii (1936), 366–68, comments on Roosevelt's sense of time, cadence, and rhythm in delivery, and (on page 367) says, "His feeling of rhythm in speech is quite exceptional. . . . His sense of rhythm is probably related to his sense of style."

An outstanding example of a combination of these methods is the conclusion of the speech of March 4, 1937, at the Democratic Victory Dinner. This combines striking parallel structure of sentences and reiteration of the word "now." Concluding devices such as summary, suggestion, and action appeal are blended into the structure.

Here is one-third of a nation ill-nourished, ill-clad, ill-housed—NOW![2]

Here are thousands upon thousands of farmers wondering whether next year's prices will meet their mortgage interest—NOW!

Here are thousands upon thousands of men and women laboring for long hours in factories for inadequate pay—NOW!

Here are thousands upon thousands of children who should be at school, working in mines and mills—NOW!

Here are strikes more far-reaching than we have ever known, costing millions of dollars—NOW!

Here are spring floods threatening to roll again down our river valleys—NOW!

Here is the dust bowl beginning to blow again—NOW!

If we would keep faith with those who had faith in us, if we would make democracy succeed, I say we must act—NOW!

In the same speech there is an example of rhythm within a sentence, through series of phrases and clauses:

a nation intact, a nation at peace, a nation prosperous, a nation clear in its knowledge of what powers it has to serve its own citzens, a nation that is in a position . . . a nation which has thus proved.

Another example of this type of rhythm within a sentence is in the speech of September 17, 1937, on the 150th anniversary of the signing of the Constitution. Two excerpts in different parts of the speech read as follows:

Fear spreads throughout the world—fear of aggression, fear of invasion, fear of revolution, fear of death.

That ideal makes understandable the demands of labor for shorter hours and higher wages, the demands of farmers for a more stable income, the demands of a great majority of business men for relief from disruptive trade practices, the demands of all.

There are several examples of rhythmic parallel sentence structure in this same speech. There is a series of four paragraphs, each containing two sentences, with each first sentence and each second sentence constructed similarly:

[2] The press copy of this speech, released from the White House, has the word NOW in heavyfaced type.

Lawyers distinguished in 1787 insisted that the Constitution itself was unconstitutional under the Articles of Confederation. But the ratifying conventions overruled them.

Lawyers distinguished in their day warned Washington and Hamilton. . . . But the Executive and the Congress overruled them.

Lawyers distinguished in their day persuaded a divided Supreme Court that the Congress had no power to govern slavery in the territories. . . . But a war between the States overruled them.

Lawyers distinguished in their day persuaded the Odd Man on the Supreme Court that the methods of financing the Civil War were unconstitutional. But a new Odd Man overruled them.

And again in the same speech,

It cost a Civil War to gain recognition of the constitutional power of the Congress to legislate for the territories.

It cost twenty years of taxation on those least able to pay to recognize the constitutional power of the Congress to levy taxes on those most able to pay.

It cost twenty years of exploitation of women's labor to recognize . . .

It had cost twenty years already . . .

In the First Inaugural we find the following structural development of a series of sentences:

The task can be helped by definite efforts . . .
It can be helped by preventing . . .
It can be helped by insistence that the . . .
It can be helped by the unifying of . . .
It can be helped by national planning . . .
It is the way to recovery.
It is the immediate way.

More recent speeches give ample evidence of the same stylistic tendency. In two speeches given on September 3, 1940, at T.V.A.'s Chickamauga Dam and at Great Smoky National Park these excerpts are found:

I had studied the washing away of the wealth of the soil . . .
I had seen water commerce impeded . . .
I had understood the waste . . .
I had seen forests denuded or burned—but worst of all, I had seen the splendid people living in parts of seven States fighting against nature instead of with nature.
We must prepare in a thousand ways. Men are not enough. They must have arms. They must learn how to use those arms. They must have skilled leaders.

The speech of September 12, 1940, contains these series of sentences:

You can remember, however, the other days . . .
You can remember when it was rare indeed . . .

You can remember when employers sought . . .
You can remember when many large employers resorted to . . .
They would seek unlimited hours of labor. They would seek lower wages. They
    would seek the cancellation of those safeguards . . .

Time for March 25, 1940, quotes a paragraph containing almost identical parallel sentence structure taken from a Roosevelt speech:

It cannot be a real peace if it fails to recognize brotherhood. It cannot be
a lasting peace if the fruit of it is oppression. . . . It cannot be a sound peace if
small nations must live in fear of powerful neighbors. It cannot be a moral
peace if freedom from invasion is sold for tribute. . . . It cannot be a righteous
peace if worship of God is denied.

This speaker's loyalty to parallel structure of idea development also
carries from speech to speech.[3] A marked similarity in his style of describing bad and good conditions in a locality is noted in the following excerpts
from two different speeches. The first is from a speech during the 1936
political campaign, delivered at Pittsburgh, October 1, 1936. This paragraph combines metaphor, imagery, alliteration, and rhythm in excellent
manner. The second paragraph is from the Chickamauga speech already
referred to:

Compare the scoreboard which you have in Pittsburgh now with the
scoreboard which you had when I stood here at second base in this field four
years ago. At that time, as I drove through these great valleys, I could see mile
after mile of this greatest mill and factory area in the world, a dead panorama
of silent black structures and smokeless stacks. I saw idleness and hunger
instead of the whirl of machinery. Today as I came north from West Virginia,
I saw mines operating, I found bustle and life, the hiss of steam, the ring of
steel on steel—the roaring song of industry.
    When I first passed this place, after my election but before my inaugura-
tion as President, there flowed here a vagrant stream, sometimes shallow and
useless, sometimes turbulent and in flood, always dark with the soil it had
washed from the eroding hills. This Chickamauga Dam, the sixth in a series
. . . is helping to give. . . . Through them we are celebrating the opening of a
new artery of commerce, new opportunities for recreation, relief from the deso-
lation of floods. . . .

From these typical examples it is evident that rhythmic structure is
not a random technique of Franklin Roosevelt. It is rather a carefully
planned and executed technique, designed as a basis for better style and
for helping to achieve rhythm and cadence in the delivery. It is an important part of Mr. Roosevelt's total rhetorical style and effectiveness as a
speaker.

[3] It is interesting to note here that the famous First Inaugural statement, "the only
thing we have to fear is fear itself," was repeated verbatim by Mr. Roosevelt in the
speech of May 27, 1941.

8

War Requested:
Wilson
and Roosevelt

Herbert L. Carson

Through comparison and contrast, this author illuminates two speeches, as well as a speech type, while drawing on biography, history, and occasion to guide a reader-listener toward a full realization of the nature of the speeches, their tone, and their intention. In a still larger sense, this tight study demonstrates that the great speech arises from a particular occasion in a particular way; there can be no "canned" approach to seemingly similar problems.

The function of the President of the United States when Congress has been called together for a declaration-of-war address is not unlike that of a high priest in a ritual. He is there as a matter of ceremonial necessity. His purpose is not necessarily to persuade, to deliberate, or to inform, but primarily to intone the words required in a democratic society faced with the necessity of waging war. The exact words of the leader, the specific manner in which he performs the ritual, may vary according to many factors, especially the circumstances surrounding the message and the distinctive personality of the Chief Executive himself.

The war messages of Woodrow Wilson and Franklin D. Roosevelt were characteristic of these similarly minded but emotionally different men. Where Wilson pondered a problem, Roosevelt uttered an exhortation. Wilson expressed his consciousness of the burden he was putting on the country, hesitating to do so, but forced to the act by the circumstances of his times. Roosevelt, on the other hand, was stirred bitterly by a surprise enemy attack, and delivered a partisan call to arms.

The differences between the two addresses are immediately apparent. Hear Wilson's sorrowful exordium:

[Herbert L. Carson is Professor of Speech at Ferris State College, Big Rapids, Michigan. This article originally appeared in the *Central States Speech Journal*, x (Autumn, 1958), 28–32, and is reprinted with the permission of the author and the Central States Speech Association.]

195

I have called the Congress into extraordinary session because there are serious, very serious, choices of policy to be made, and made immediately, which it was neither right nor constitutionally permissible that I should assume the responsibility of making.

The tone implies deliberation.

Compare to this measured statement Roosevelt's indignant opening: "Yesterday, December 7, 1941—a date which will live in infamy—the United States of America was suddenly and deliberately attacked by naval and air forces of the Empire of Japan." The tone implies retaliation.

Thus it is that war formally begins as a matter of words, chief among which are those used to carry out the ceremonial obligation of proclaiming the hostilities. The exact nature of such ritualistic utterances not only may reveal to a reader the speaker's character, but also may be indicative of the circumstances which prompted the address.

I

The circumstances of April 2, 1917, were favorable to quiet deliberation. Europe had been at war for three years. The contending nations had continually sought American support during this period. American aid to Britain and her embattled allies had brought forth belligerent retaliation from Germany. Sabotage of American plants had aroused bitterness toward the German government. Resumption of German submarine attacks on American ships convinced Wilson, shortly after his second inauguration, to call Congress into joint session. With the elected representatives, he undertook the ceremony of declaring war.

Since there were many factors which had made the ceremony inevitable, Wilson had the opportunity to make a reasoned although occasionally emotional appeal. He used this occasion to explain the circumstances behind his decision to ask for a declaration of war, to justify the act, and to distinguish the cause for which the war was to be fought. The German resumption of submarine warfare was cited for its "reckless lack of compassion or principle." Compassion because "Even hospital ships and ships carrying relief to the sorely bereaved and stricken people of Belgium" were not immune to attack. Principle because "No nation had the right of dominion [over the seas] . . . where lay the free highways of the world." Thus, by "throwing to the winds all scruples of humanity or of respect for the understandings that were supposed to underlie the intercourse of the world," the German government was engaged in "a war against all nations."

Wilson then discussed his measures of the twenty-sixth of February, when Congress had authorized him to arm American merchant ships, and the lack of effect that such armed neutrality had. The failure of the German government to recognize this attempt as legitimate meant that the United States was in the position of either submitting to maritime restrictions or of accepting "the status of belligerent which has thus been thrust upon it." Having built to this alternation, Wilson discussed the latter of the two choices, stressing the necessity for cooperation, organization, and mobilization. He then went on to the reasons behind this act of war: "Let us be very clear, and make clear to all the world what our motives and objects are." The aim of this war was

to vindicate the principles of peace and justice in the life of the world as against selfish and autocratic power and to set up amongst the really free and self-governed peoples of the world such a concert of purpose and of action as will henceforth insure the observance of those principles.

Wilson clarified this goal by observing, "We have no quarrel with the German people. We have no feeling towards them but one of sympathy and friendship. It was not upon their impulse that their government acted in entering this war." The quarrel, rather, was with the powers of autocracy, those totalitarian forces that deny the rights of their peoples. Such a government can never become allied with free countries in an attempt at peace. "A steadfast concern for peace can never be maintained except by a partnership of democratic nations." This aim, this "partnership of opinion [for peace]," as Wilson called it, was the ultimate mark of the war effort. Citing the fall of the Russian aristocracy as a good sign in the development toward free nations, Wilson referred to a "League of Honor." Here was the direction of the effort, a target that depended upon a war fought with purpose but not with "rancour . . . [or] selfish object." Such a grand war demanded "a high spirit of right and fairness." The fight was for "a universal dominion of right by such a concert of free peoples as shall bring peace and safety to all nations and make the world itself at last free. With God's help, no other direction can be taken."

The emotional and ideological effect of Wilson's speech was conveyed by a variety of factors, especially language, meter, and general tone (or mood). These elements are always difficult to segregate. In Wilson's speech, they blend into a solemn and affecting unity. The analogy between the President and the priest used earlier serves well to describe this total effect. Using sentence patterns of an intricate variety, Wilson achieved the air of a pontiff serving at a serious and weighty function. He conveyed the importance of the occasion by the lengthy and involved metrical structure of his sentences and by the repetition of key words. Further power came from Wilson's avoidance of hysteria. He made little use of slanted language, stating the situation almost objectively. Wilson was not only the head of a state, but also he was an historian. The two roles combined in his sober appraisal of a taut situation.

Not that Wilson avoided all emotion in the address. Such a move would have negated the ceremonial purpose of his talk. One requirement of the ritual is the use of dramatic simplification—the black-versus-white nature of the conflict. Thus, Wilson's words were used to arouse emotion as well as to convey ideals. The German government was ruthless, reckless, and lawless. Opposed to such powers of evil were the forces of peace, honor, and legitimacy.[1] The United States was justified in accepting the extreme of war. It had to defend its own freedom and that of the entire world. Wilson's remarks however, were generally more reasonable than emotional.

In preparing a speech which he knew his countrymen wanted to hear, Wilson sought to achieve a level of purpose which would give moral meaning to the war hysteria. Free of the necessity to push or persuade Congress into heeding his call to arms, Wilson attempted to make the request a chance to state the principles, procedures, and goals of such belligerency. Among the many important ideas included in this message to Congress were those which stressed the distinction between a people (potentially friendly) and their erring government, the ideal that all American citizens would unite in the great aim of this war (regardless of their national origins), the need to aid this nation's allies in the battle, the necessity of using a higher tax base in order to avoid undue debt, and the great goal of "honor"—that league of free nations which Wilson hoped would result from the successful conclusion of the war, and which would serve as a deterrent to future aggression by any power.

The professor had seen an opportunity to combine the ritual of war with the deliberation of the lecture platform—in doing so he delivered a war address that distinguished itself by its clear appraisal of the necessity for war, by its lucid discussion of the obligations of war, and by its idealistic expression of the aims of war. The ritual is rarely performed so well. Few leaders do more than unify a nation into mass hatred. Wilson's character was such that he took the occasion to elevate mankind even in the act of sending it into battle.

II

The circumstances of December 8, 1941 (the date on which Roosevelt delivered his war message), were different from those in which Wilson had formulated his appeal. In addition to the characters of Wilson and Roosevelt, one must consider the exigencies of the moment, the differences of situation. Wilson had capped a slow development of tension between

[1] The exact wording here is mine, although Wilson does use either these words or forms of them in parts of his address.

this country and Germany with a brilliant elucidation of circumstances and aims. Roosevelt was addressing a people in whom earlier tensions had been replaced by a state of horrified shock and disbelief. Whether or not the intelligence service of the United States had any knowledge of the Japanese plans for an offensive in the Pacific is unimportant in this context, for certainly the people of the United States (and their elected representatives) were innocent of such awareness. The events of December 7, 1941, were cataclysmic to a nation which, while emotionally attuned to the prospect of war, had been encrusted with enough of the isolationist ideal to believe itself free from attack and to hope that war could be averted. While Japanese planes hovered over American bases, releasing their explosives on the unprepared forces below, the American people were awaiting the results of peace talks even then being terminated in Washington.

Roosevelt's address was much more emotionally charged than Wilson's. Peace and good will were hard to remember in the pre-Christmas weeks of 1941. It was simpler to think in terms of "a date which will live in infamy." Thus, Roosevelt's speech had less of a deliberative quality than Wilson's. It was a direct, forceful, and emotional expression of conditions and necessities, with no mention of any goals except such immediate ones as defense and ultimate victory.

Roosevelt's message, after its statement of the attack's "infamy," mentioned the fact that even during the attack the Japanese ministers in Washington were discontinuing the diplomatic negotiations with no "threat or hint of war or of armed attack." Roosevelt then pointed out that the nature of the bombardment and the distance of the targets from Japanese home bases made it apparent that the operation had been planned "days or even weeks ago." The result of the attack was mentioned in general terms ("severe damage"), and a list of other offensives and belligerent measures by Japanese forces were cited. The obvious implications were not stressed or specified by Roosevelt, who characteristically explained that he had taken the necessary measures. The need to "not only defend ourselves to the uttermost but ... [also to] make it very certain that this form of treachery shall never again endanger us" was emphasized. A few more abstract comments on "danger" and "inevitable triumph" were followed by Roosevelt's request for a proclamation of war by Congress.

Nothing in Roosevelt's brief remarks can be compared to the dialectical awareness of Wilson's sober account. Almost of necessity, such a talk as Roosevelt's must be limited to simplified details. But these details still are capable of conveying important information as well as great inspiration. Roosevelt's address was calculated to unite an enflamed and frightened nation/for the cause of victory. He made no attempt to do more. There were no fine distinctions drawn between the enemy nation and its people, no long-range goals discussed in idealistic terms.[2] The message incited without uplifting. It was a bitter and forthright talk, somewhat reassuring because of its emotional tone, but devoid of anything resembling the balanced reasoning in Wilson's speech.

As already mentioned, the circumstances helped to justify Roosevelt's approach. The fears and horrors of a nation could not have been assuaged by such a speech as Wilson's, whose objective tone would have been out of place in the particular situation of December 8, 1941. Roosevelt calmed the nation with a reassurance that he too was angered by the "infamy" of the Japanese. Thus, the President's indignation probably sought to justify the nation's wrath, and his emotion may have helped to quiet its fears. The grim tone of the speech conveyed a feeling of urgency that turned hysteria into purpose. By the accumulation of details about the surprise Japanese offensives in the Pacific area, Roosevelt suggested the needs of the moment:

Yesterday the Japanese government also launched an attack against Malaya.

Last night Japanese forces attacked Hong Kong.

Last night Japanese forces attacked Guam.

Last night Japanese forces attacked the Philippine Islands.

Last night the Japanese attacked Wake Island.

And this morning the Japanese attacked Midway Island.

Japan has, therefore, undertaken a surprise offensive extending throughout the Pacific area. . . . The people of the United States . . . well understand the implications to the very life and safety of our Nation.

The necessities of defense overcame numbed horror, so that the nation was able to go about its new business—that of waging war.

III

Time dims circumstances. The emotional pitch of that day in 1941 is difficult to recall; its necessities are now gone. Roosevelt's message helps

---

[2] One point of interest here is the echo, without development, of Wilson's war-to-end-war idea. Wilson speaks of a "fight . . . for the ultimate peace of the world," and "a concert of free peoples as shall bring peace and safety to all nations." Without further explication, Roosevelt mentions the necessity not of defense alone but also of making it "very certain that this form of treachery shall never again endanger us."

The quotations from Wilson's addresses were taken from the text printed in *The Literature of the United States*, edited by Walter Blair, Theodore Hornberger, and Randall Stewart, second volume, published in Chicago (1953), pages 795–800.

The quotations from Roosevelt's address were taken from the text printed in *The Public Papers and Addresses of Franklin D. Roosevelt, 1941 Volume*, published in New York (1950), pages 514 and 515.

General historical background was supplied by Ralph Volney Harlow's *The United States*, published in New York (1949).

evoke those emotions because Roosevelt was an astute man who had gauged the temper of the people and had understood the necessities of the moment. Where Wilson had responded to war pressures with a statement of ideal principles and aims, Roosevelt had placated the fright of a nation wounded in the field and in the heart. Both addresses reveal the characters of the speakers. Both were appropriate to their temporal context. Wilson, in admitting the necessity of war, expressed man's sorrow at the recognition of his own weakness. Roosevelt, in exclaiming anger at the need for war, expressed man's hurt at the treachery of his fellows. Both speeches will have meaning as long as wars are present realities rather than past history.

9

War Message, December 8, 1941: An Approach to Language

Hermann G. Stelzner

Since the speaker, occasion, and audience of a speech are so important for an understanding of that speech, the critic of public address is likely to direct most of his effort toward informing his reader of these conditions—and all but ignore the workings of the speech itself. In this extremely important and only apparently difficult study, the author adopts a "poetics" and offers a careful reading of a single speech as "it is, not how it came to be." He attempts to discipline and to bind together his various observations on language mainly by showing the importance of past, present, and future time in the speech's internal development. As something of a New Critic, he accepts the address as an artistic whole and then justifies the speaker's choices within the action of that address.

One interesting though dangerous approach is to posit hypothetical alternate readings and then attempt to demonstrate their inadequacies. Too often these rejections appear simply personal, since their adoption would not weaken the larger order (see the discussions of lines 4 and 5, 7, 8 and 9.) Perhaps more damaging is the loose application of such terms as "formal—informal" and "concrete—general," which is at best whimsical and demonstrates, again, the difficulty of establishing clear and objective critical terminology.

Section III as a study of cultural context warrants special attention independently of the whole article.

" Time, Narrative + Language in FDR's ... "

I

Two recent books[1] are responses to an uneasiness with much rhetorical criticism which has appeared in print. In raising questions the authors hope to stimulate more meaningful and insightful analyses of rhetorical activities and processes. They goad critics to experiment, to describe and to evaluate in ways heretofore little practiced. Both authors ask that "beginnings" be made.

Reviewers have pointed to difficulties. Arnold's review of Nichols' work asks for a sample of the criticism "I am exhorted to produce." He feels that Nichols "does not illustrate in pointed ways how criticism may, in practice, resolve the . . . issues raised."[2] Responding to Black's work, Ehninger agrees with Black's assessment of much criticism but believes Black's alternatives "are not worked out in enough detail to be viable." The "ingredients . . . are not developed into anything approaching a critical method" nor are "characteristics and possibilities . . . systematized into a program of attack and procedure which the critic . . . may apply."[3] Yet neither Black nor Nichols set out to develop systems. Black observes:

We have not evolved any system of rhetorical criticism, but only, at best, an orientation to it. An orientation, together with taste and intelligence, is all that a critic needs. If his criticism is fruitful, he may end with a system, but he should not, in our present state of knowledge, begin with one. We simply do not know enough yet about rhetorical discourse to place our faith in systems, and it is only through imaginative criticism that we are to learn more.[4]

Concluding her remarks on I. A. Richards, Nichols states:

One of the most useful things about I. A. Richards . . . is his demonstration of the possibility of finding an orderly methodology. . . . I do not mean that Richards' method should be adopted. . . . What I do mean is that we also should be looking for an orderly methodology.[5]

The thrust of Nichols' and Black's analyses is macrocosmic. Most criticism, Black states, is limited to "an estimate of the historically factual effects of the discourse on its relatively immediate audience."[6] He argues

[Hermann G. Stelzner is Professor of Speech at the University of Massachusetts. This article originally appeared in *Speech Monographs*, xxxiii (November 1966), 419–37, and is reprinted with the permission of both the author and the Speech Association of America.]
[1] Marie Hochmuth Nichols, *Rhetoric and Criticism* (Baton Rouge, La., 1963); Edwin Black, *Rhetorical Criticism* (New York, 1965).
[2] Carroll C. Arnold, review of *Rhetoric and Criticism* in *Southern Speech Journal*, xxx (Fall, 1964), 62.
[3] Douglas Ehninger, "Rhetoric and the Critic," *Western Speech*, xxix (Fall 1965), 231.
[4] Black, p. 177.
[5] Nichols, pp. 106–7.
[6] Black, p. 48.

for enlargement, for an "interpretation of the discourse that realizes all that is in it and that aims 'to see the object as it really is'. . . ."[7]

A rhetorical act is both rich and complex. To probe it fully requires all the critical postures, approaches, and talents described by Stanley Hyman in his portrait of an "ideal" critic.[8] Full disclosure is the ideal.

The posture of this study is microcosmic. We center on the language of Franklin D. Roosevelt's "War Message" to Congress, December 8, 1941. The analysis is motivated by the treatment of language found in much traditional criticism. Often critics fragment discourse, investigate chosen samples of language as independent variables and draw conclusions. One analyst, after studying Stevenson's 1952 campaign addresses, reported that Stevenson has a "middle" style, "neither plain nor grand."[9] To the traditional procedures, Nichols has responded: "Hoary with age."[10] She believes that the usual approaches have failed to treat language adequately: "Year after year, language, if it is handled at all, gets a few words about rhetorical questions, antithesis, and metaphors."[11] Ehninger's description of existing criticism includes like comments:

Instead of describing what is going on in a discourse as it works to achieve its ends, they [critics] focus on how the discourse came into being, on the circumstances under which it was delivered, and on the reactions or results it produced. Analysis of the speech itself not only is scanted, but to the extent that it is present it tends to consist of a classification of certain grosser properties, cast under the heads of the traditional modes and canons—to be a mechanical accounting or summing up of how well the speech fits an *a priori* mold.[12]

The present approach to Franklin D. Roosevelt's "War Message" is "topographical." The speech is the "particular place" and, to assess the configurations of its language, its "roads," "rivers," "cities," "lakes," and "relief" are examined. To shift the figure, fragments of language are not selected from the speech and regarded as the dominant lights, independent and autonomous. The concern is with the constellation, not the major star alone. Interest centers on the order, movement, meanings, and interrelations of the language; the object is to discover not only what goes on, but how it goes on. The aim is full disclosure.

We explicate. We try, inductively, a kind of "statistical inspection"[13] to find out what goes on and how the "on-going" is generated. We note development *"from what through what to what."*[14] shifting from grammar to syntax to diction to logic to rhythm to figure or whatever, when the

[7] *Ibid.*
[8] Stanley Edgar Hyman, *The Armed Vision* (New York, 1955), pp. 386–91.
[9] Nichols, p. 107   [10] *Ibid.*   [11] *Ibid.*   [12] Ehninger, p. 230.
[13] Kenneth Burke, *The Philosophy of Literary Form* (New York, 1957), p. 59; on p. 75 Burke refers to the examination as an "inductive inspection."
[14] *Ibid.*, p. 60; italics his.

speech itself demands a shift to account for the totality of tensions in the language. Speeches, including those of the expository genre, are more than collections of statements. Explicating is more than paraphrasing. It is "the ex*plicit*ation of the implicit."[15] We explore the lexical possibilities of words and word combinations. As a way of demonstrating what is going on in a speech, explication is analogous to Hyman's description of Burke's mode: "Use All There Is to Use," which means "the rather disorganized organizing principle of investigating every possible line of significance."[16]

The speech provides the clues. The available drafts of Roosevelt's address have been examined and, when variations in the drafts bear on the analysis, we cite them.[17] However, the primary purpose is not to trace the *development* of the "War Message" of December 8, 1941. How the speech *is*, not how it came to be, is the concern.

We do not suggest that Roosevelt himself consciously structured the relationships we explore and evaluate. It "cannot be said too often that a poet does not fully know what is the poem he is writing until he has written it"[18] applies to all composition. Burke argues it is not until "*after the completion* of the work"[19] that interrelationships in it can be analyzed; analysis of these involves both "quantitative and qualitative considerations":[20]

Now, the work of every writer contains a set of implicit equations. . . . And though he be perfectly conscious of the act of writing, . . . he cannot possibly be conscious of the interrelationships among all these equations. . . . The motivation out of which he writes is synonymous with the structural way in which he puts events and values together when he writes; and however consciously he may go about such work, there is a kind of generalization about these interrelations that he could not have been conscious of, since the generalization could be made by the kind of inspection that is possible only *after the completion* of the work.[21]

Because this analysis is limited to the language of a single speech, we cannot generalize from it to "style." The inability to generalize from a single example presents the reverse of a difficulty which reviewers saw in Nichols' and Black's macrocosmic postures: the difficulty of implementa-

---

[15] W. K. Wimsatt, Jr., *The Verbal Icon* (Lexington, Ky., 1954), p. 249; italics his.
[16] Hyman, p. 390.
[17] The Franklin D. Roosevelt Library, Hyde Park, N.Y., has four drafts of this message. They were examined and are referred to by number. Changes from draft to draft are not extensive. Grace Tully, Roosevelt's secretary, indicates that the address was delivered in almost the identical form in which it was originally dictated to her by the President. See Grace Tully, *F.D.R., My Boss* (New York, 1949), p. 256.
[18] C. Day Lewis, *The Poetic Image* (London, 1947), p. 71.
[19] Burke, p. 18; italics his.
[20] *Ibid.*, p. 59.
[21] *Ibid.*, p. 18; italics his.

tion. And microscopic analysis, no matter how successful, does not shed much light on discourse in general. Yet William E. Leuchtenburg's insightful essay, "The New Deal and the Analogue of War,"[22] offers possibilities for extending the analysis undertaken in these pages. He points out that much New Deal policy was accomplished through the figure of war. Roosevelt himself often applied the topic, "war," to social and economic problems. In a sense his December 8, 1941 "War Message" was but another treatment of that topic. Scrutiny of a number of his addresses might provide insights into his use of language, his "style," on the topic "war"; generalization would then be possible. Speaking to the point of generalization, Burke states that it is first necessary to trace down the "interrelationships as revealed by the objective structure of the book itself":

The first step . . . requires us to get our equations inductively, by tracing down the interrelationships as revealed by the objective structure of the book itself. [Eventually one may] . . . offer "generalizations atop generalizations" whereby different modes of concrete imagery may be classed together. That is, one book may give us "into the night" imagery; another "to the bottom of the sea" imagery; another the "apoplectic" imagery . . . and we may propose some over-all category . . . that would justify us in classing all these works together on the basis of a common strategy despite differences in concrete imagery.[23]

The objective structure of a speech, as well as of a book, is a composite of subtly balanced meanings; all language is weighted toward something, hence away from something; for something, hence opposed to something. A "statistical inspection" of a speech reveals what the speaker talked about, and from that knowledge the balance of his meanings can be established. For example, in the "War Message" of December 8, 1941 "time" is central to Roosevelt's discussion. He uses the future and the past, even as he speaks in, about, and to the present. Future is balanced against Past; these are poles of a continuum along which "goods" and their opposites balance antithetically. The past is given negative valence in Roosevelt's address; and in like manner other concepts, entities, and conditions are antithetically balanced. The balanced meanings are listed below. Those on the left have "positive" quality; those on the right are "negative." Successive balances emerge as the speech advances and they, hence, constitute a structural pattern according to which analysis of the address may proceed.

[22] William E. Leuchtenburg, "The New Deal and the Analogue of War," in *Change and Continuity in Twentieth-Century America*, ed. John Braeman (Columbus, Ohio, 1964), pp. 81–143.
[23] Burke, p. 59.

Future time	Past time
God	"Devil"
United States	Japan
government	government
military	military
people	people
Absence of danger (presence of peace)	Presence of danger (absence of peace)
International involvement	Isolationistic non-involvement
"I" of address	Non-"I"[24]

An arrangement of the balanced meanings of an address, such as the arrangement just set forth, describes the relationships of the topics discussed by the speaker; the arrangement does not, however, explicate these relationships. There remains the task of revealing not only the weight of each pole in a particular balance of meaning but how the weighting, hence relationship, was rhetorically achieved.

We may turn now to the text of Roosevelt's address:[25]

1   Yesterday, December 7, 1941—a date which will live in infamy—the United

2   States of America was suddenly and deliberately attacked by naval and air forces of

3   the Empire of Japan.

4   The United States was at peace with that nation and, at the solicitation of

5   Japan, was still in conversation with its Government and its Emperor looking toward

6   the maintenance of peace in the Pacific.

7   Indeed, one hour after Japanese air squadrons had commenced bombing in the

8   American island of Oahu, the Japanese Ambassador to the United States and his colleague

9   delivered to our Secretary of State a formal reply to a recent American message. And

10   while this reply stated that it seemed useless to continue the existing diplomatic

11   negotiations, it contained no threat or hint of war or of armed attack.

12   It will be recorded that the distance of Hawaii from Japan makes it obvious that

[24] In a speech situation, the speaker, the "I," is never wholly absent. Listeners may respond to his voice and/or his physical presence even when he handles materials largely denotative and expository in character. The continuum of "presence-absence" is one of convenience, establishing poles and making possible relative weighting.

[25] This text is the transcript of the message as delivered. Text from Franklin D. Roosevelt Library, Hyde Park, N.Y.

13   the attack was deliberately planned many days or even weeks ago. During the inter-

14   vening time the Japanese Government has deliberately sought to deceive the United

15   States by false statements and expressions of hope for continued peace.

16   The attack yesterday on the Hawaiian Islands has caused severe damage to American

17   naval and military forces. I regret to tell you that very many American lives have

18   been lost. In addition American ships have been reported torpedoed on the high seas

19   between San Francisco and Honolulu.

20   Yesterday the Japanese Government also launched an attack against Malaya.

21   Last night Japanese forces attacked Hong Kong.

22   Last night Japanese forces attacked Guam.

23   Last night Japanese forces attacked the Philippine Islands.

24   Last night the Japanese attacked Wake Island.

25   And this morning the Japanese attacked Midway Island.

26   Japan has, therefore, undertaken a surprise offensive extending throughout the

27   Pacific area. The facts of yesterday and today speak for themselves. The

28   people of the United States have already formed their opinions and well understand the impli-

29   cations to the very life and safety of our nation.

30   As Commander-in-Chief of the Army and Navy I have directed that all measures

31   be taken for our defense. But always will our whole nation remember the character

32   of the onslaught against us.

33   No matter how long it may take us to overcome this premeditated invasion, the

34   American people in their righteous might will win through to absolute victory.

35   I believe that I interpret the will of the Congress and of the people when I

36   assert that we will not only defend ourselves to the uttermost but will make it

37   very certain that this form of treachery shall never again endanger us.

38   Hostilities exist. There is no blinking at the fact that our people, our

39   territory and our interests are in grave danger.

40   With confidence in our armed forces, with the unbounding determination of our

41   people, we will gain the inevitable triumph—so help us God.

42   I ask that the Congress declare that since the unprovoked and dastardly

43   attack by Japan on Sunday, December 7, 1941, a state of war has
            existed between the
44   United States and the Japanese Empire.

II

The man who writes or speaks of an "anticipated war ... must select his
material out of the past and the present."[26] He is committed to speak in
some fashion about history. On December 7, 1941, history was made suddenly and directly. The equally direct, initial, verbal response (1–3) parallels the historical facts which made statement necessary. Moreover, the
mass media had described fully the international activities of December 7,
1941, and listeners could easily fit the speaker's initial statement into a
larger and ordered background.

"Yesterday" quickly anchors the address to the immediate historical
past, to the events of December 7th. It suggests that the speaker does not
intend to go deeply into the past or to discuss it as part of the recommendations he will ultimately make.[27] The meaning of the immediate past
was clearly less important than the present and the future. This placement
of yesterday contributes to the overall past-present-future structure of the
address and to the connotative values of "time" in it. The direct
announcement (1–3) ruptures "yesterday," a time of reasonable stability
and peace. That mind which wished to wander even fleetingly back over
time, is restrained and controlled by the appositive, December 7, 1941.
The speaker acknowledges that his listeners understood (27–29) the "leisure," the peaceful "timelessness" of yesterday had gone; but he impresses
the point upon them.

The appositive, December 7, 1941, not only defines the specific yesterday among the potentially many. It establishes the date, which for historical purposes is more important than the day, Sunday, here omitted. The
personal value judgment—"a date which will live in infamy"—colors the
appositive and introduces the future into the discussion. Introduced as an
"aside," the future already acts, offering judgments about the present. The
matter is carefully handled. The speaker did not say: the date will live in
infamy. A shift from the indefinite to the definite article and the excision
of the relative pronoun *which* makes the speaker's personal judgment cate-

[26] Burke, p. 203.

[27] Tully, p. 256, reports that when the message was being prepared, Roosevelt called
Secretary of State Cordell Hull to the White House to examine a draft. "The Secretary brought with him an alternative message drafted by Sumner Welles, longer and
more comprehensive in its review of the circumstances leading to the state of war. It
was rejected by the Boss."

gorical, forcing on the historical future a value judgment which only the historical future can rightfully make.

That a sense of and a sensitivity to history operates[28] can be seen by testing alternatives: *Yesterday, a day which will live in infamy.* . . . Here the appositive is omitted, a possibility because it was unlikely that any member of the immediate audience would have been unaware of the date. History, however, catalogues dates, not yesterdays or days; the date is supplied. Omitting the appositive also makes necessary the revision of "a date which" to "a day which"; the former is somewhat more precise and sustains better the historical overtones of the initial announcement (1–3). Thus, the first twelve words of Roosevelt's address join past and future; the present is represented by speaker and audience. And the immediate present—unsettled, disrupted, and anxiety-provoking—is somewhat stabilized by the past-future continuum which provides a sense of continuity. In the speaker's judgmental aside, the future renders a verdict on present activities which favors us; implicatively the future is on "our side."

The passive voice of the initial announcement makes possible some specific relationships between time, the actors in time, and the judgmental aside about the time. Though the statement's subject is the naval and air forces of the Empire of Japan, in the passive voice the subject becomes a marginal, omissible part of the sentence and its sense. The speaker could have said: . . . *the United States of America was suddenly and deliberately attacked.* But as delivered, the first statement treats the Japanese Empire as "marginal," subordinate. The passive emphasizes the United States as receiver of the action on a specific date, a day of peace until the attack which was infamous in character. The interrelationship of the three allows the immediate audience and history to record these facts. The initial statement might have been active: *Yesterday, December 7, 1941, a date which will live in infamy, naval and air forces of the Empire of Japan suddenly and deliberately attacked the United States.* Not only would the Japanese Empire have become central and active, but the United States would have been removed from its relationship to time. Yet time is essential to the well-being of the country. Past times treated her badly; future time (33–34, 40–41) will heal her wounds.

Even as yesterday was ruptured, the formal, settled, and trusted diplomatic conventions (4–6) were in process. These, too, will be broken (9–15) as the speaker particularizes some of the specific details in the deliberations. The formal and elevated diplomatic language describes.

[28] Roosevelt "regarded history as an imposing drama and himself as a conspicuous actor. Again and again he carefully staged a historic scene: as when, going before Congress on December 8, 1941, to call for a recognition of war with Japan, he took pains to see that Mrs. Woodrow Wilson accompanied Mrs. Roosevelt to the Capitol, thus linking the First and Second World Wars." Allan Nevins, "The Place of Franklin D. Roosevelt in History," *American Heritage*, xvii (June 1966), 12.

"Nation" (4) is more formal and concrete than a possible alternative, *country*. "Solicitation" (4) is more formal than *request*, and "conversation" (5) is more formal than *discussion* or *conference*. Consistent with the formality of the language is its loose, alliterative quality, more pronounced here than in any section of the address. "Peace" (4, 6) opens and closes the section, its sound sense somewhat reinforced by a weak alliterative echo: "Pacific." Between these points, "nation,' "solicitation,' "conversation," occur in rapid order; "maintenance," modifies the pattern by introducing a different, though not wholly dissimilar, sound tension.

Time remains central to the development. "The United States was at peace"[29]—past, "still in conversation"—present, "looking toward the maintenance"—future. The actors in the drama are polarized. Responding to a Japanese "solicitation," we were still concerned with tomorrow, even as they were not. The formal, diplomatic language (4–6) symbolizes a mask behind which duplicity is hidden. The duplicity, one dimension of a key term, "infamous" (1), is woven into the texture of the address. For example, the close relationship of "yesterday" (1, 16, 20) to the repeated "deliberately" (2, 13, 14) intensifies and supports the duplicity or infamy. The formal language (4–6) foreshadows the recital of specific events (7–11).

"Indeed," injecting emphasis and force, begins the recitation and colors the neutrality of formal, diplomatic language. Not *yet, still, but,* nor *however* would have functioned as well to introduce the formal, but false, overtures of the Japanese. "Indeed" imprints a reaction of the individual "I" on the yet-to-be-stated particulars. Moreover, "indeed" gains force and support from the earlier "yesterday," "infamy," "deliberately," "at peace," "still in conversation," and "maintenance of peace." Following the expletive, the speaker says "one hour after" (7), not merely *after*. "One hour after" makes time concrete, supports the emotional dimensions of "indeed," and forecasts the brazen, formal action of the Japanese Ambassador and the duplicity behind his formality. Also supporting duplicity is a subdued temporal pattern (7–11): after Japanese air squadrons attacked—past, the Ambassador delivers his reply—present, concerning *future* relationships.

"Japanese air squadrons" (7) were the instruments of attack. The phrase might have been rendered: *after the Japanese air force* or *after Jap-*

[29] In drafts I, II, and III the line reads: "The United States was at the moment at peace." The "at the moment" phrase emphasizes time unnecessarily; it contributes little to clarity or sense, and its excision is merited. Further, its excision diminishes the possibility of the immediate listeners' setting up the balance: was at the moment —is at the moment. "At this moment" (i.e., the moment of the address) the United States was in practical terms at war. Yet the President was speaking formally to the Congress to whom the legal right formally to declare war belonged. "At this moment" we were "legally" still at peace. Excision of "at the moment" diminished the possibility of a mistaken response by either the Congressional or the general audience.

anese air forces. These alternatives parallel better the first reference to the Japanese military (1); but therein lies a weakness. The modified repetition provides some variety. More important is the matter of image. *Air force* and *air forces* denote and connote mass, a large quantity which blankets a sky. Such a mass moves, but in droning and lumbering fashion. "Air squadrons" is a sharper, definable form of the force, as an image in the mind's eye. The image is of small groups, of well-defined patterns in the total mass, of tightly knit units sweeping in and out over the target.

"Air squadrons" is quantitative, definitive, and repetitive. To the extent that squadrons are patterns, the image presents formal patterns inflicting damage. Formal patterns are the enemy: of the past—"one hour after" (7), as well as the near present—"the Japanese Ambassador . . . delivered" (8–9). The formality of pattern connoted by "Japanese air squadrons" is also explicitly denoted of the Ambassador's act; he delivers a "formal reply" (9), which is contrasted to a slightly less formal "American message" (9). Had the description been of an *American note*, it would have been overly informal. Slightly more formal and rigid than "our Secretary of State" (9) is "the Japanese Ambassador" (8). If there is in these lines a heightened sense of the "formal" and if formality marks the enemy, all formality becomes symbolic—a mask—for duplicity and infamy. The closed, distant, difficult-to-read "formal" opposes the somewhat easier-to-read, open "informality." Such suggestion is consistent with the Western, especially American, stereotype of the Orient and Oriental, circa 1941. Duplicity masked by formality is thus further intensified. On first glance the construction of line 11[30] appears anticlimactic. "War" (11) is more encompassing and potentially more dangerous than "armed attack." However, "war" connotes a formal, open declaration of conflict. The Japanese dispensed with that formality, favoring "armed attack," an action outside the conventions of diplomacy.

Thus far no objective evidence has been offered to support the charge of duplicity. The speaker has been reporting diplomatic relationships (4–6) which the listeners themselves cannot verify; they are dependent upon him. But the shift is now to a geographical relationship (12) which supports the charge. "It will be recorded. . . ." By whom? The immediate audience certainly, but the historical audience as well. The verb "record" alters the speaker's stance and the passive "will be recorded" his perspective. The speaker's verb refers to, points to, the intellectual activity of man. Together, in concert, the speaker and the listeners function as

[30] In draft II lines 10–11 read: "This reply contained a statement that it seemed useless to continue the diplomatic negotiations, but it contained no threat nor hint of war or of armed attack." Drafts III and IV are consistent with the final text. The draft II version is a compound sentence and fails to stress the "no threat nor hint of war." The revision, a dependent-independent arrangement, emphasizes the "no threat nor hint of war." It emphasizes duplicity.

detached observers—they measure mileage—and as commentators. "Makes it obvious" (12) is a phrase which befits such activity—of seeing, of reasoning, of understanding. The passive allows the evidence to be offered in dependent clauses, which contain the signs upon which the conclusion depends; it provides the "distance" necessary to detached, intellectual analysis. All the signs, and especially the final, objective, mileage sign, which is positioned nearest the conclusion which all signs support, contribute to one judgment: infamous duplicity. Finally, "the distance of Hawaii from Japan" (12), a particular sign, is embedded in a sentence which itself spans syntactical distance.

The passive construction makes possible analysis of events which are outside the direct experience of the speaker. Events of the more immediate past (14–15) are handled differently; they are not in dependent clauses and the subject of detached, intellectual analysis. Of these events, the speaker has direct knowledge, and he shifts to the active voice. Japan acts. The language which responds is categorical and conclusive: "deliberately sought to deceive the United States by false statements and expressions of hope . . ." (14–15). Was the deception successful? The ambiguous "sought" leaves the question open, even as the speaker's emphasis on Japan's deliberateness and falsity tend to forestall the asking of it.

As further details are enumerated, time shifts slightly in importance. In "the attack yesterday" (16), the act is more important than the time. The emphasis on time could have been maintained: *yesterday's attack*. The new arrangement is less emphatic. The shift in emphasis does not however alter the basic time-act or act-time relationship. A legitimate alternative would have considerably weakened, if not broken, it: *the attack on the Hawaiian Islands yesterday*. . . .

From the description the personal "I" (17) emerges to link the speaker with the "blackest" event yet—the specific human tragedy. Both the "I" and the tragedy gain stature from the relationship. Had the "I" chosen a compound sentence, he could have avoided announcing the loss of life: the attack . . . *caused* . . . *damage to* . . . *forces* and very many *American lives have been lost*. Or he might have said simply: *Very many American lives have been lost*. These choices diminish both the ethical posture of the "I" and the dignity of the men who lost their lives. The "I" reveals (17–18), explicitly and implicitly, something of his regard for life—he separates it from the materials of war—and of his concept of duty, as a human being and as President and Commander-in-Chief. He demonstrates his understanding of and his respect for the conventions of tragic announcement. Moreover, he emerges "to tell" (17) his listeners. The direct, common verb suggests closeness—he to them and they to him. A close relationship must exist between the bearer and the receivers of tragic tidings for the verb "tell" to operate. When there is distance the tendency

good

is toward formality, neutrality, and elevation: to *inform*, to *report*, or to *announce*.

"In addition" (18) adds still another detail. Is it of equal, more, or less importance than others? That depends upon the reaction of the listener to the total configuration. But the speaker by his placement of it reveals his assessment of its importance. Japanese submarines have approached the United States; they act not at far-off Hawaii, but nearer home. For an already upset nation the news is serious and distressing. The distress is minimized somewhat by placing it following the announcement of the loss of life, which absorbed most, if not all, emotional energies. The statement which follows the news helps to minimize the danger from the submarines. Attention and concern are diverted by the quick, crisp movement to Malaya (20)—about as far as danger could be removed.

Additional forces further diminish the submarine threat; distance is achieved by having the ships torpedoed on the high seas between San Francisco and Honolulu. The language moves danger "away from" the shores of the United States. The proper nouns, San Francisco and Honolulu (19), are necessary to the overall effect. Let the speaker say: *In addition, American ships have been reported torpedoed on the high seas.* Responses become: Where? Everywhere? Close to the United States? How close? Distant? How distant? The proper nouns meet some of the questions. Where? On a direct path between San Francisco and Honolulu. One can almost see it on the wall map of the mind—the narrow, well-defined shipping route. Close? How close? Ambiguously the image suggests movement *away from*. One may speculate on the range of possible responses had the speaker said, *on the high seas between Honolulu and San Francisco*, or merely *on the high seas*.

The choice and arrangement of the proper noun diminish danger; a vague term in the same sentence (18–19) functions similarly. "Have been reported torpedoed" said the speaker. "Reported" has truth-value, but relative to source and circumstance. Reports of that time were somewhat chaotic and unreliable. The speaker hints at doubt and uncertainty. The weight of the office of President and Commander-in-Chief does not support the reports. An alternative could diminish doubt: *American ships have been torpedoed.* The specific and the concrete joined in the same sentence to the vague and ambiguous moderate danger.

The announcement of the attack against Malaya (20), which partially relieved concern for the movement of Japanese submarines, has another function. It quietly extends the conflict, joining the United States as partner and ally of the British. The United States' involvement is not to be limited; it will become global. "Also" (20) signals this extension, though "Malaya" and "Hong Kong" must be heard to make the idea meaningful.

The concluding generalization, "a surprise offensive extending throughout the Pacific area" (26–27), also quietly involves the country with allies and quietly prepares it for total involvement without the speaker's need to expend ethos to stress the necessity of an international commitment.[31]

The announcement of the attack against Malaya (20) also introduces a shift in the movement and tone of the address. The former will be quickened, the latter be made emphatic. The statement of the attack against Malaya parallels in substance lines 1–3; it begins "yesterday"; its subject is Japanese activity. However, its voice is active; it has neither qualifiers nor dependent clauses; its verb is simple past tense. No other statement in the address thus far is as compressed or moves as quickly.

The "yesterday" which introduces the attack against Malaya concludes a compression among the yesterdays; note only the distance between them (1, 16, 20). This compression occurring over time and distance foreshadows, even as it is counterbalanced by, the tightly compressed "last night" series (21–24), including as well the modified restatement of time: "this morning" (25). These compressions of time herald the end of discussion about events in the immediate past. Attention will soon be directed (27–29) to what must be done today and tomorrow.

The tonalities of the "last night" series (21–25) are controlled by line 20 which begins formally: "the Japanese Government." The verb, "launched," quickly tarnishes the formal recognition. Rather than "launched," why not *began, commenced,* or still simpler *attacked?* None of these verbs reinforces or sustains as well as the connotations of "suddenly and deliberately attacked" (2) and "deliberately planned" (13), which emphasize the Japanese activities were outside the conventions of diplomacy. Had they been within those conventions, "launch" might have been an inappropriate description. A verb of strong thrust and impulse, "launch" has sufficient energy to encompass all remaining action (21–25).

Formal agents and agencies, "Japanese forces" (21–23), advance the action. Soon the less formal and somewhat ambiguous "the Japanese" (24–25) forward it. Is the referent only the Japanese Government and/or its agents? Or has there been a subtle expansion to include the citizens of Japan, as well? The choice of "Japan" (26) suggests the latter explanation. "Japan"—not the Empire of Japan, nor the Emperor, nor the Ambassador, nor the Government—merely Japan; the common term describes the nation. The Government and its agents are the explicit enemy; by implication the people are also numbered among the enemy. Nowhere before has

---

[31] James Reston, *New York Times,* December 9, 1941, p. 5, wrote: "Two facts seemed to impress this gathering [Congress] more perhaps than the simple words of the speech. By not the slightest inflection did he suggest that the facts of the world situation had finally justified his policy, as even his opponents were admitting today he might very well have done."

the term, Japan, been used in this naked fashion. The "Japan" of line 5 occurs within the context of elevated, diplomatic language; in line 12 the reference is a straightforward, geographical one. The common term is later repeated (43) and tarnished completely by "unprovoked and dastardly" (42). The national name is finally too good to serve to describe the country. Reduction of Japan is effected by carefully controlled and disciplined language. Men in the street could and did say "Japs." The speaker could not. To have done so would have diminished not only the stature of the office of President but also the occasion and the place, the formal chambers in which affairs of state were conducted. Equally important, to have said 'Japs" would have reduced the leader to the level of the led; distance, however defined, is necessary to effective leadership.

The "last night" series (21–24) supports the pace and quality of the attacks. Logically, last night, a part of yesterday, is illogical. The compressed "last nights," figuratively ticking off the clock, bring yesterday to a climactic end. The three "yesterdays" (1, 16, 20) spanned time and space; the night and the events in the night move faster. Simple declarative sentences present facts—actor, action, acted upon. The lengthy iteration is necessary to establish the magnitude of the Japanese thrust. However, had it been extended by the addition of only a few details, it would have been compromised, having its force, pace, and energy enervated. Finally, the verb "launched" more than attacks; it launches a series of sentences which structurally (i.e., in form) harmonize with the acts embedded in them. The actions (i.e., their substance) and the manner of describing them (form) are one. The syntax is itself symbolic of the fast moving military operations.

The connotations from the cluster of "last nights" do more than support the emotional responses rising from "in the quiet of the night when all were abed and defenseless." The cluster is the turning point in a chain of emotive phrases. Prior to the "last night" series, descriptions are relatively mild and basically denotative: "suddenly and deliberately" (2), "deliberately planned," (13), "deliberately sought to deceive" (14), and "false statements" (15). Following the cluster and supported by it is a chain of increasingly stronger phrases: a mild "surprise offensive" (26), a slightly stronger "premeditated invasion" (33), the strong "this form of treachery" (37), and the vehement "unprovoked and dastardly" (42). As the descriptions of the Japanese actions become stronger, so also does the language which responds. Later shifts in verb and voice which describe the response of the United States will be noted.

Finally, the stress which the language contributes, sustains and intensifies the general emphasis of the "last night" passage (20–25). "Yesterday" has three syllables, the first being accented. The phrase "last night" has two accented syllables, relatively equal in stress. Each "last night" is encircled by "attack" or "attacked." This stress pattern of the language is a bombardment. The final line (25) begins with a conjunction which readies the listener for the final "to top it all off." Thus, "and," too, is a term of some stress and strength. "And this morning," a phrase of four syllables, the first three accented, concludes the bombardment.

How all this discourse is managed is seen best by examining some alternatives. Compare "Last night Japanese forces attacked Hong Kong" (21) with: (a) *Japanese forces attacked Hong Kong last night,* or (b) *last night Hong Kong was attacked by Japanese forces.* Alternative (a) maintains the active voice, emphasizing Japanese forces. But the immediacy of "last night" is lost when the phrase concludes the thought. The arrangement also negates the effect produced by accent and stress. "Japanese" contains three syllables, relative stress being unaccented, unaccented, accented. Bombardment by stress is weaker. Further, alternative (a) significantly changes the range of the connotative values of "last night," which now modifies Hong Kong and which divides the emotional response. Sympathy goes out to the people of Hong Kong who experienced catastrophe during the night, yet this relieves somewhat the intensity of the negative emotional response centered on the Japanese, the central actors in the night. Alternative (b) is also unable to capitalize fully on the connotative values of "last night." The passive construction of (b) slows the pace; it also makes the subject, "Japanese forces," a marginal part of the sense. Yet the "last night" series (20–25) is the speaker's final statement about yesterday's activities. He soon directs his listeners (27–29) to respond positively. Their active responses are directed to and focused on something central, not marginal.

Finally, the passive construction of alternative (b) puts the places attacked prior to the act of attack and the attacking forces. Place names, Malaya, Hong Kong, Guam, are presented to the listener first, and though the places are scattered over geography, mentioning them first tends to fix them within a general geographical framework. Anchoring the place names makes the image somewhat static. In the active construction (20–25), the image has more movement. The attacks push on places which are in turn pushed over geographical distance enlarging the area of the conflict. The image thus better foreshadows the concluding, explicit reference to a surprise offensive "extending throughout the Pacific area" (26–27).

Roosevelt's conclusion is introduced by the formal, logical sign, "therefore" (26). His demonstration concluded, the speaker again shifts posture, removing himself altogether from the discussion. He chooses to let a transcendental power suggest action. He personifies: "The facts . . . speak for themselves" (27). The information could have been conveyed in other ways: *the facts . . . are clear; the facts . . . are obvious; the facts . . . are self-evident; the facts . . . are self-explanatory.* But, "facts . . .

speak. . . ." To whom? Directly, which none of the alternatives above manage quite as well, to "the people of the United States," the subject of the following sentence. How do the people respond? What do they do? Verbs (28) indicate that they use their intellects and power to reason. They have "formed their opinions and well understand." So powerful were the facts that they spoke; so reasoned were the pople that they needed no guidance to arrive at a conclusion. No intermediary stands between the facts and the people of intellect. What conclusion had the people "already" (28) reached? To support the action which the speaker announces he has "already" taken (30–32).

The people of the United States are presented as acting on the danger before their Government. Though the danger is not well defined, they understand the "implications" and react positively. When the speaker first mentions the danger, he embeds it in his statement about the people (27–29). Their positive response envelops danger, thereby minimizing it.

The speaker's treatment of the situation and the course of action asserts a commonplace of democratic decision making: the people (27–29), the President (30), the troops (30–31) act jointly. Though they act jointly, the people are presented as having the power to effect decisions.[32] The point is demonstrated by rearranging the speaker's language so that it violates the commonplace:

The facts of yesterday and today speak for themselves. As Commander-in-Chief of the Army and Navy, I have directed that all measures be taken for our defense. The people of the United States, understanding well the implications to the very life and safety of our nation, have already formed their opinions as to the necessity of this action.

To take the action which the logic of the people demanded, man must act. The speaker shifts stance to act in their behalf: "directed" (30)

[32] The power structure upon which the democracy rests compares favorably with that of the enemy; the Emperor, the troops, the people, the latter recognized by their omission. Two reasons partially explain the absence of any formal recognition of the Japanese people, thereby implicatively numbering them among the enemy. First, the conflict does not become one between people; the enemy scapegoat is clearly displayed and well-defined to allow reactions to center on it. Second, the people have to be handled as a totality, as an entity. Even were it possible to define some as "enemy" and others as "friend" the difficulties would have been great. Fine distinctions would have necessitated logical and legalistic development which would have slowed and weakened the movement of the address. The problem would have been only slightly less difficult had the speaker said categorically: The United States has no quarrel with the Japanese people. (Substitute the word German for Japanese in this sentence and it becomes Woodrow Wilson's position in his "War Message" on April 2, 1917. Roosevelt's treatment of the Japanese *people* is quite different from Wilson's treatment of the German *people*). Quite apart from the fact that the Japanese had made American citizens part of the conflict, the speaker, perhaps ahead of the mass of men, realized that such a statement, with its overtone of righteousness, had no place in the mid-twentieth century. War was total. To have said publicly that the people of Japan were not a part of the conflict would have involved the speaker in an untruth, at worst, or in "mere rhetoric," at best. These charges he had earlier levied against Japan.

and "taken" (31) indicate reinvolvement with immediate circumstances. He has been reporting. Now he leads: "I direct" (31), "I believe" (35), "I interpret" (35), "I assert" (36), "I ask" (42). Henceforth energies are marshaled and thrust upon the circumstances which face the country. In the prepositional phrase of interrelation and interaction, "between the United States and the Japanese Empire" (43–44), the United States is mentioned first, giving an additional sense of thrust to our energies. After the speaker announces that the "facts of yesterday . . . speak for themselves," the United States becomes active and positive in its response to those facts. The shift in movement is marked when compared to earlier activity, lines 1–3 being but one example.

The turning point in this address having been reached, the events of yesterday now sustain and support the energy of the country. "That always will our whole nation remember the character of the onslaught against us" (31–32)[33] is in a syntactically dependent position. Though the clause is somewhat awkward and forced, it does foreshadow the first comment about the ultimate outcome (33-34): "no matter how long it may take" (33) which tempers hopes of a quick conclusion. The introductory qualification needs its present emphasis so that listeners' hopes may not be falsely supported. Had the speaker said: *the American people . . . will win through to absolute victory, no matter how long it may take*, listeners might have missed the qualification. Patience, determination, and fortitude are connoted to counterbalance the zeal with which the people, who had "already" (28) reached a judgment, meet the challange. The zeal is not destroyed, but protected; zeal often becomes impatient when detours or setbacks delay progress. The "righteous might" (34) not only provides alliteration and balance for "premeditated invasion" (33), but also triggers a new chain of images: from "righteous might" (34) to "God" (41) to "Sunday" (43). "God" in medial position reflects backward and forward.

Though the specific "I" has emerged to act, his actions vary. What he is and what he does are partially revealed by the choice of verbs. Three verbs (35–37) point to intellectual activity: "I believe," "I interpret," "I assert." Having earlier "directed" and "taken" (30–31), he now becomes an observer of evidence and a commentator thereon. A slow reading of lines 35–37 reveals the tentative, cautious, distant quality of the prose. These lines contain three dependent clauses; no other lines in the address contain as many. Moving through the clauses, the speaker searches for and

[33] In drafts I, II, and III this line reads: "Long will we remember the character of the onslaught against us." In draft III "long" is struck and "always" substituted. "Always," positive and categorical, is stronger than "long," a relative term. "Always" also better suits the historical overtones in the address and the emphasis on future time. "Long" appears again in line 33, but the repetition serves no rhetorical purpose.

examines present signs as a basis for his "assertion" (36): "that this form
of treachery shall never again endanger us."[34]

Following this intellectual-activity statement, long in the sense of distance and tone and by word count the longest in the address, Roosevelt
shifts posture again, jolting listeners to a blunt recognition of present
difficulty. "Hostilities exist" (38) is his shortest and most direct statement.
Yet so mild, so objective, and so matter-of-fact is it that it functions as
understatement. Responses spill out and over it; reactions are some variant
of "that puts it mildly." Emotional responses to the events are stronger
than this statement about the events. Thus, some response spills into lines
38–39 finding resolution in, and providing support for, the judgment,
"grave danger" (39).

"Hostilities exist" has another function. Though the future is of concern, listeners could not long tolerate intellectual analysis of the present
and future. They might allow the speaker to speculate, but their impulses
were for direct action, having "already" (28) reached a judgment. Yet the
distant quality of understated assessments dulls somewhat the listener's
emotional edge, taking his mind momentarily off the present; it rests the
mind before that mind has to accept the judgment of "grave danger"
(39). When the speaker turns from intellectual analysis to the present, he
indicates that he has not forgotten immediate concerns. He meets the
present head-on.

Earlier the facts spoke to the people. They must now look directly at
the facts: "There is no blinking at the fact that our people, our territory
and our interests are in grave danger" (38–39). In the first three drafts,
this line read: "There is no mincing the fact. . . ." The revision is clearer
and stronger. To give "no mincing" meaning, an auditor might have to find
a context which helped explain it; for example, I'll not mince words.
"Blinking at" is clearer; its meaning is rooted in a common physiological
process and in common usage. Moreover, a sound-sense equivalent to
"blinking at" is "winking at"; and if sense were a problem the latter would
easily furnish it. A sound-sense equivalent to "mincing" is "wincing"; the
listener who sought meaning analogically would be misled.

The degree of danger is finally stated explicitly. Though "grave" (39)

---

[34] In drafts I, II, and III line 35 begins: "I speak the will of the Congress and of the
people." This construction is much more emphatic and direct than what the speaker
actually said, and he would not have been inaccurate had he said it. Yet his actual
statement better suits the commonplace of democracy which holds that the President
speaks as a result of what the people and their representatives will. He does not say:
I *speak your will*; but rather, "as a result of your will, I speak." And he gives the
appearance of "sounding out" the will and responding to it, even as he knows what
that will is. Also in drafts I, II, and III, lines 36–37, "but will make it very certain"
read "but will see to it." The latter expresses the tone of determination but not the
finality of the result. The actual statement is categorical in a way which "see to it" is
not; moreover "see to it" is somewhat more colloquial than "make it very certain."

is judgmental, it stands as "fact" (38). Heretofore "grave danger" has been suggested in various ways: "character of the onslaught against us," "premeditated invasion." The statement, "There is no blinking at the fact that our people, our territory and our interests are in grave danger," is a modified repetition and an extension of "The people of the United States have already formed their opinions and well understand the implications to the very life and safety of our nation." New meaning is given to "implications." They are "grave."

However, the gravity (38–39) is tempered by its position in the general pattern. It is preceded by the statement which indicates that we shall respond so that this "form of treachery shall never again endanger us" (35–37) and followed by a statement prophesying "inevitable triumph" (40–41). The tensions created by gravity are counterbalanced by terms of positive outlook and mounting force: "confidence," "unbounding determination," "inevitable triumph," "God" are positive, categorical, and absolute. The swing of the pendulum of construction is longer, stronger, and more forceful than the swing of destruction. Contributing to the strength of the categorical language of lines 40–41 is the loose, but recognizable and felt, iambic meter, which moves firmly to the inevitable triumph, "so help us God."

"With confidence in our armed forces, with the unbounding determination of our people, we will gain the inevitable triumph, so help us God" is the leader-speaker's oath, publicly taken.[35] So commonplace is its structure, diction, and rhythm that once underway the line cannot be turned nor resisted. Its sweep catches all. The well-being of the country is set in the timeless future. Rearranging the structure, diction and rhythm upsets the sweep of the statement and weakens it as an article of faith: *We have confidence in our armed forces; our people have unbounding determination; we will gain the inevitable triumph, so help us God.*

The oath taken, no further thematic development is necessary. Only the formal declaration of war (42–44) remains.[36] However, additional modified repetitions woven into the formal declaration enlarge and emphasize thoughts, values, and feelings in the address. "Unprovoked and das-

[35] Lines 40–41 do not appear in drafts I, II, and III. Harry Hopkins suggested the additions, though his second phrase read: "with faith in our people"; Roosevelt altered this to "with the unbounding determination of our people." Since Roosevelt's entire statement (40–41) is a confession of faith, the excision of "faith" in Hopkins' second phrase is appropriate. Too, "faith" has but one syllable, making Hopkins' second phrase shorter than his first and third and restricting somewhat the "swelling" movement of the entire confession. Roosevelt's "the unbounding determination of" is not only phonetically more expansive, but the additional syllables support better the rhythmical movement to the climactic "so help us God."

[36] In drafts I, II, and III line 42 begins: "I, therefore, ask that . . . " The formal, logical sign is unnecessary; Roosevelt's logical and rhetorical conclusion was lines 40–41; lines 42–44 are a formal, ceremonial statement dictated by the nature of the occasion and the place.

tardly" (42) not only balances but also intensifies and enlarges "suddenly and deliberately" (1). The common "Japan" (43) is elevated to the "Japanese Empire" (44) which parallels the formality of "Empire of Japan" (3). The final elevation is one of form only: "dastardly Japan" is the subject. The day, as well as the date, has value. "Sunday" (43) extends and reinforces the connotations of "last night"; its proximity to "dastardly" (43) intensifies the connotations of that term, even as "Sunday" itself gains value and support from its relationship to "God" (41).

The generic negation, the Devil term, is "dastardly" (42).[37] Its appearance is surprising; its choice, apt. Though not a term of the vernacular, it is clear, conveying a dimension of the speaker's moral indignation. As the Devil term, it stands in antithesis to "righteous might" (34), "Sunday" (43), and "God" (41). It has another function. It is as close as the President, speaking to the country in a public chamber, could come to profanity. The movement from "dastardly" to "bastardly" is slight and swift: the latter epitomizes one dimension of the public mood on December 8, 1941. Infamous duplicity has become bastardly duplicity. The leader-speaker controls his emotions before his public and again maintains his distance from his public. Yet the adroit and adept rhetorical choice effects a public catharsis.

The dependent clauses in the final statement (42–44) allow the speaker his judgment of "unprovoked and dastardly" and permit a return to the past: "a state of war has existed." Though the safe and settled formal language of diplomacy and the settled and safe historical past are upset and sundered by the declaration, its formality suggests that the United States respects the conventions of diplomacy even when confronted by dastardly actions outside the accepted conventions. Formality marks the conclusion as well as the beginning. The address has come full circle.

III

Elements of the "War Message," which sets forth Roosevelt's doctrine of demonology, need to be placed in the larger context of culture. We do not suggest that a direct, causal relationship exists between the speech and events in the culture. Cultural conditions have multiple causes; only rarely have they single causes. We do maintain that an address helps to create and sustain a "climate" which justifies activities, even though the speech itself is not *the* cause of any activity. The language of an address by the President of the United States in a time of crisis helps to create and sus-

[37] For an interesting observation on the word "dastardly," which bears on the discussion here, see Barbara W. Tuchman, "History by the Ounce," *Harper's*, ccxxxi (July 1965), 74.

tain a "climate." It also begins to pattern the perceptions and the behaviors of those who hear it. Optimum language bears on perceptions and behaviors in a cohesive way.

The emphasis which Roosevelt gave to topics in his address provided his listeners an orientation to the Japanese and to the nature of the conflict; (these had immediate and long-range consequences.) He emphasized the infamous duplicity behind the Japanese attacks; they carefully and deliberately prepared their military onslaught, masking their preparations behind neutral and formal diplomatic negotiations. American political folklore and the folklore of the people generally hold such behavior in low esteem; the regard is revealed by popular maxims: the man who wears two hats; the man who works both sides of the street; the man who talks out of both sides of his mouth. Roosevelt's portrayal of the Japanese and their activities fits the sense of such widely known and well-understood commonplaces.

Too, the people of the United States generally knew little about the Orient, and stereotypes were associated with it and the Oriental long before December 7, 1941. Even in California, Washington, Oregon, and Arizona, where most of the Japanese in the United States lived, they were little known. The "War Message" enlarged and intensified the stereotypes. These long-standing cultural raw data were supported. On December 7–8, 1941, additional raw data came to the country from the news reports of the conflict. The latter data especially were confusing and anxiety-provoking. To them, Roosevelt gave meaning as he structured a climate of opinion and orientation.

The President's description of the Japanese Government as marginal, fraudulent, dangerous, and capable of dastardly-bastardly behavior has its parallels in the treatment of the Japanese people in the United States. For example, the Commanding General of the Western Defense Command, John L. DeWitt, agreed, as did others, that the Japanese on the West Coast had not engaged in any sabotage after Pearl Harbor. Yet on February 14, 1942, General DeWitt publicly cited the absence of sabotage as "a disturbing and confirming indication that such action will be taken."[38]

On February 6, 1942 in Los Angeles, Mayor Fletcher Brown, "an able and honest public official,"[39] said in a radio broadcast: "If there is intrigue going on, and it is reasonably certain that there is, right here is the hot bed, the nerve center of the spy system, of planning for sabotage." The Mayor recommended "removal of the entire Japanese population—alien and native born—inland for several hundred miles."[40] Ultimately Japa-

[38] Carey McWilliams, *Prejudice: Japanese-Americans, Symbol of Racial Intolerance* (Boston, 1945), p. 110; Dorothy S. Thomas and Richard S. Nishimoto, *The Spoilage* (Berkeley, Calif., 1946), p. 6.
[39] McWilliams, p. 252.
[40] Alexander H. Leighton, *The Governing of Men* (New York, 1964), p. 20.

nese were removed to relocation centers, but those details lie outside the present concern.

United States military policy toward Nisei, American citizens of Japanese-American ancestry, reflected Roosevelt's portrayal of the Japanese in his "War Message." Nisei inducted into military service before Pearl Harbor were, shortly after December 7, 1941, given honorable discharges, with no specification of cause of dismissal. In March, 1942, potential Nisei inductees were arbitrarily assigned IV-F, ineligible for service because of physical defects; on September 1, 1942, this classification was changed to IV-C, the category ordinarily used for enemy aliens.[41]

Not until January 8, 1943, were Japanese-American citizens eligible for military service on the same basis as other citizens. President Roosevelt publicly approved, saying "no . . . citizen of the United States should be denied the democratic right to exercise the responsibilities of his citizenship, regardless of his ancestry."[42]

Of course the general anxiety of the civilian population immediately after December 7, 1941 contributed to development of hostility toward Japanese-Americans. It also made the civilian population susceptible to the rantings of professional patriots, witch hunters, alien haters, and others with private aims, who used the cover of wartime patriotism to achieve what they wanted to do in peace time—rid the West Coast of the Japanese.

Numerous private citizens and officials of Government sought to redress such attacks upon the Japanese-Americans. For example, the San Francisco *Chronicle*, December 9, 1941, said editorially: "The roundup of Japanese citizens in various parts of the country . . . is not a call for volunteer spy hunters to go into action. Neither is it a reason to lift an eyebrow at a Japanese, whether American-born or not."[43] On balance, the voices of tolerance and fair play were the weaker.

President Roosevelt's "War Message" prepared the United States for a long military operation against the Japanese Empire. The nature of the political and military enemy abroad was clear. Indirectly, he supported a civilian army, equally anxious to do its duty, in its march against the civilian "enemy" at home. The "War Message" offered no protection to Japanese-Americans. In the terms of the analysis here presented these people were given "no weight." Two phrases, "the people of the United States" (27–28) and "the American people" (33–34), only implicitly recognize this group, and as a group they were a minority and a marginal part of the culture. Moreover, the two phrases do not contain positive terms; they

[41] Thomas and Nishimoto, p. 56.
[42] *Ibid.*
[43] *Ibid.*, pp. 17–18. Also see McWilliams, pp. 271–273.

contain dialectical terms, which reflect value judgments.[44] In this connection, note that Roosevelt's public statement in support of the induction of Nisei into the military service did contain the positive term, "citizen," which transcends even as it anchors such dialectical phrases as "the American people."

We do not suggest that had the "War Message" contained and emphasized the term, citizen, the address itself would have diminished attacks upon Japanese-Americans in the United States. We note only the absence of any protection, a matter of weighting, and thus conclude that the address contributed to the development of a climate for the attacks by strengthening the attitudes of those who, for whatever reasons, wished to attack. Equally important, those wishing to counter such attacks could find in the "War Message" of the President little to support them and the Japanese-Americans.

Though the primary concern of this analysis has been the language of the "War Message," we have in the paragraphs above extended the analysis and speculated upon possible cultural effects. We have done so because the major elements of any speech work on listeners' perceptions and when other factors, rhetorical and non-rhetorical, are present, perceptions become translated into behavior.

IV

We have centered on the language of an address because in much published criticism language has been neglected in favor of analysis of other factors in the rhetorical environment. What goes on in a speech? has been the question. To say that the "last night" series (20–25) is parallel and repetitive, thus contributing force and energy, is to say too little. We have tried to link the section with preceding and following configurations of language and to analyze closely the section itself. The "last night" series is not in the active voice merely because the active voice is clear, direct, and emphatic, among other things. Had the series been structured differently, the image would have become static and less able to sustain the speaker's conclusion about the magnitude of Japanese activity: "a surprise offensive extending throughout the Pacific area" (26–27). The "last night" series is the turning point in the address; following it the United States becomes active, reacting to the events of yesterday. Had the series been structured differently, the Japanese actors would have become less central and the reaction of the United States more difficult to direct and focus.

[44] Richard M. Weaver, *The Ethics of Rhetoric* (Chicago, 1953), pp. 16, 187–188.

Though it makes sense for the speaker to choose to handle the Japanese Empire as "marginal" in his first recognition of the enemy (1–3), it makes equal sense for him to place the Japanese in a central position in the "last night" series. To expose linguistic strategies of rhetoric one needs thus to see language as "moving," as "linking," and as "ordering a hierarchy."

The critical posture here has been microcosmic; the analysis, microscopic. Such analysis does not reveal much about discourse in general. Yet it may be helpful to those who search for orderly methodologies for dealing with all rhetorical activities and processes. The interplay of the microcosmic and the macrocosmic may yield insights which will lead to more fruitful and productive rhetorical criticism.

STUDIES OF A SPEECH: DOUGLAS MacARTHUR'S "ADDRESS TO CONGRESS"

These critiques of MacArthur's "Address to Congress" establish the excitement and the problems of the more immediate reaction. There seemed to be no middle ground, and sides were violently taken and held. But the man, his personality, his ideas, and his language, all became enmeshed in the moment of history, and the problem of distinguishing among the man, the issues, and the speech—and one's own general political position—should have been the work of only the coolest analysts. All these studies must be considered general in that they touch many different aspects of the situation and speech and defy neat categories. They can serve as prefaces to more particular papers, which, hopefully, will be developed.

The Symposium is a gathering of widely differing reactions by responsible critics in politics, journalism, and education. Because the statements are frustrating in both variety and brevity, they are difficult to accept and equally difficult to challenge. But they see certain directions worth following while demonstrating the intensity of the reaction to MacArthur's speech.

Wylie, with more room, challenges MacArthur's logic and unexplored consequences of policy and, more importantly, demands arguments the General did not use. In replying to Wylie, Beall rightly and heatedly emphasizes the immediate context in judging the soundness of the speech, but he slides away from most of the issues Wylie raises.

Beaven presents, by indirection, something of an interim report on Mac-Arthur's speeches. Attempting the even tones of an objective critic, he praises MacArthur as speaker but prudently notes the limited evidence the General used to support the issues.

Wallace, some two years after the speech, gives quick summaries of previous opinions, as well as both direct and indirect judgments of those opinions. But he says, "My purpose is not to enter the lists as a critic of MacArthur's speech. Rather I intend to function here only as a student of rhetorical criticism; to observe critics at work, and to comment on what I find." He is asking, in part, what has been gained by the published reactions? What are the limits of rhetorical criticism? Along with Wylie he is concerned in particular with

227

examining the possible lines of argument as well as the ones actually used and with scrutinizing the structure of the speech itself.

Obviously more needs to be said on MacArthur as both thinker and speaker and on his "Address to Congress." The genuinely surprising first observation is that no speech journal has carried any article on that speech in all these years since Wallace's indirect observations of 1953. There has been no attempt to account for the earlier interpretations, to study his preparation or describe his delivery, to analyze his ideas or his audience, to face directly the structure and language of this speech, a clearly significant one if only as a sociological phenomenon. If these gaps in our understanding of the "Address to Congress" should perhaps not be filled, we need to know why. The evidence of these collected reactions and of the issues they raise indicates that we do need to know more, that this speech could serve as a test case for critics. What happened, what did it mean, and what does it mean?

Two inexpensive paperbacks of documents and analyses could serve as the next step: The Truman-MacArthur Controversy, edited by Richard Lowit,[1] and The MacArthur Controversy and American Foreign Policy, edited by Richard Rovere and Arthur M. Schlesinger, Jr.[2]

[1] Chicago: Rand McNally, 1963 (Berkeley Readings in American History Series, No. 17).
[2] New York: Farrar, Straus & Giroux, 1965.

10

General
MacArthur's
Speech:
A Symposium
of Critical
Comment

Frederick W. Haberman

The forty-nine million Americans who composed the radio, television, and face-to-face audience that heard General Douglas MacArthur's address to the Joint Session of Congress on April 19, 1951, became speech critics overnight. Their criticism had quantity and it had intensity. It ranged from Representative Dewey Short's statement in the *Congressional Record* (April 19, p. 4238): "We saw a great hunk of God in the flesh, and we heard the voice of God" to the opinion that the speech was Satanic in its power to evoke chaos. Like these two examples, much of the criticism was a blend of happy emotionalism and the urge to formulate dicta; but much of it was aesthetic and philosophical. To gather a set of comments on this extraordinary speech and to obtain some samples of contemporary criticism, I invited critics from three groups to contribute to this symposium.

[Frederick W. Haberman is Professor of Speech and Chairman of the Department at the University of Wisconsin. This article originally appeared in the *Quarterly Journal of Speech*, xxxvii (October 1951), 321–31, and is reprinted with the permission of the author and the Speech Association of America.]

The Congressional critics include Joseph W. Martin, Jr., Minority Leader of the House of Representatives; Senator Robert S. Kerr, of Oklahoma; Senator Karl E. Mundt, of South Dakota (formerly Professor of Speech); Senator Hubert H. Humphrey, of Minnesota; Senator Alexander Wiley, of Wisconsin; and Representative Robert J. Corbett, of Pennsylvania (formerly a coach of forensics). The journalist critics include Richard H. Rovere, contributor to *The New Yorker*; Quincy Howe, School of Journalism and Communications, University of Illinois; and William T. Evjue, editor and publisher of *The Capital Times*, Madison, Wisconsin. Included in the third group—the academic critics—are W. Norwood Brigance, Wabash College; Herbert A. Wichelns, Cornell University; Wilbur Samuel Howell, Princeton University; Henry L. Ewbank, University of Wisconsin; and A. Craig Baird, State University of Iowa. In my letter of invitation to these critics, I made one suggestion—that the commentary be brief.

I. CONGRESSIONAL CRITICS

Joseph W. Martin, Jr.

In politics, the effectiveness of a speech is measured by its ability to strengthen friendships and win converts. Usually the most effective political speeches contain comprehensive thought, breadth of viewpoint, humor, warmth of words, and emotional impact. All too frequently, political addresses "sound" better than they "read."

The address of General MacArthur to the Joint Meeting of Congress was a masterpiece of context and delivery, possibly the great address of our times, certainly surpassing, in my opinion, the first Roosevelt Inaugural speech in 1933 and the Winston Churchill address to the Joint Session of Congress in 1942. When a speech moves Members of Congress to tears, its impact cannot be denied. In my 27 years in Congress, there has been nothing to equal it.

The MacArthur address not only "sounded" in a masterful fashion, it "reads" even better. Each sentence is freighted with thought; each word is at work. Its logic, its simple directness, its clear-cut statement of the issues, and its orderly exposition make the structure of the speech a model for all to follow.

It was a monumental effort.

Robert S. Kerr

I listened earnestly and carefully to General MacArthur's speech. I looked for unity. I didn't find it. I watched for an acknowledgment of the necessity to maintain the integrity of civilian control of the military power. It was not there. I searched for language that would give hope of a limited conflict and a purpose to prevent the spread into world-wide conflagration. He did not provide it.

I listened for words which would promote cooperation between this nation and our allies for collective security. Those words were not spoken. I expected him who had been in command of the United Nations forces to acknowledge and report on his stewardship and tell how to strengthen the common front. He did not even mention the United Nations or a single ally.

I hoped he would show the way to promote peace and prevent more or larger war. He was not looking in that direction.

Instead, if I understood him, he sounded a call for an expanded war, a second front for sure, and a third front, if it came. The General spoke sadly, but I was much sadder because I was convinced that his plan would not lead us upward to the goal of peace, but would hurl us downward to the awful road of total war.

Karl E. Mundt

The speech Douglas MacArthur delivered to the joint meeting of the House of Congress upon his return from Korea seems destined to become one of the classics of the English language.

Sitting as I did about twenty feet directly in front of General Mac-Arthur as he stood at the front of the chamber of the House of Representatives I had an opportunity to view at close range the presentation of an oratorical masterpiece which was excelled in its composition only by the skillful prowess with which it was delivered to those who heard it in person and to the many millions who gave it their rapt attention via radio and television. Without any apparent oratorical effort, MacArthur from the very beginning and by the very force of his sincerity and his magnetic personality held the intense attention of the audience he was to go on to inspire and captivate. He was the complete master of the occasion all the way.

What were the superb qualities of the great speaker that MacArthur so vividly exemplified? High on the list of factors contributing to MacArthur's mastery of the situation was the sincerity and the obvious earnestness he radiated. His choice of vivid words, his balanced phraseology, his great reserve power, his facial expression, and the eye contact he managed to maintain with the audience without doing violence to his manuscript all contributed to the excellence of his delivery and the convincing impact of his message. Even those who were later to disagree with him and to criticize his recommendations were caught in the magnetism of the occasion;

there were very few who had temerity enough to offer quick rejoinder to the arguments presented.

My experience as a college speech teacher impelled me to rate Churchill, Roosevelt, and Madame Chiang Kai-shek—in that order—as the most impressive speakers I had heard before joint meetings of the Congress in my fourteen years there prior to the MacArthur speech. Without question, and by general agreement of most of us who had heard all four of them in person, Douglas MacArthur stood out spectacularly above them all.

Perhaps it was the near perfect control of his inflections, perhaps his impressive posture and actions, perhaps the emphasis with which he stressed his points without ever appearing to approximate his full powers of expression—whatever it was, no other speaker in our generation has moved strong men of politics to open tears and caused even those who disagreed with his position to praise his oratorical ability with unhesitating superlatives. In brief, the MacArthur address to Congress demonstrated once again the prowess of the spoken word; it gave new proof that men can still be moved and policies determined by those who excel in the arts of speech.

Hubert H. Humphrey

General MacArthur's speech was a masterful presentation by a persuasive man rising at a dramatic occasion to give reason and justification for his life's work and life's reputation. There is no doubt that it affected every member of the Congress who heard him. His manner, poise, language, and the strength of his voice helped create an impression favorable to him and consistent with the myth associated with him and carefully developed over the past few years.

The issues represented by General MacArthur's speech, however, are far more important than the personality questions involved and more significant than the techniques of speech he has so artistically developed. It is to those issues I enter my dissent.

In my judgment, the basic issue involved in the controversy is one of civilian versus military control over our foreign policy. In a democracy, the elected representatives of the people are responsible for determining foreign policy, and this responsibility is not vested in the military leaders. This is one of the essential elements of our historical tradition. It is part of our Constitution. In dismissing General MacArthur, President Truman, as Commander-in-Chief under our Constitution, had no choice. The General—a brilliant and able military leader—disagreed with our government's foreign policy and with the recommendations of General Marshall and the Joint Chiefs of Staff. No government can exist so divided in policy, since no government can be guided by two inconsistent foreign programs. General MacArthur, as an individual, has a perfect right to disagree with our Government's foreign policy but he has no right and no prerogative as a military commander to formulate his own policy in opposition to policy established by our Government.

I welcomed General MacArthur's arrival in the United States and his address to the Congress. It brought with it a complete re-examination of our foreign policy, particularly as it affected the Far East. There is no doubt in my mind that at the conclusion of the debate, with the fading away of emotions and the supremacy of reason, the American people will come to see that President Truman was correct in removing General MacArthur. It is my hope that, even as they come to disagree with the General's policies and regret his human failings, they will not allow it to interfere with their judgment of him as a great military leader.

Alexander Wiley

The basic standard by which to evaluate a speech is whether or not it actually succeeds in its objective. Does it sell the speaker's ideas, the speaker's personality? Does it win the audience?

Based on that standard, General MacArthur's address to the Congress and to the American people was a masterpiece of effectiveness. It has been stated that at many times during his speech there was hardly a dry eye in the entire audience—so emotional was its impact.

It should be remembered that although the General had the sympathetic admiration of practically all Americans in view of his fifty-two years of honored military service, he faced a seen and unseen audience which was sharply divided (then as now) as to the major policy points he was recommending. Many members of Congress particularly on the Democratic side of the aisle knew that their every favorable manifestation—applause, cheers, etc.,—might be interpreted as an implied slap at their Chief Executive, the head of the Democratic party. Nevertheless, they gave themselves almost unrestrainedly in rousing general support of the General even though they did not completely reflect Republican enthusiasm for MacArthur's specific suggestions.

Rarely has a divided audience been so attentive to a speech. Judged from every technical standpoint, the General's comments came across with brilliant diction, masterly timing, keen logical sequence, splendid choice of words. Because he was the thorough master of his subject and of the specific phrasing of his speech, he could look up at the television cameras and at the audience in such a way as to maintain perfect rapport.

MacArthur's speech helped, moreover, to disprove many false ideas about him. To those individuals who had swallowed the false line about MacArthur's arrogance, he came to be respected as a man of great humility. To those individuals who were convinced that he was anxious to precipitate a partisan controversy, he emerged as a true statesman who avoided all references to personalities and who gallantly accepted the cruel dismissal action. To other individuals who had assaulted his basic motives, MacArthur's objective approach knocked the ground from under them. Douglas MacArthur, in summary, made an historic address which will be reviewed by future generations as one of the great expositions in the history of oratory.

It should be remembered that not just any individual could have made a speech of such stature. It was a great speech, delivered by a great American, at a great time in the history of our country and of the world. Assuming that combination of circumstances, the speech was a masterpiece. Had it been offered by any individual other than MacArthur, and at any other time, under any other circumstances, it would not have "come off." As it is, it has become a classic in American history.

Robert J. Corbett

The address of General of the Army Douglas MacArthur to the Joint Meeting of Congress was one of the outstanding speeches of modern history. This is true, not because of extraordinary eloquence, excellent delivery, masterful phrasing, or thought-compelling philosophy. The speech was great because it met the situation exactly as it was designed to do.

The situation was as tense and drama-packed as any that ever happened. Tens of millions had waited since the hour of his dismissal for this moment. Few had ever seen or listened to this almost mythical person. Here at last he stood in the halls of Congress after years of absence from the country, and after a long trip, punctuated with tremendous receptions and covered in minutest detail in the press and on the radio. He could fall or triumph. His case could be lost completely. His whole career could end in a sorry flop. Seldom has so much depended on a single speech.

The speech was great because it met that tremendous situation with unbelievable perfection. The speech did what it was supposed to do. It explained the General's point of view clearly and persuasively. It said what was necessary to say and little more. It matched and multiplied the tense emotional feeling that gripped the nation. The speech was the test of the whole man and his whole career. He and it measured up.

I do not believe that MacArthur's speech should be dissected and analyzed. It can't be studied as a thing apart from the whole circumstance with any hope of understanding or appreciation. It was a great speech because it did a great job.

II. JOURNALIST CRITICS

Richard H. Rovere

As a literary critic and political observer, I view the speech solely from the literary and political points of view. I am not qualified to criticize oratory or elocution.

As a piece of composition, the speech seemed to me a good deal but not a great deal better than the general run of public prose in the United States today. MacArthur has eloquence of a kind, but it strikes me as a rather coarse eloquence. He never shades his meanings, never introduces a note of humor, never gives the feeling that he is one man, only one, addressing himself to other men. His language is never flat and bloodless; neither is it flabby and loose-jointed, as so much writing of this sort is. But to me there is rather a fetid air about it. It does not leave me with the impression that a cool and candid mind has been at work on difficult matters of universal concern. Instead, it leaves me with the impression that a closed and in a sense a rather frantic mind has been at work to the end of making an appeal to history—not neglecting to use any of the rule-book hints on how to do it. I think not of history but of second-rate historians as I read the speech.

Form and content are, if not inseparable, very closely related. Politically, MacArthur's speech seemed extremely weak to me. This is not, I think, because I am opposed to his politics; I believe he could have made out a much stronger case for himself. But he never came to grips with the issues. For example, he wanted to have it that he was being persecuted for "entertaining" his particular views. This, of course, is rubbish. He got into trouble not for the political and military views he entertained (no doubt he was right in saying they were entertained by many of his colleagues) but for seeking to usurp the diplomatic function. He never sought to answer the objections to his position that rest on political and economic facts recognized by both sides: that if we followed him, we would be abandoned by several allies; that if Russia invaded Europe, which he has admitted might be an early consequence of his policy, the industrial balance would favor the Communist world; that, like it or not, American power does have its limitations. MacArthur's policy may be sounder than Truman's. But this contention cannot be sustained without facing these stubborn facts about the world today. MacArthur, in his speech, never faced them.

Quincy Howe

In a period that produced Winston Churchill and Franklin D. Roosevelt, General MacArthur stands out as perhaps the greatest actor of them all.

Churchill and Roosevelt knew how to express many different moods. MacArthur has less versatility, but greater power within his own field. It is perhaps no accident that his first wife chose as her second husband the professional actor, Lionel Atwill, for MacArthur might also have made a great career for himself on the stage. But he had wider interests and abilities and chose soldiering instead. Finally, at the tragic climax of a dramatic career, he found himself called upon to play before both Houses of Congress the part of the old soldier who did his duty as God gave him to see that duty. By a coincidence, rare in the history of drama, the man who acted the part of the old soldier happened himself to be an old soldier whose experiences precisely resembled the experiences of the old soldier whose part he was enacting. The result was a fusion of man and actor, of reality and illusion, unique in the history of politics and drama. The qualities that make a man a great actor require a student of the drama to define. But the student of history with any experience or interest outside his special field can hardly fail to recognize that MacArthur certainly belongs in the company of Edwin Booth and William Jennings Bryan. His position as a statesman seems to this observer measurably lower than that of Harry S. Truman.

William T. Evjue

An injustice is being done to Abraham Lincoln by those who are claiming that General MacArthur's speech to the Congress is "another Gettysburg address." There is a great difference in the two speeches, as there is a great difference in the two men. One was a humble, sincere, and warmly human man of the people. The other is a mighty warrior, a showman conscious of the part he is playing and the destiny which he seeks to fashion for himself. The climax of Lincoln's greatest speech was a deathless expression of the ideal of democracy. The center of Douglas MacArthur's speech was Douglas MacArthur. The climax was a plea for sympathy for an "old soldier" "fading away."

There is a vast difference between the beautiful simplicity of Lincoln's address and the straining for colorful expression found in MacArthur. Some of it is downright hammy and some would not pass muster in a college freshman theme. For example, MacArthur's statement that the last words of the Korean people to him were: "Don't scuttle the Pacific," belongs in the department of statements that were never made. This is corn. In developing his hunch that the Russians would not enter a war on the side of the Chinese, MacArthur said: "Like the cobra, any new enemy will more likely strike whenever it feels that the relativity in military or other potential is in its favor on a worldwide basis." The simile reveals a striving for effect that makes the thought ridiculous. It conjures up the ludicrous picture of a cobra looking over reports from its intelligence service before it strikes to make sure that the "relativity in military or other potential is in its favor on a worldwide basis."

Outstanding in MacArthur's address was the obvious and amazing lack of knowledge of China. The General in the past has been given to speaking of the "Oriental mind"—an expression, incidentally, of which the Orientals deeply disapprove. It is a concept without foundation; just as much as the "Occidental mind," or the "American mind," or the "Wisconsin mind," or the "Madison mind" is baseless in social psychology.

In his speech the General said that the Asian people seek "friendly guidance . . . not imperious direction." But in a letter to the V.F.W. on August 28, 1950, he wrote that it is "in the pattern of the Oriental psychology to respect and follow aggressive, resolute and dynamic leadership." The general said that sixty percent of the world's resources lie in Asia. Does he include the inaccessible coal and the non-existent steel? He said that the "war-making tendency [up to 50 years ago] was almost non-existent, as they still followed the tenets of the Confucian ideal of pacifist culture." Any student of Chinese history knows that this "pacifist culture" was chiefly marked by centuries of bloody strife between competing war lords. Actually Confucianism is no more pacifist than Christianity. Would a Chinese speaker be right if he told his people that the Christian nations did not make war because Christ taught the ways of peace?

Students of Chinese history are shocked that the General in his discussion of the unification of China failed to mention the name of Sun Yat-sen. MacArthur gave credit to Chang Tso-lin, thus choosing a Manchurian warlord in preference to Dr. Sun, who was a great scholar and statesman and whose dream was the establishment of a progressive democracy for his people.

In short, it is inconceivable that his address, with its obvious shortcomings in knowledge of essential historical background, its attention to easy and empty sociological concepts, its emotional preoccupation with vainglory and its regrettable theatrics, could even be compared to any of Lincoln's great masterpieces.

III.   ACADEMIC CRITICS

W. Norwood Brigance

Three times within the past 15 years high army commanders have found themselves in disagreement with their chief executives. The first, Francisco Franco, led the army against the government, overthrew it by civil war, and set up himself as dictator. The second, Erwin Rommel, was handed a pistol by the executive's agent and told to shoot himself, else he with his family would be executed. The third, Douglas MacArthur, returned from the field of action and presented his case to Congress and to the American people without reprisal or threat of reprisal from the Chief Executive. This is the larger setting for MacArthur's speech. It was not merely a momentous speech. It was not merely the first momentous speech to be delivered to a combined television and radio audience in America. It was also a demonstration of public address as a force in a free society.

MacArthur's audience might be classified into four groups. First was the noncritical mass of people to whom he was an abused war hero. Second were the Republicans—until now hopelessly divided on foreign policy, with Hoover's American Gibraltar wing at one end and the Dulles' world leadership wing at the other—who suddenly and unexpectedly found an issue and a man behind whom they could unite. Third were the Democrats, stunned by the public fury over MacArthur's dismissal, definitely on the defensive, yet hoping that MacArthur would discredit himself before Congress and the nation. Finally were a few thinking critical people who respected MacArthur as a great military leader, but who were half convinced that many years in the Far East had conditioned him to think of issues primarily in terms of Asia only.

Within the first 10 minutes, the Democrats knew that they were in a fight for their survival as a majority party. In a voice that sometimes rasped, seldom rose from a low flat pitch, yet swelled with resonant confidence, he came almost at once to the ultimate issue in the minds of critical listeners. "The issues are global . . . there are those who claim our own strength is inadequate to protect on both fronts, that we cannot divide our effort. I can think of no greater expression of defeatism."

Interrupted by applause some thirty times, he marched with a soldier's precision from point to point . . . the Asiatic background, the Korean invasion, his call for reinforcements and for political decisions, a resulting military campaign that "forbade victory."

The climax of "old soldiers never die" was perhaps overdone for critics who heard the speech by radio. Some sneered at it as "corn." To those who saw it on television, however, it was emotionally effective, if not indeed spine-tingling and "beyond the limits of ordinary present-day oratory."

The President was probably right in his decision to dismiss MacArthur. MacArthur was probably wrong in his claim that his position was supported by the Joint Chiefs of Staff. In the immediate aftermath of the speech neither of these important issues counted for much. By this speech MacArthur had seized the initiative even as he had done by the audacious landing at Inchon.

Herbert A. Wichelns

Demosthenes had the problem, too: how much to spell out, how formal and explicit to make his proposals. At times Demosthenes judged it best not to "make a motion" but merely to offer comment and advice at large. MacArthur made a similar choice. In the main he chose not to debate, in the sense of formulating proposals and defending them in full. Instead he indicated the heads for debate, leaving no doubt as to the direction of his policy. Definite proposals were few, and sharply limited to Formosa and Korea. Supporting reasons were very sparingly given, and sometimes confined to bare assertions (as on the extent of China's present military commitment and Russia's probable course). But the call for a harder and more aggressive policy is plain from the beginning ("no greater expression of defeatism"). The chief support for that policy is neither logical argument nor emotional appeal, but the self-portrait of the speaker as conveyed by the speech.

It is an arresting portrait. Certain colors are of course mandatory. The speaker respects Congress and the power of this nation for good in the world. He is free from partisanship or personal rancor. He sympathizes with the South Koreans and with his embattled troops. He prefers victory to appeasement. He seeks only his country's good. He hates war, has long hated it. If these strokes are conventional, they take little time, except for the last, on which the speaker feels he must defend himself.

More subtle characterizing strokes are found in the "brief insight into the surrounding area" which forms a good half of the speech. Here the General swiftly surveys the nature of the revolution in Asia, the island-frontier concept and Formosa's place in the island-chain, the imperialistic character of the Chinese communities, the regeneration of Japan under his auspices, the outlook for the Philippines, and the present government of Formosa. All this before reaching Korea. Most of these passages have no argumentative force. But all together they set up for us the image of a leader of global vision, comprehending in his gaze nations, races, continents. The tone is firmest on Japan ("I know of no nation more serene, orderly and industrious"), least sure on the Philippines, but always positive.

Rarely indeed have the American people heard a speech so strong in the tone of personal authority. "While I was not consulted . . . that decision . . . proved a sound one." "Their last words to me"—it is the Korean people with whom the General has been talking. "My soldiers." The conduct of "your fighting sons" receives a sentence. A paragraph follows on the General's labors and anxieties on their behalf. The pace at which the thought moves, too, is proconsular; this is no fireside chat. Illustration and amplification are sparingly used; the consciously simple vocabulary of the home-grown politician is rejected. The housewife who "understood every word" was mistaken; she missed on *epicenter* and *recrudescence* and some others. But having by the fanfare been jarred into full attention, she understood quite well both the main proposition of the speech—a harder policy—and the main support offered—the picture of a masterful man of unique experience and global outlook, wearing authority as to the manner born.

Wilbur Samuel Howell

No prominent speech of the post-war era has contained so strong an appeal to emotion as MacArthur's did. Here was the old soldier in the fading twilight of life still seeking at the end of a career of fifty-two years in the Army to serve his country, even though she had deprived him of command, even though he was the reluctant advocate of an expanded war. Here was the veteran warrior recalling his boyish hopes and dreams on the plain at West Point a half-century earlier, and concluding his speech in part from the words of a popular barracks ballad of his youth and in part from the celebrated accents of Lincoln in the peroration of the Second Inaugural Address.

But these dominant and recurrent appeals would have been more persuasive if they had not clashed with that which he more briefly developed when he spoke of America's fighting sons in Korea. "I can report to you without reservation," he said, "that they are splendid in every way." He then mentioned his own anguish and anxiety at the growing bloodshed of the savage conflict in Korea. Such words would have the effect of arousing similar anguish and anxiety in his audience, and these powerful sympathies would cancel out those which he was bent upon creating towards himself as part of his program of advocacy of what might produce still greater bloodshed.

Ethical ambiguities in his speech tend also to weaken the effect he wanted to have. The only one of these that I shall deal with is so plainly at work that one wonders why he or his political advisers did not correct its injurious influence in advance. Those who listened to him on April 19 may have shared in part at least my feeling of elation when he urged America not to pursue "a course blind to the reality that the colonial era is now past and the Asian peoples covet the right to shape their own free destiny." Here is an ethical standard to which the wise and just can repair. But hardly had these words reached our ears when he declared that from our island chain between the Aleutians and the Marianas "we can dominate with sea and air power every Asiatic port from Vladivostok to Singapore." We do not have to be Asiatics ourselves to feel at this point that in MacArthur's denunciation of colonialism the voice is Jacob's voice, but in his assertion of our power to threaten Asia the hands are the hands of Esau.

As for logic, MacArthur's speech tends to expand into propositions that are easy to grasp and hard to defend. One of these is that all-out war with Communist China should be risked at once, not avoided as long as we can. MacArthur discounts this risk in eleven words—"China is already engaging with the maximum power it can commit." Does not the General miscalculate his rhetorical strategy when he allots so few troops to such a crucial position? An even more crucial position which his strategy requires him to occupy is that America should deliberately risk war with Soviet Russia at this time. But again he does not man the position in strength. He sees that his four recommendations might cause Russia to intervene on the side of China; and then he deals with that grim eventuality so as to discount its possibility, not to calculate its final result. He merely says, "The Soviet will not necessarily mesh its actions with our moves." Even if this is right so far as it goes, it gives our moves a significance that we as a nation have to estimate in terms more exact than those used by the General. Thus it may happen that, with the applause now over and done with, the General's thesis will seem less and less attractive as time goes on.

Henry L. Ewbank

It is difficult to imagine a more dramatic speech situation. A great military hero and speaker of unusual power, just relieved from his command for reasons not generally understood, broadcasts over all major networks his criticisms of the Department of State and the President. It couldn't happen in Russia. We are glad it can happen here.

This speech is part of a "great debate" on our foreign policy and who should determine it. In the main, MacArthur stuck to the issues, labeled his opinions as such, avoided *ad hominem* attacks, and presented his case with poise and dignity.

By way of objective analysis I applied Rudolf Flesch's criteria of readability. He has devised two scales: one measuring "ease of reading," the other "human interest." The reading ease score is based on sentence length and the number of syllables per hundred words. Possible scores range from zero (practically unreadable) to 100 (easy for any literate person). MacArthur's average sentence length is 24.5 words. The shortest has 6; the longest, 80. The number of syllables per hundred words ranges from 130 to 190; the average is 161. His score is 46 (difficult) compared with 70 (fairly easy) for the Gettysburg Address. The human interest score is based on the percentages of "personal words" and "personal sentences." Possible scores range from zero (very dull) to 100 (of dramatic interest). MacArthur's score is 20, on the borderline between "mildly interesting" and "interesting." Listeners who rated the speech higher in clarity and interestingness were probably reacting to the speaker's prestige, the content of his speech, and the excellence of his delivery.

The style is uneven. There are direct skillfully constructed sentences: "It assumes instead the friendly aspect of a peaceful lake"; "We have had our last chance"; "They are blind to history's clear lesson."; "In war there can be no substitute for victory"; "These gallant men will remain often in my thoughts and in my prayers always."

But there are a few words strangers to the average listener, an occasional awkward phrase and some sentences whose precise meaning is not readily apparent: "The whole epicenter of world affairs rotates back toward the area whence it started"; "These political-social conditions . . . form a backdrop to contemporary planning which must be thoughtfully considered if we are to avoid the pitfalls of unrealism"; "China . . . was completely non-homogeneous, being compartmented into groups"; "Efforts toward greater homogeneity produced the start of a nationalist urge"; "I formally cautioned as follows"; "The problem . . . involves a spiritual recrudescence."

One must, it seems, say something about the concluding paragraph. It does not fit our stereotyped picture of Douglas MacArthur, nor has he just faded away. But let him who has not waxed sentimental as he bade his fraternity brothers farewell, or reached the end of his professional career, cast the first stone.

In many ways this was, and is, a great speech. But it will not find an enduring place in our literature as a model of speech composition.

A. Craig Baird

General Douglas MacArthur will be ranked as one of America's outstanding military orators. Partly because of disciplinary and strategic restraints, few modern soldiers have achieved reputations as outstanding speakers. Exceptions occur when military command and political leadership have merged, or when American public opinion of the present decade has invited nationwide, untrammeled reports from such five-star heroes as George Marshall, Dwight Eisenhower, and Douglas MacArthur.

General of the Army MacArthur, before the Joint Session of Congress, on April 19, 1951, was deeply eloquent in his Apologia. His defense was in the tradition of Robert Emmet, before the Dublin court that had condemned him.

The General adequately fulfilled the speaking demands of the situation, with its expectancy of powerful eloquence that should exist "in the man, in the subject, and in the occasion." He is an orator by temperament, by habit, and by long exercise. Before Congress he realized Webster's criterion of the orator as one who possesses boldness, manliness, and energy.

The mode of his discourse, in spite of its logical texture, was primarily personal and ethical—a vindication of his intellectual integrity, wisdom, and good will. The historical-philosophical overview, the delineation of the new strategic frontier in the Pacific, the speech structure and movement, the language at times somewhat Churchillian—all these exalted the mature judgment and common sense of the speaker. The general's understanding of the vast Eastern populations, his sympathy for them, his implications of his own destiny strongly enforced his assumptions about his own character.

MacArthur in this dramatic setting was heroic in his bearing, movements, and gestures. His voice was by turns self-confident, convincing, stern, scornful, righteous.

What were his limitations? His sonorous delivery, occasional volatile phrasing, and calculated peroration were defects due to Asian rather than to Attic style. Pericles would presumably have composed and delivered this oration with more artistic subtlety, sense of order, freedom from extravagance, with more intellectual severity and emotional balance.

If MacArthur had not been a soldier for the past fifty-two years, he could have become a statesman of stature. For he has much of the parliamentary grand manner and an eloquence that the age has not outgrown.

11

Medievalism
and the
MacArthurian
Legend

Philip Wylie

On April 19th, 1951, General Douglas MacArthur stood before the Congress of the United States of America to make a speech which perhaps enjoyed greater advance prestige than any previous human utterance. The General was regarded by millions as America's foremost hero; his eloquence was renowned; his military genius was thought by multitudes to have won the Pacific War; as a statesman he was deemed to have performed in Japan almost overnight the perfect revolution—bloodless, ennobling, and irreversible; as a man, he was handsome and charming, magnetic, persuasive, domineering (but only as a good leader must be), and above all *colorful* in a way that took the breath and stung the eyes of legions of his fellow citizens.

The civilized world was electronically connected with the rostrum from which the General spoke. He had been the Light of the West in Asia—and he had just been recalled from that service to his country by a President whom millions regarded as so inferior that the very reason for the recall—repeated insubordination—merely added further outrage to their fury. It was confidently predicted that what MacArthur was about to

[Philip Wylie, the noted polemicist, is the author of A *Generation of Vipers* and many other works. This article originally appeared in the *Quarterly Journal of Speech*, xxxvii (December 1951), 473–78, and is reprinted with the permission of the author and the Speech Association of America.]

say would take a place beside Washington's Farewell Address and Lincoln's short speech at Gettysburg. "School children," murmured one Senator, with tears in his eyes, "will commit to memory the words we are about to hear."

Then MacArthur spoke—and a week later no one could accurately recall a paragraph.

He began with a homily on the psychology of Oriental peoples wherein he soon commenced to contradict himself. He next recommended a defensive system in the Pacific similar to the one which had calamitously failed when he was in command of it. He followed with a report on Japan which, in view of naked fact, sounded like quotations from Pollyanna. He asked for an extension of our military frontiers in the Korean struggle and offered an unsupported opinion that such enlargements of the fronts would not precipitate war with Russia. He executed what has become a necessary gambit, these days, for every military leader: a staunch assertion of hatred for war. And he concluded with what should have been a most appealing reminder: that he had served his country for fifty-two years.

Amidst cheering and weeping, he sat down.

Unfortunately for him, the speech was immediately set in print, where men could study it without emotion. It then appeared that the one moving portion of his address, the part that referred to fifty-two years of service and tendered his adieus, was not "great" or even dignified; it was rather a composition of a sort less sonorous men call "corn"; and its thesis that he had done his duty and would "fade away" was belied by his rush to a hundred-dollar-a-day suite in New York's most lavish hotel and a tour of America's cities comparable to a victorious Caesar's home-coming.

Nothing for schoolchildren to remember appeared in the speech. Not a single new principle or concept was added to those in current discussion. No vivid turn of phrase gave fresh content to the ancient ideals. Indeed, as oratory, the talk contained many sentences that would have been stricken from a high school theme. Here is an example: "Like a cobra any new enemy will more likely strike wherever it feels that the relativity in military or other potential is in its favor on a world-wide basis." Sententious, awkward, absurd in its simile, such talk may in truth be "purple" but that is all.

Millions expected MacArthur to show the way out of the "Korean mess." The same millions, by and large, feared and detested all fighting. They were left—when, finally, they stopped to think about it—with the gnawing worry that what the General had proposed might get them swiftly into conflict a thousand times worse. Americans who are obliged to make plans concerning the world (not just extravagant gestures toward Asians) found no new bearings behind the ringing timbre of authority. For our dilemma could not be worldwide as MacArthur stated and at the same time depend wholly upon Asia, as he insisted. Even the Chinese, of whom he spoke with such assurance, could not be two kinds of people at once: "There is little of the ideological concept either one way or another in the Chinese make-up," he said. But he had said, one paragraph before, of China, that it had become in fifty years, "militarized in ... concepts and ideals ... a new and dominant power ... allied with Soviet Russia but ... in its own concepts and methods ... aggressively imperialistic with a lust for expansion."

Now, either the Chinese are non-ideological and mainly interested in a better living standard, as MacArthur asserted, or they are imperialistic and communistic as he described them. They cannot be both.

What emerged, in sum, was an intellectual chaos, alarming in one so highly placed and in one with so relevant a background. MacArthur's views on Asia were not acceptable because they were incoherent.

A second sort of self-delusion is to be seen in his statements about the Japanese who, under his regime, have erected "an edifice dedicated to the primacy of individual liberty and personal dignity." He went on to say that "politically, economically and socially Japan is now abreast of many free nations of the earth and will not again fail the universal trust." Such talk has here been cited to the Pollyanna school; a better word for it is hogwash. At present, Japan depends upon American largesse for mere survival. Japan's economic future under any other aegis is inscrutable, since it would turn upon recapturing the markets of China, currently communist. In the longer range of time, Japan's plight seems hopeless. For the Japanese birth rate is rapidly lowering the standard of living and setting up the same situation that keeps India a human shambles: too many mouths for the food supply.

How any honest intelligence could ignore such fundamental factors is impossible to imagine. But the General waved them aside.

He waved aside Europe. Subsequently, during his long interrogation, it appeared that he felt himself ill-equipped to "think" about Europe. Hence, the effect of all he said on some two hundred millions of our most industrialized and best educated associates in the struggle against communism was one of absolute shock and utter horror. By ignoring them, the General had written them off: Asia must be salvaged but America can neglect England, France, Italy, the Benelux countries, Germany, the Near East, and so on. MacArthur talked like a man on a ship who felt that if he worked to keep his half afloat it did not matter if the other half foundered. He called the crisis "global" but the globe, to MacArthur, is limited to the area he knows.

Those are some of the conspicuous examples of his faulty logic and his disdain of fact. Many more could be noted. Concerning America's military security he asserted flatly, "Any predatory attack from Asia must be an amphibious effort." It is interesting to remember that, although Japan was approached by "amphibious efforts," the main islands fell without such onslaught. Even while MacArthur spoke, vast American agencies were being formed, funds were being levied, and the laws of all forty-eight states were being changed, to make ready for a "predatory" atomic attack upon the U.S.A. by air alone. Indeed, the most bizarre blank in the General's "thinking" (and in his address) was the absence of any consideration of the new-style, atomic attack that certainly will occur if war becomes global. What is at the very least a consummate hazard for America as a whole—not just as a military establishment—was ignored by MacArthur.

The fact is that—if he were a man of imagination and insight—rather than to exploit the confused causes of distant Asia he might well have chosen to discuss the failure of Congressional leaders to prepare the American people for atomic bombardment.

The probable nature of any next war is, in this author's opinion, our most critical current problem; it could and should be visualized for all the people and for that majority of their representatives who are too ill-educated to understand. The next war may be won or lost, not with troops or navies or airplanes, but in the streets of cities and through the valor or the panic of opposed civilians under assault by weapons of mass destruction and terror. MacArthur, alas, seems incapable even of considering such a possibility. The name he has given it publicly is "hysteria." That term in its two principal senses of inappropriate reaction or absence of required reaction, seems to fit not those who are informed and anxious but the General himself. He must be unable to understand the august scientific problems involved, since he ignores them—even conceives them to be emotional.

His speech gave one clue to the nature of his intellectual quandary. Thoughtful men see the world in the midst of a terrible conflict between men who want to be free and men who want to impose a "system." But, to MacArthur, *The problem basically is theological."*

If that is so, we are probably doomed. For, in America, it is the constitutional right of each person to take whatever "theological" view he sees fit and none has the right to impose his dogma on the rest. Only the communists have an absolute and international "theology," with Marx as its God-head, Lenin as its Savior, Stalin as its High Priest, the Manifesto as its creed, and a power to impose identical belief by physical means transcending even the frenzy of that "Christian" anomaly, the Inquisition. Among men still largely free, or hoping again to be free, this is not the time for "theological" propaganda. Such a use of the word by a potential American leader will shock all who understand what liberty has meant here for two centuries. If we cannot agree that we are endeavoring to establish a free world and imagine, instead, we are seeking a "theology," the communists, who have a perfected brand, will surely undo us for not knowing what we are trying to do! The obeisance MacArthur later paid the Catholic Church in the person of Cardinal Spellman sharply emphasized the General's sense of "theology" as distinguished from freedom.

Of such notions spoke MacArthur, sabotaging the best opportunity for a speech ever offered in history. His words startled many of the people who until then had almost revered him. They touched off a nation-wide squabble about policy which soon faded away. The speech in Washington was followed by equally confused and confusing harangues on domestic matters—words of a man who had been away from home for half a generation. Yet crowds still yelled for him and one Representative, after the address, insisted he had just listened to "a large hunk of God."

The question raised by the speech is thus not limited to the speech itself. The only praise an honest man can give the address is that it was well-delivered. The important aspect is the impact of MacArthur himself upon so many of his fellow-citizens. Even after cold type had revealed the faults and flaws and grievous gulfs in the old soldier's thought processes, many millions of plain people still believed him the next thing to God, and many leading politicians behaved as if they agreed—because at the moment, it seemed expedient. Perhaps only the President, who had dealt so long with the General and who was regarded by so many as his measureless inferior, knew enough to anticipate what would happen. He could have silenced MacArthur with a sentence; instead, he let him talk. He is supposed to have said, rather wryly, that by talking, the General would soon disillusion all but his blindest followers. And, of course, MacArthur has done just that: where now is his boom for President?

Two factors, in the opinion of this writer, are responsible for the fast-tarnishing "MacArthur legend."

In the first place, the legend was handmade by the General himself. Throughout the war his lurid statements warmed the hearts of the simple-minded majority even when they threw no light whatever on the military situation. But his censorship was sometimes as strict as the late Doctor Goebbels'. The officers around him, including his press officers, were selected for "personal loyalty"—a total adulation achieved at the expense of detachment and by the extirpation of the critical function. It was "loyalty" such as Hitler once demanded and Stalin requires today. Among men who regard "equality" as an ideal—even among many military men—such an attitude seemed pompous, ego-maniacal, the very essence of what is "un-American." Nevertheless the requirement of total adulation served to insure that whatever got through to the American public about MacArthur from his headquarters enlarged his personal grandeur. Contrary opinion and contrary fact were discouraged, brushed aside, denied, and ignored. Their purveyors were punished if possible. Correspondents with the "Dugout Doug" slant, those who wondered aloud about the General's private fortune, those who resisted policies-in-contradiction-to-reality, were sometimes sent back to the U.S.A. A legend was ruthlessly nourished. Only when the General himself came home to save the country was it sadly, almost shamefully, apparent that the press-agentry had created mere myth.

Historians alone can judge MacArthur's competence—and his failings—as a military man. But one quality he had: color. In an age of Trumans and Tafts, a post-Roosevelt age, color is the aspect least visible in national leadership. Beside MacArthur all the other generals, including even Eisenhower, pale. And color, above other qualities, is what the American people "buy," whether in packaged goods, motor cars, or leaders. The hat, the bravura of "I shall return," the carefully screened aspect of jauntiness, the orotund defiance, the profile, the voice—those qualities were vivid precisely when and where other men were merely efficient and effective, brave without a halo of self-congratulation. MacArthur often seemed great when he was merely grandiose—or gaudy.

In our dark years, moreover, he shone not only through contrast but because we so desperately and truly needed greatness in our leadership. During all such Toynbeean times of trouble the mob invariably invents what it needs but lacks; MacArthur knew the need and abetted the invention but he did not and cannot fill the lack.

The fable of the king whose tailor cut for him a suit of thin air, in which His Highness paraded for the admiration of all his subjects save one honest-eyed boy, is not just a fable; it states a basic principle of mass psychology. Lincoln said it another way; and for a while, MacArthur fooled nearly all the people. Illusion and delusion are universal properties of the senses and of so-called reason (as the psychologists at Princeton and Dartmouth have just expensively and rather redundantly proved). MacArthur staged illusions for a vast body of people who, lacking the real thing, were emotionally in a state to accept the ersatz. In the last analysis, that condition of the public, not the intellectual immaturity of the General, is the real hazard.

Our nation is presumably founded upon a principle which makes one special and peculiar leader unnecessary. Leading ourselves is a right and a duty we refuse jealously to transfer to any individual. However, during the past decades, we have unwittingly abdicated many of our rights and duties, under freedom. The long tenure of Roosevelt, whether in itself good or bad, was psychologically evil from this standpoint: half a generation grew up under political stasis. We have abandoned the core of freedom—freedom of knowledge—owing to duress; today, neither the public nor its elected representatives are privy to the mere knowledge which shapes national policy, consumes our resources, uses up our tax monies, and so on. The secrecy of the atom bomb has become an ubiquitous secrecy; the first concern of our government is military and unknowable. In a philosophical sense we are a partial military dictatorship, however temporary; in a literal sense we are all currently disenfranchised.

We have abrogated rights and values in other categories. The ultimate result of the Depression in the Thirties has been a substitution of the chimera of "security" for the old value of independence. This exchange—in an age of upheaval—is psychologically shaky because it is properly felt to be both unworthy and inadequate. And two thirds of us live, in conscious or unconscious uneasiness, under the menace of the sudden and hideous effects of atomic bombardment. Such circumstances, along with others too many and varied to mention here, have inclined the American people, in my opinion, much farther away from our valid principles than we realize and have, inevitably, made us prey to the sentiments of any near-panicky mob, to the yielding up of personal responsibility, and to the yearning for a leader, a responsibility-taker, a papa, a large hunk of God personified.

But all the "men on horseback" in history, once unhorsed, are seen to have been riding for no greater cause than the childish cravings of the masses and their fears, whether real or synthetic. We may then regard as a hopeful sign the fact that, when Americans saw the General close up, they decided they were not "going his way." For a free people cannot be dominated by any one man or by his theology; and no man who understands liberty can have such an ambition.

12

Viper-Crusher
Turns
Dragon-Slayer

Paul R. Beall

A popular fable of India chronicles the derring-do of a flea who, riding on the back of an elephant, traversed a dangerous chasm over a rickety vine suspension bridge. "We certainly made that old bridge shake, didn't we!" said the flea. Now fleas, as all men who have associated with them know, are embarrassingly perceptive and have a sycophantic sense of humor. It is only reasonable to conclude that the wily jungle flea was playing for laughs.

Similarly, in Mr. Philip Wylie's recent excoriation of General Douglas MacArthur,[1] it is impossible not to suspect that he, at least in some wee degree, was having fun with his own extensive and enthusiastic public. Also, although author Wylie would never stoop to chicanery, he probably knows that, although the most fortunate thing that can happen to a popular writer is to be banned in Boston, the second most bountiful event that may befall him is for a press-wide debate to result in response to his publication of such shockers as (in paraphrased ellipsis) "MacArthur's dignity is corny . . . his English sententious, awkward, absurd in its simile . . . his logic is faulty . . . his appraisal of Japan is Pollyannaish (or 'hogwash') . . . he discouraged correspondents with the 'dugout Doug' slant, thus establishing himself as an egomaniac with the 'loyalty' standards of Hitler

[Paul R. Beall is a commercial consultant in industry and military management in Georgia. This article originally appeared in the *Quarterly Journal of Speech*, xxxviii (February 1952), 51–56, and is reprinted with the permission of the author and the Speech Association of America.]
[1] Philip Wylie, "Medievalism and the MacArthurian Legend," *QJS*, xxxvii (December 1951), 473–478. [Reprinted in this text, pp. 244–50.]

and Stalin . . . he does not know his business—does not understand modern scientific warfare . . . and the General is intellectually immature."[2]

Let such frivolous exacerbation be publicly joined and rejoined for a few rounds, and a sizable bloc of Wylie's "simple-minded majority"[3] will queue up at the book counter. For example, I have already been to the drug store and laid out fifty cents for two Wylie bestsellers to be read for background.

The *Symposium of Critical Comment*[4] on General MacArthur's speech has now reached the stage where critic B is criticizing the criticism of critic A's criticism of the speech, and the end may not be yet. At this point two matters stand clearly: (a) perspicacious and distinguished critics have been in the fray (Congressional critics Martin, Kerr, Mundt, Humphrey, Wiley, and Corbett; journalists Rovere, Howe, and Evjue; speech professors Brigance, Wichelns, Howell, Ewbank, and Baird)[5] and (b) on every known criterion for the judgment of the worth of public address (even including Ewbank's application of Flesch's magic-numbers formula)[6] at least two competent critics stand diametrically in opposition to each other. How far this debate should go in a staid and dignified family publication like *The Quarterly Journal of Speech* is difficult to say. I felt Wylie's piece to be an opinionated rant, *hogwash* (since he finds that euphemism a meaningful critical term), or even *sheep dip*. However, I enjoyed the entire blast hugely, complimented Editor Aly on its publication, and urged that Mr. Westbrook Pegler be invited to write a rejoinder. Instead Professor Aly has asked me to sit in for a hand, and if the readers suffer he must bear the blame.

In concurrence with Senator Mundt[7] and countless others, my rebuttal thesis is that the General's address will become an English language classic—even a world classic in oratory.

Although Rovere[8] feels that his adverse judgments on the speech are uninfluenced by his personal opposition to the General's politics, I must confess that my appraisal of the address is influenced by the fact that I sympathize with the General. But, even admitting the bent of my sympathies (which show in every critic, whether he admits it or not—nothing sillier in letters has been evolved than the concept of "objective criticism," at least when a critic is doing the criticizing), I think that Wylie's argument *in toto*, as well as each issue separately, can be reasonably negated.

[2] *Ibid.*
[3] *Ibid.*, p. 476.
[4] Frederick W. Haberman, "General MacArthur's Speech: A Symposium of Critical Comment," xxxvii (October 1951), 321–331. [Reprinted in this text, pp. 229–43.]
[5] *Ibid.*
[6] *Ibid.*
[7] *Ibid.*, p. 322.
[8] *Ibid.*, p. 325.

The "corn" issue is a heated one. It is interesting how exact a meaning this connotative colloquialism seems lately to have acquired. Contemporaneously (though not originally) from "corn-fed," hence hickish, yokelish, rustic, the word now semantically indicates the subtle boundary or point of departure beyond which an emotional performance or expression that is artistically acceptable becomes emotionalism made ridiculous by its poor taste and obviousness.

The judgment of corniness may be subtle and is always subjective, yet whole social groups with a reasonable degree of intellectual and cultural homogeneity are frequently in agreement on corn issues. For example, an educated audience of English-speaking people accepts the balcony scene in *Romeo and Juliet* as convincing, yet an audience of Tibetans or Aleuts might howl at it. American school boys find nothing corny in the heroic defiance, "My only regret is that I have but one life to give for my country," but had Wylie, or I myself for that matter, reported for the *London Public Advertiser* the hanging that prompted the statement, my every instinct tells me we would have played up the contemporaneous equivalent of *corn*, perhaps *fustian* or *bombast*.

The whole point of corn is that it depends upon who you are and how old you are and where you happen to be sitting. *Uncle Tom's Cabin* is played nowadays only as a hilarious burlesque, but I have heard a distinguished historian assert that, had the book never been written, the controversy between the North and South might have been settled around the conference table.

Wylie, sitting on his porch in Florida, may yowl when he reads MacArthur's Philippines landing speech:

People of the Philippines, I have returned. By the grace of Almighty God, our forces stand again on Philippine soil. . . . Rally to me. Let the indomitable spirit of Bataan and Corregidor lead on. As the lines of battle roll forward to bring you within the zone of operations, arise and strike! . . . For your homes and hearths, strike! In the name of your sacred dead, strike! Let no heart be faint. Let every arm be steeled. The guidance of Divine God points the way. Follow in His Name to the Holy Grail of righteous victory.[9]

This is prose of the brightest purple, but the Filipinos to whom it was addressed were not sitting on porches; many were cowering in caves where they had subsisted for painful and weary years. My prophecy is that as long as American children read, "Give me liberty or give me death!" Filipino school children will be reading and declaiming the General's victory exhortation.

Conceding no modern writer to be Wylie's peer as an authority on or

[9] General George C. Kenney, *The MacArthur I Know* (New York: Duell, Sloan and Pearce, 1951), pp. 96–97.

producer of corn, I am nonetheless confident that MacArthur's high emotional periods meet Quintilian's ideal, "Public speaking is a virtue; its excellencies are sourced in man's moral nature; and its criterion is appropriateness." The future will not judge the General's public address to have been corny.

Lambasting the General's English style as "sententious, awkward, absurd in its simile,"[10] Wylie, by a coincidence, uses the same quotation (which he misquotes, substituting *wherever* for *whenever*) that editor Evjue, in the preceding issue of the *QJS*, had employed to support his own adverse opinion of MacArthur's English usage.[11] The sentence, "Like a cobra, any new enemy will more likely strike whenever it feels that the relativity in military or other potential is in its favor on a world-wide basis,"[12] is sub-college freshman work, according to Evjue, and would fail to pass in a high school theme, according to Wylie. From this I conclude that neither Evjue nor Wylie has recently corrected any college or high school English papers. The "cobra" sentence is "terse and energetic in expression, pithy"—*sententious* indeed, as Mr. Webster defines it, although I am aware that Wylie intends a connotative derogation. I have the impression that writer Wylie composes with ease and speed, a skill and competency to be envied rather than deprecated, but perhaps a manner ill suited to rhetorical criticism. Any one who avers that "*hogwash*" labels an alleged exaggeration better than the figure "of the Pollyanna school"[13] should hesitate to designate as awkward a simile which compares a new enemy to a cobra looking for the opportune time to strike. General MacArthur's vocabulary, style, and total speech structure all make their necessary contributions to the wholeness of his great address before the two Houses.

Alleging many examples of faulty logic in the General's talk, Mr. Wylie cites as particularly illogical his assertion, "Any predatory attack from Asia must be an amphibious effort."[14] Such a statement is foolish, says Wylie, in view of the fact that Japan proper fell without an amphibious onslaught. There is poor logic here, but it is in Wylie's criticism rather than the General's statement. (Wylie must both write and *read* rapidly.) Talk of MacArthur's ignorance of the possibilities of atomic attack is nonsense too absurd to refute. Although no man is perfect in being able always to use the exact word, the General is not a loose writer; he does not

---

[10] Wylie, p. 474.
[11] Evjue, in Haberman, *op. cit.*, p. 326.
[12] Senate Document No. 36, *Address of General of the Army Douglas MacArthur, at a Joint Meeting of the Two Houses, in the Hall of the House of Representatives, April 19, 1951* (82nd Congress, 1st Session) (U.S. Govt. Printing Office, Washington, 1951), p. 6. [Reprinted in this text, pp. 88–95.]
[13] Wylie, p. 474.
[14] *Ibid.*, p. 329.

throw language around. To be *predatory* means "to plunder," to "move in and destroy," to "rob," to "carry things away." Certainly no Asiatic power can move in on us without an amphibious effort. The language of the "predatory" quotation is exact and the logic is exquisite. A *careful* reading shows the whole argument of the speech to be logical.

Scholarly Dr. Howell points out an "ethical ambiguity" of the General's that more fairly supports the contention of poor logic. Professor Howell notes that MacArthur says we must recognize the end of the colonial era, only to add later that, in control of the island chain from the Aleutians to the Marianas, "we can dominate with sea and air power every Asiatic port from Vladivostok to Singapore.'[15] For better ethos the General might well have explained that our only purpose in such a blockade would be to keep *ourselves* from being colonized (or pulverized)—not to further Asiatic colonization.

I am only contending that the General made a great speech, not a perfect one. Howell also wonders that the General's political advisers did not caution him to correct the above-mentioned "ethical ambiguity." This wonderment pays the General an unintended compliment. Before the Old Warrior stood up all alone at a joint meeting of the two Houses to defend himself, he sat down all alone and wrote out his defense. No one has suggested that a logographer[16] helped him. If this be a fault, it is a fault of rare uncommonness these days. A more frequent response to a passable piece of public address is, "I wonder who ghosted it."

Mr. Wylie is critical of the General's "self delusion" in presuming to say that the Japanese, during the term of his office as Supreme Allied Commander for occupied Japan, had erected "an edifice dedicated to the primacy of individual liberty and personal dignity" and saying further that "politically, economically and socially Japan is now abreast of many free nations of the earth and will not again fail the universal trust."[17]

Such talk Wylie dismisses as *hogwash*. In his opinion Japan's survival depends upon American largesse and the recapturing of Chinese markets; Japan's plight is probably hopeless anyway because her rapidly rising birthrate will probably force living standards of the island people to the human-shambles level of India.[18] All this may be true; but as criticism it is a *non sequitur*. Some day Fujiyama may come to life, erupt, and kill everyone on its island, although the General didn't mention this possibility either. The critical device of pointing out what a speaker does *not* say is unlimited, but public address commonly lives or dies with the current issues of the dailies upon the basis of what the speaker *does* say.

[15] Howell, *QJS*, xxxviii (October 1951), 329.
[16] *Logographer*: Greek for "spook."
[17] Wylie, p. 474.
[18] *Ibid.*, p. 474.

I have talked with many people who have visited Japan or worked there during the term of MacArthur's administration. Military leaders, economists, educators, and industrialists have all spoken favorably of the General's success in rehabilitating the morale of the Japanese people as well as their economy. Similar favorable reports have been and still are commonplace in the press. Wylie's opinion on this issue stands rather shakily alone.

In one of his back-stabbing criticisms Wylie hoists himself on his own poniard. Lamenting the General's "pompous and ego-maniacal" conduct in allegedly being responsible for sending home correspondents who had the " 'Dugout Doug' slant,"[19] Mr. Wylie seems inadvertently to lend support to an unsavory journalistic practice. As I comprehend the meaning of free-dom of the press, it involves an idealism that winces at dishonest propa-ganda lines as perverting freedom to the level of license.

For all of Wylie's lament, it must be noted that the slanted corre-spondents were not throttled. The slant seems still to be coming through. There are, however, limitations to the successful use of the propaganda technic of the Big Lie. The General's reputation for personal bravery during his life as a soldier hazards no danger from the efforts of the little men with the "Dugout Doug" slant. On this issue the best rejoinder is from General George C. Kenney, "Perhaps the term 'Dugout Doug' is meant to emphasize an entirely opposite characteristic of the man—like calling a fat man 'Skinny.' "[20]

Arguing that the General does not know his professional business, Wylie again makes a big point of criticizing him for things he did not say. Wylie says that since he did not talk about the dangers of mass civilian atomic bombing it may be concluded that the General "must be unable to understand the august scientific problems involved."[21] The terrible tech-nic of war does not fit exact or limited formulae. During his allotted speak-ing time the General necessarily was limited in the aspects of his subject he could cover. Wylie thinks he selected his issues unwisely bceause he failed to talk about the atomic bomb. Others have said that he should have referred to the problems of antisubmarine warfare, guided missiles, chemical warfare, and what not. I have not, however, heard any other person, civilian or military, avow that the General is ignorant of scientific warfare. On this point his military career from his days at West Point, where he earned the highest four-year average ever recorded at the Acad-emy, through his progress to youngest Chief of Staff of the United States Army and, indeed, all of his life as a soldier speak eloquently of his mili-tary acumen.

[19] *Ibid.*, p. 476.

[20] Kenney, p. 135.

[21] Wylie, p. 475.

After reading a number of author Wylie's stimulating and successful books I have the impression that no cultural facet of civilization incites him to rave as passionately as does the idea of a theology. Personally I do not wish to be a Gnostic. I share, I think with Wylie, the ideal recently voiced by Bertrand Russell and formerly expressed by many others, that a wise man should not feel absolutely certain of anything. The first conclusion following this precept, it seems to me, is that it may be unwise to be uncertain of everything. Indeed, there may be many of "the simple-minded majority" who are unsophisticated in their acceptance of a theological dogma. However, this is one of the things I am uncertain of, and I shudder to think what our world might be like if the mass of people believed in nothing. One needs only to look at the speech to see that General MacArthur did not, as Wylie with word-twisting viciousness contends, say or imply that the solution to the problems of the war-weary world is for the world's free people to let themselves be dominated "by any one man or his theology."[22]

With profoundest intellectual maturity the General, quoting from his talk made on the occasion of the Japanese surrender on the battleship *Missouri*, said:

Military alliances, balances of power, leagues of nations, all in turn failed, leaving the only path to be by way of the crucible of war. The utter destructiveness of war now blots out this alternative. We have had our last chance. If we will not devise some greater and more equitable system, Armageddon will be at our door. The problem basically is theological and involves a spiritual recrudescence and improvement of human character that will synchronize with our almost matchless advances in science, art, literature, and all material and cultural developments of the past 2,000 years. It must be of the spirit if we are to save the flesh.[23]

The word *theological* in the context of this quotation is obviously not used to refer to religious dogma. The General meant "spiritual recrudescence." Such language is not the talk of a "man on horseback."

The Congressional members of both parties responded with enthusiasm to the force of General MacArthur's address before the two Houses on April 19, 1951. Most of those in the radio and television audience were deeply moved. With this writing almost nine months after the event, critics are still discussing the speech. For the second successive year the general has been voted Man of the Year by Associated Press editors in a nationwide year-end poll. A great man delivered a significant message on a memorable occasion. Surely the speech will not be forgotten in the years to come.

[22] *Ibid.*, p. 478.
[23] MacArthur, Senate Document No. 36, p. 5.

13

Douglas MacArthur

Winton H. Beaven

Probably no man in America in modern times has made a more dramatic speech than the one General MacArthur delivered before the Joint Session of the Congress in April, 1951. Certainly none has inspired so much "criticism," in the broad sense of the term.[1] And because that speech has been so thoroughly discussed, it is, perhaps, wise in evaluating the speaking effectiveness of the General in the campaign year to ignore it altogether.

During the fifteen months between his homecoming speech and the Republican National Convention in July, MacArthur delivered seven major addresses in such widely scattered cities as Houston, Boston, Cleveland, Jackson, Mississippi, and Lansing, Michigan. For all of them he appeared in full uniform and read from carefully prepared manuscript. He limited himself to one major speech in any particular area. Many of the concepts and ideas which appeared in his defense before Congress reappeared in these major addresses, although rarely in the same words. Throughout these speeches seemed to appear a definite progression of increasing bitterness toward the Administration and of an increasing partisan political attitude. However, at no time before the convention in any of his addresses did he definitely and irrevocably label himself a Republican.

[Winton H. Beaven is the President of Columbia Union College, Takoma Park, Maryland, as well as Professor of Speech. This article originally appeared in the *Quarterly Journal of Speech*, xxxviii (October 1952), 270–72, and is reprinted with the permission of both the author and the Speech Association of America.]
[1] Frederick Haberman, "General MacArthur's Speech: A Symposium of Critical Comment," *QJS*, xxxvii (October 1951), 321–31. [Reprinted in this text, pp. 229–43.] Philip Wylie, "Medievalism and the MacArthurian Legend," *QJS*, xxxvii (December 1951), 473–78. [Reprinted in this text, pp. 244–50.] Paul R. Beall, "Viper-Crusher Turns Dragon-Slayer," *QJS*, xxxviii (February 1952), 51–6. [Reprinted in this text, pp. 251–57.]

In his keynote speech in civilian garb for the first time he confessed to a lifelong allegiance to the Republican party.

In assessing the speaking effectiveness of General MacArthur, to separate the "speaking" from the bias of the listeners is almost impossible. From a certain minority in almost all areas of the country he inspired a fanatic loyalty and response. Others considered him an autocratic general whose every action was suspect. Personal observation, both in face-to-face speaking and over television, seemed to indicate a much more favorable response from the older generation than the younger.

Certain characteristics of MacArthur's speaking seem incontrovertible. In delivery, he is a master. With very little gesture he reads from manuscript with great skill and power. Occasionally he lifts a hand with a half-arm gesture or taps a finger or a hand. But always he makes effective use of his microphone. So perfect was his reading skill that he never made a significant stumble; so well did he familiarize himself with his manuscript that he was always in absolute control of his delivery and maintained eye-contact with his audience as much as half the time during an address. In his keynote address he was ready for each burst of applause; it appeared to have been practiced. His voice was deep and clear on most occasions, though a slight huskiness characterized the convention address. Always it carried strong emotional overtones capable of producing strong emotional responses. A flexible instrument capable of varied shades of meaning, it was particularly effective in the lower registers. Emphasis was always subdued and controlled but vigorous; the General gave the impression of speaking from the depths of strong feeling held under vigorous control. Plosives were particularly emphatic; words such as *stagger, whiplash, flaunted, proved,* and the like, fairly crackled as they exploded. For particular emphasis he used two devices: one was a vigorous repeated side to side shake of the head with such words as "those reckless men," the other a pumping motion of the upper torso from the waist, executed on the balls of the feet and repeated six to eight times in rapid succession as the General reached a climax. The pace was always measured. The only noticeable delivery weakness was a tendency on some words to an s-whistle. In the main, so excellent was the delivery that even political enemies praised it.

In style and arrangement of his speeches MacArthur excelled. Introductions were brief, usually personal. Conclusions were equally short, often merely two or three sentences. Never were they summaries; always they were suggestive appeals to action, and often the Deity was mentioned. Composition could be described as tight or compact; rarely was a word wasted. Transitions were clear, even when implied. Certain stylistic devices were particularly notable. The use of refrain was especially effective; for instance, in the keynote speech successive paragraphs began with "they view with dismay"; later successive sentences began "it ignores—it ignores." Parallel construction was also apparent; successive phrases began "we practically invited—we deliberately withdrew—we recklessly yielded." These devices, rather than appearing forced, served to heighten the address and to produce greater impact of idea. As a coiner of powerful phrases the General has thus far been unequaled in this election year. Rhythm of composition was particularly noticeable; it was not "Churchillian" but possessed a quality all its own. Undoubtedly it was produced with great care; yet as delivered it did not "smell of the lamp."[2] Very long sentences, a paragraph in length, are typical of the MacArthur style, yet so carefully are they constructed that as delivered their meaning is immediately transparent. Balance and proportion are notable both in composition of sentences and in the overall composition and arrangement of the entire speech. The choice of words indicated at times a military background; the language was not always simple, but understanding of ideas did not seem impaired. The style approaches eloquence.

In the area of invention the critic finds his greatest difficulty. The problem is magnified by the fact that all phases of invention are involved; and all divisions of invention in this case are affected by the ethical appeal of the speaker.

No more controversial character lives in America today than Douglas MacArthur. He is undoubtedly a brilliant man; he has an excellent military record. Beyond that all is chaos. To his adherents he is magnetic, handsome, charming, colorful, persuasive, a military genius and prophet, a statesman without peer. Douglas MacArthur speaks with a strong tone of personal authority, poise, and dignity. For those who believe in him, his ethical and pathetic appeals are unmatched by those of any living speaker.

On the other hand, for those who believe the General to be an egomaniac with a "God" complex, an authoritarian who strives for the sole spotlight and who tolerates no disagreement, his ethical appeal is entirely negative and his emotional appeals are considered to be merely acting. He has been described as a consummate "ham."

For most people, there seems to be little middle ground in the controversy. Historically, MacArthur's career has demonstrated all the aforementioned qualities in varying degrees. If one accepts him as sincere, then his speeches, which have strong moral and religious overtones, are persuasive rallying cries to a people seeking a leader. If one believes him to be seeking high office as a wronged man, then his appeals are meaningless.

In the realm of logic, MacArthur's speaking is subject to question. All his speeches cover vast areas of subject matter. They are filled with gener-

---

[2] A United Press Dispatch of July 2 indicated that the first draft of the keynote address was written in longhand at least a week before its delivery and thereafter polished and revised.

alizations, seldom supported by evidence, and by personal assertions which apparently are to be accepted because of the prestige of the speaker. Apparent inconsistencies and contradictions arise, such as calls for a return to the good old days of peace and tranquillity, and at the same time advocacy of a policy in Korea that apparently would spread a local into a global war. But most of the definitive criticism of the General's ideas would seem to depend on the course of history to prove him right or wrong. Certainly, since his defense before Congress, his ideas relative to the Far East have stood up as well as those of his critics.

In his keynote speech MacArthur demonstrated his ability to handle a specialized kind of public address. Traditionally such a speech has as its purpose the unification of the party. The keynote speaker normally accomplishes this feat by pointing out all the sins of the opposing party and outlining all the virtues of his own. General MacArthur presented a thoroughly comprehensive indictment of the Democratic Party and, at least temporarily, focused the attention of the Republicans upon their common enemy. He did not, however, extoll the Republican Party. Although the speech was not as dramatic as his defense before Congress, it was a partisan address calculated to stir party enthusiasm, and at the same time produce a patriotic appeal. It did not appear calculated to advance the cause of any particular candidate for the nomination. It was not as overwhelmingly successful as, for instance, Alben Barkley's speech at Philadelphia in 1948, but it produced an excellent response.

The final evaluation of MacArthur as a speaker in 1952 cannot yet be written. Undoubtedly his ideas have found a dramatic response in the hearts of many. Certainly his style and delivery have interested, even captivated, many listeners. Without question he has been an effective spokesman against the Administration and has served to vitalize and focus the Republican attack upon the Democratic Party.

14

On the Criticism
of the MacArthur
Speech

Karl R. Wallace

One of Professor Beall's prophetic judgments may some day be tested by events. In December, 1951, he wrote: "The *Symposium of Critical Comment* on General MacArthur's speech has now reached the stage where critic B is criticizing the criticism of critic A's criticism of the speech, and the end may not be yet." Doubtless the end of critical study of MacArthur as a speaker is not yet; it is at least another generation away. Some student of public address twenty years hence may be able to view MacArthur's "eloquence" in measured perspective. He will be remote from the drama, glamour, and emotional partisanship enveloping MacArthur's oration to Congress. When he comes to the final tasks of the critic, assaying the immediate and ultimate effect of the speech and assigning it a place among similar productions, he will discover, in the pages of the *Quarterly Journal of Speech*, contempoary critics making sweeping value-judgments with which he must deal.[1] His interpretation of the judgments should not be difficult, for some are plainly marked with political and ideological bias, most reveal uncritical enthusiasm, and only one shows judicial restraint.

[Karl R. Wallace is Professor of Speech and Head of the Department of Speech at the University of Massachusetts. This article originally appeared in the *Quarterly Journal of Speech*, xxxix (February 1953), 69–74, and is reprinted with the permission of both the author and the Speech Asssociation of America.]
[1] Frederick W. Haberman, "General MacArthur's Speech: A Symposium of Critical Comment," xxxvii (October 1951), 321–331 [reprinted in this text, pp. 229–43]; Philip Wylie, "Medievalism and the MacArthurian Legend," xxxvii (December 1951), 473–478 [reprinted in this text, pp. 244–50]; Paul R. Beall, "Viper-Crusher Turns Dragon-Slayer," xxxviii (February 1952), 51–56 [reprinted in this text, pp. 251–57].

Among the six Congressional critics appearing in Professor Haberman's *Symposium* is Mr. Martin, who regards the address as "certainly surpassing" the Roosevelt Inaugural of 1933 and the Churchill address of 1942. "In my 27 years in Congress, there has been nothing to equal it."[2] "Its logic, its simple directness, its clear-cut statement of the issues, and its orderly exposition make the structure of the speech a model for all to follow."[3] Whereas Senator Kerr simply found the speech unconvincing to him and Senator Humphrey was content to record that it "affected every member of the Congress,"[4] Senator Mundt—a former teacher of public address—averred that the speech "seems destined to become one of the classics of the English language."[5] Mundt had heard Roosevelt, Churchill, and Madame Chiang Kai-shek address Congress, but "without question Douglas MacArthur stood out spectacularly above them all."[6] Senator Wiley, reporting "hardly a dry eye in the entire audience" and remarking that even Democrats gave applause and cheers, believed that MacArthur emerged as a man of "great humility" and a "true statesman" in an address "which will be reviewed by future generations as one of the great expositions in the history of oratory."[7] A "masterpiece of effectiveness" which no other man could have made, "it has become a classic in American history."[8]

The journalistic critics appearing in the *Quarterly Journal* are less enthusiastic than the Congressional observers. Rovere thought that "politically" the speech seemed "extremely weak";[9] Howe saw it as a good job of acting, quite in character with man and legend; and Evjue was shocked that anyone should presume to compare the speech with any of Lincoln's speeches, above all with the Gettysburg Address.

The academic or professional critics of public address, like the journalists, are for the most part less eager to give the speech high rank in history. Baird predicts that MacArthur "will be ranked as one of America's outstanding military orators,"[10] but he thus drastically limits the field of comparison. Beall, however, permits himself to say that "the general's address will become an English language classic—even a world classic in oratory."[11] Compared to this is Ewbank's judgment: "In many ways this was, and is, a great speech. But it will not find an enduring place in our literature as a model of speech composition."[12]

[2] Haberman, p. 321.
[3] *Ibid.*, p. 322.
[4] *Ibid.*, p. 323.
[5] *Ibid.*, p. 322.
[6] *Ibid.*, p. 323.
[7] *Ibid.*, p. 324.
[8] *Ibid.*
[9] *Ibid.*, p. 325.
[10] *Ibid.*, p. 331.
[11] Beall, p. 52.
[12] Haberman, p. 331.

As is doubtless evident, my purpose is not to enter the lists as a critic of MacArthur's speech. Rather, I intend to function here only as a student of rhetorical criticism: to observe critics at work, and to comment on what I find. The materials for observation are limited to Haberman's *Symposium* and to the subsequent articles by Philip Wylie and Paul Beall. From such examples of critics at work can be drawn a few observations which may underline the fundamentals of rhetorical criticism.

The first observation has already been made, i.e., a critic is unwise to assign to a contemporaneous product values which can best be assessed, if at all, by history. Let him be content with recording such facts as he can about the immediate reaction to a speech and let the critic of tomorrow try to decide whether an oration or an orator has become classic.

The second observation may prompt some disagreement among students of rhetorical criticism. How central to criticism are judgments about the appropriateness of the basic ideas in a speech? Has the speaker shown good judgment in selecting his purpose, in choosing the ideas and lines of explanation or of argument through which he expects to secure his effect? If he be engaged in argument or persuasion, has he seen the issues and presented as good a case as could be reasonably expected of an informed and competent speaker? The appropriateness of a speaker's chief ideas, first to the immediate and larger context of the subject in controversy, and second to the knowledge, motives, and emotions of his audience, would seem to be of prime consideration to criticism. Judgments about "appropriateness" are fundamental and essential if the critic is to do more than explain and interpret methods and techniques, if the critic is to tell *his* audience how to take the speech.

What we have in mind here is well illustrated by a comparison of the professional critics with the non-professionals. Evjue, the journalist, says, "It is inconceivable that his address, with its obvious shortcomings in knowledge of essential historical background, its attention to easy and empty sociological concepts ... could even be compared to any of Lincoln's great masterpieces."[13] Evjue specifically singles out the references to the Chinese and tries to show swiftly that the speaker either did not know Chinese history and culture or had distorted it to serve his purposes. Much of Philip Wylie's article blasts MacArthur for ignorance, inconsistency, or misleading tactics with regard to the Chinese, the Japanese economy, and the Russian menace in Europe. Although his animus vitiates much of his criticism, Wylie at least invites the reader to evaluate the speaker's knowledge and judgment. Another journalist, Rovere, points to the problem any speaker faces, that of analyzing his resources of argument and selecting his case: The speech, he says, "seemed extremely weak to me ... I believe he could have made out a much stronger case for himself. But he never came

[13] *Ibid.*, p. 327.

to grips with the issues."[14] It remains for Senator Kerr, however, to point out the possibilities of alternative argument and strategy:

I watched for an acknowledgment of the necessity to maintain the integrity of civilian control of the military power. It was not there. I searched for language that would give hope of a limited conflict and a purpose to prevent the spread into world-wide conflagration. He did not provide it.

I listened for words which would promote cooperation between this nation and our allies for collective security. Those words were not spoken. I expected him who had been in command of the United Nations forces to acknowledge and report on his stewardship and tell how to strengthen the common front. He did not even mention the United Nations or a single ally.

I hoped he would show the way to promote peace and prevent more or larger war. He was not looking in that direction.[15]

Such comments undoubtedly help in appraising the speech, for they point to the grounds of analysis from which the speaker must select his case.

The professional critics of public address, in contrast, pay little attention to appropriateness of ideas, issues, and arguments. Brigance, despite limitations of space, points out the dominant groups in the audience and suggests their attitudes towards MacArthur and towards the conflicts in the current debate over foreign policy. Accordingly, one expects either an explanation or an appraisal of how the speaker's ideas and his method of treating them constituted appropriate adaptation to group attitudes. That expectation, however, is not fulfilled beyond the statement that "the Democrats knew that they were in a fight" and that MacArthur recognized the "ultimate issue in the minds of critical listeners."[16] Wichelns suggests that MacArthur was conscious of alternative methods of advancing his position (a "call for a harder and more aggressive policy") and, like Demosthenes at times, decided not to debate but to suggest the heads for debate. The speaker then supported his suggestions chiefly by painting an arresting self-portrait. This is good interpretation; and Wichelns' account of the way MacArthur drew and colored his portrait should be carefully studied by students of criticism. Yet Wichelns is concerned with the speaker's *method of presentation* and means of support; he raises no questions over the speaker's basic position and case, as Senator Kerr does. Howell indicates ambiguities in MacArthur's self-portrait and shows that the speaker's four proposals for success in the East receive inadequate logical support. The speech "tends to expand into propositions that are easy to grasp and hard to defend."[17] Ewbank deals principally with the style of the speech, by subjecting it to Flesch's criteria for ease of reading and human interest.

[14] *Ibid.*, p. 325.
[15] *Ibid.*, p. 322.
[16] *Ibid.*, p. 328.
[17] *Ibid.*, p. 330.

Baird's appraisal is in its essentials similar to that of Wichelns, although he goes beyond Wichelns by commenting briefly on delivery, style, and taste. In brief, it seems fair to say that the academic critics, in the examples at hand, show less concern for "invention" in the traditional sense than do the journalists and members of Congress.

Why did not the professional critics deal more fully with "invention"? At least three reasons should be recognized. First, Haberman's demand for brevity is cramping. To attempt analysis in terms of the context of the controversy, the occasion and the audience (both seen and unseen) requires space. If one makes the attempt, he does nothing else, as both Humphrey and Evjue clearly demonstrate. Second, perhaps our critics feel that the critic should grant the speaker his purpose, his subject, and his case and that criticism chiefly consists in interpreting means and methods of securing effect. If this were the view, value-judgments would be limited to techniques of presenting, supporting, and developing materials, and modern rhetoric would concede invention to the logician, the historian, and the political scientist. I doubt whether this view is widely held. Yet among our examples is some evidence that confusion exists. Note Rovere's opening paragraph:

As a literary critic and political observer, I view the speech solely from the literary and political points of view. I am not qualified to criticize oratory or elocution.[18]

Clearly here is a man with a literary background who is suggesting that literature, politics, and oratory somehow have strict provinces and exclude each other. (Does he suggest, also, that oratory and elocution are the same?) And despite his assertion that "form and content are, if not inseparable, very closely related," when he criticizes MacArthur for inadequate analysis, he takes care to speak as a political man, not as a literary man. Professor Beall seems uncertain whether a critic of speech-making may consider what a speaker does not say. He complains that the device is "unlimited,"[19] and rightly censures Wylie for making too much of what MacArthur might have said and did not. How relevant to the circumstances and context of occasion and subject is Wylie's suggestion that MacArthur, rather than take the line he did, might better have prepared the American people for atomic bombardment? If the rhetorical critic is not to be emasculated, he must claim the right, and have the equipment, to make reasonable judgments about a speaker's "invention."

A third reason for the critic's failure to make much of invention springs from the speech itself. Can one be sure of the purpose of the speech—of the effect intended, either immediate or ultimate? The speaker

[18] *Ibid.*, p. 325.
[19] Beall, p. 54.

himself was not explicit. Does the speech reveal a definite point of view, a proposition—stated or clearly implied—and structurally-related lines of development? Unless the critic is able to say yes or no with some firmness to these questions, he can scarcely weigh the appropriateness of the speaker's purpose, his case, and his chief lines of support. It appears plain to me that the critics before us had difficulty in answering such questions. Among the Congressional group, Kerr believes that MacArthur "sounded a call for an expanded war," yet he can find no unity.[20] Corbett declares that the speech "met the situation exactly as it was designed to do"; "it explained the General's point of view clearly and persuasively"; it was a "test of the whole man and his whole career."[21] Senator Wiley talks somewhat vaguely about "objective,"[22] and Martin, after stating the general purpose of all political speeches as the strengthening of friendships and winning of converts, refers casually to "its orderly exposition," "its logic," and "its clear-cut statement of the issues," without explanation of any of these phrases.[23] Mundt is virtually silent, but Humphrey is explicit and seems confident. MacArthur's purpose, he says, is to "give reason and justification for his life's work and ... reputation";[24] but when he states that "the basic issue ... in the controversy is one of civilian versus military control over our foreign policy," whether he has in mind the speech or its context is not clear.[25] The three journalists are pretty certain that Mac-Arthur aimed primarily at exalting himself. Uncharitable Mr. Howe thinks that the speech gives the great actor another chance to act the part of the hero; and Evjue states flatly that "the center of Douglas MacArthur's speech was Douglas MacArthur."[26] Rovere believes that MacArthur spoke "to the end of making an appeal to history," yet "never came to grips with the issues."[27] Of the six academic critics, only one attempts to pin down the purpose of the speech; he asserts that the address is an "Apologia," a defense of the speaker himself.[28] In harmony with this assertion is the undeveloped judgment that among other qualities of the address, "the speech structure and movement ... exalted the mature judgment and common sense of the speaker."[29] Howell simply alludes to MacArthur's "advocacy of what might produce still greater" war,[30] and Wichelns alone, as we have seen, discovers a central proposition clearly implied—a

[20] Haberman, p. 322.
[21] Ibid., pp. 324–325.
[22] Ibid., pp. 323–324.
[23] Ibid., pp. 321–322.
[24] Ibid., p. 323.
[25] Ibid.
[26] Ibid., p. 326.
[27] Ibid., p. 325.
[28] Ibid., p. 331.
[29] Ibid.
[30] Ibid., p. 329.

call for a harder and more aggressive policy. It appears, accordingly, that the speech itself may evade the kind of rhetorical analysis necessary if the dispassionate critic is to deal confidently with the logic of invention. Our professional critics were probably aware that a contemporary observer is wise to limit himself to interpretations of rhetorical methods and techniques. Indeed, this is what they did.

Other aspects of the critics' work deserve at least general consideration. First, two of the academicians reflect the confusion implicit in some of the traditional rhetorical categories. Consider Wichelns and Howell, for the moment, the first saying that the line of support for MacArthur's policy is neither logical argument nor emotional appeal, but the speaker's self-portrait—his character or ethos. Howell, on the other hand, builds his entire comment on the statement, "No prominent speech of the post-war era has contained so strong an appeal to emotion as MacArthur's did:"[31] The two interpreters then employ the same material, for the most part, to support their points of view, one seeing in the materials evidence of ethos, the other, evidence of pathos. Although this may be entirely proper and may be managed with consistency, a thoughtful student will raise the question: Can such categories of "proof" or support be given sufficiently precise meanings when close, scholarly criticism is at issue? Are these traditional concepts, in times past acceptable enough, satisfactory to an age whose scientists and scholars call for symbols with precise meaning? The same questions can be raised with respect to another venerable category, style. Its meanings are almost legion, ranging from the manner of presenting the speech (including all the verbal, visible, and audible components of the complete whole) to word choice and word order. The larger meaning Wichelns may have in mind when he refers to the tone and movement of the speech; the narrower meanings are evident in Ewbank's use of the Flesch formula, in the controversy between Beall and Wylie over the cobra metaphor, *predatory*, and *corny*.

In closing, we should direct attention to what we usually have in mind when we talk about the form, structure, or arrangement of the speech. Form is as necessary to the being of a speech as it is to any artistic production, aesthetic or utilitarian. Yet in the examples of criticism before us, the treatment of structure is almost casual. When form is mentioned at all, it is by phrase or single sentence; sometimes it is vaguely recognized by implication. Such judgments as are evident are unsupported and undeveloped, at times even ambiguous and conflicting. Beall thinks that the "total speech structure" made a "necessary" contribution to the "wholeness" of the speech.[32] Philip Wylie refers to the "intellectual chaos" of the address,[33] but he may have in mind not structure, but the instances of

---

[31] *Ibid.*
[32] Beall, p. 53.
[33] Wylie, p. 474.

faulty logic and inconsistency which he uncovers. Martin says that the "orderly exposition" makes the speech a model, but Ewbank, as we have seen, cannot regard it as an enduring model of speech composition. Baird alludes to "its logical texture" and holds that "the speech structure and movement" favorably impress the listener with the speaker's "mature judgment and common sense." Senator Wiley uses the phrase, "keen logical sequence," yet Kerr "looked for unity" and didn't find it. Mundt believes that the "oratorical masterpiece" was "excelled in its composition" only by the "skillful prowess" of the speaker's delivery.[34] And Rovere, in his literary role, writes: "As a piece of composition, the speech seemed to me a good deal but not a great deal better than the general run of public prose in the United States today."[35] In view of this mosaic of interpretative comment, a critic of the critics is almost bound to wonder whether the structure of public address is today being taken for granted and therefore not worthy of more than passing reference.

[34] Haberman, p. 322.
[35] *Ibid.*, p. 325.